# Be Exultant

## WARREN W. WIERSBE

## *Victor*®

*The Bible Teacher's Teacher*

COOK COMMUNICATIONS MINISTRIES
Colorado Springs, Colorado   •   Paris, Ontario
KINGSWAY COMMUNICATIONS LTD
Eastbourne, England

Victor® is an imprint of
Cook Communications Ministries, Colorado Springs, CO 80918
Cook Communications, Paris, Ontario
Kingsway Communications, Eastbourne, England

Be Exultant
© 2004 by Warren W. Wiersbe

First printing, 2004
Printed in the United States of America

3 4 5 6 7 8 9 10  Printing/Year  10 09 08 07 06

Editor: Craig Bubeck
Cover photo: © Photo Disc Collection/Getty Images

Library of Congress Cataloging-in-Publication
Wiersbe, Warren W.
 Be exultant / by Warren W. Wiersbe.--1st ed.
   p.  cm.
 ISBN-13: 978-0-7814-4101-8
 ISBN-10: 0-7814-4101-3(pbk.)
 1. Bible. O.T. Psalms–Commentaries.  I. Title
   BS1430.53.W534 2004
   223'.207--dc22

                                    2004002871

# CONTENTS

# PREFACE

The *Be* series had a modest beginning in 1972 when Victor Books published my commentary on 1 John and called it *Be Real*. Nobody remembers who named the book, but for me it was the beginning of three decades of intensive Bible study as I wrote additional commentaries, all of them with *Be* in the title. It took twenty-three books to cover the New Testament, and they were published in two bound volumes in 1989. Then I started the Old Testament *Be* series, and *Be Obedient*, on the life of Abraham, was published in 1991. Over twenty books are now available in the Old Testament series, and the Lord willing, I hope to complete the Old Testament within a year.

I owe a great debt of gratitude to the editorial staff for their encouragement and cooperation these many years, including Mark Sweeney, Jim Adair, Lloyd Cory, Greg Clouse, and Craig Bubeck. These men have been faithful to "shepherd" me through book after book, and I appreciate the friendship and ministry of each more and more. Every author should be as fortunate as I've been to work with such dedicated, skillful people who always take a personal interest in their authors. To the best of my knowledge, during these years we've ministered together, we've never had a cross word or a serious misunderstanding.

I especially want to thank the Lord for His kindness and mercy in allowing me to minister in this way through the printed page. I can think of many of my friends who could have done a far better job than I in this series, but the Lord graciously gave the privilege to me. He also gave me the wisdom and strength to get each book written on time—and sometimes ahead of time—in the midst of a very busy life as a husband and father, a pastor, a radio Bible teacher, a seminary instructor, and a conference speaker.

This leads me to say that I couldn't have done it without the loving care of my wife, Betty. She manages our household affairs so well and takes such good care of me that I've always had the time needed for studying and writing. When I started this series, our four children were all at home. Now they're all married, and my wife and I have eight wonderful grandchildren! Time flies when you're checking proofs!

The numerous readers of the *Be* series have been a great source of encouragement to me, even when they have written to disagree with me! I have received letters from many parts of the world, written by people in various walks of life, and they have gladdened my heart. Unless a writer hears from his readers, his writing becomes a one-way street, and he never knows if what he wrote did anybody any good. I want to thank the pastors, missionaries, Sunday school teachers, and other students of the Word who have been kind enough to write. We could compile a book of letters telling what God has done in the lives of people who have studied the *Be* series. To God be the glory!

As I close, there are some other people who ought to be thanked. Dr. Donald Burdick taught me New Testament at Northern Baptist Seminary and showed me how to study the Word of God. Dr. Lloyd Perry and the late Dr. Charles W. Koller both taught me how to "unlock" a Scripture passage and organize an exposition that was understandable and practical. I recommend their books on preaching to any preacher or teacher who wants to better organize his or her material.

For ten happy years, I was privileged to pastor the Calvary Baptist Church in Covington, Kentucky, just across the river from Cincinnati. One of my happy duties was writing Bible study notes for "The Whole Bible Study Course," which was developed by the late Dr. D.B. Eastep, who pastored the church for thirty-five fruitful years. No church I have ever visited or ministered to has a greater love for the Bible or a deeper hunger for spiritual truth than the dear people at Calvary Baptist. The *Be* series is, in many respects, a by-product of Dr. Eastep's kindness in sharing his ministry with me, and the church's love and encouragement while I was their pastor. I honor his memory and thank God for their continued friendship and prayer support.

To you who study God's Word with me, "I commend you to God, and to the word of his grace, which is able to build you up, and to give you an inheritance among all them which are sanctified" (Acts 20:32).

Warren W. Wiersbe

# ONE

## INTRODUCTION
## TO THE BOOK OF PSALMS

# *Psalms*

The book of Psalms has been and still is the irreplaceable devotional guide, prayer book, and hymnal of the people of God. The Hebrew title is "the book of praises" (*tehillim*). The Greek translation of the Old Testament (the Septuagint) used *psalmos* for *tehillim*; the word means "a song sung to the accompaniment of a stringed instrument." The Vulgate followed the Septuagint and used *psalmorum*, from the Latin *psalterium*, "a stringed instrument." *The King James* adopted the word, and thus we have the book of Psalms.

**Writers.** The writers of about two-thirds of the psalms are identified in the superscriptions. David leads the way with 73 psalms. He was Israel's "beloved singer of songs" (2 Sam. 23:1 NIV) and the man who organized the temple ministry, including the singers (1 Chron. 15:16; 16:7; 25:1). The sons of Korah, who served as musicians in the temple (1 Chron. 6:31ff; 15:17ff; 2 Chron. 20:19), wrote 11 psalms (42–49, 84, 85, 87), Asaph 12 psalms, King Solomon two (Pss. 72 and 127), Ethan wrote one (Ps. 89), and Moses one (Ps. 90). However, not all scholars give equal value to the titles of the psalms.

**Organization.** The book of Psalms is divided into five books, perhaps in imitation of the Five Books of Moses (Gen.–Deut.): 1–41, 42–72, 73–89, 90–106, 107–150. Each of the first three books ends with a double "amen," the fourth ends with an "amen" and a "hallelujah," and the last book closes the entire collection with a "hallelujah." The book of Psalms grew over the years as the Holy Spirit directed different writers and editors to compose and compile these songs and poems. David wrote 37 of the 41 psalms in Book I, so this was the beginning of the collection. Books II and III may have been collected by "the men of Hezekiah" (Prov. 25:1), a literary guild in King Hezekiah's day that copied and preserved precious Old Testament manuscripts. Hezekiah himself was a writer of sacred poetry (Isa. 38). Books IV and V were probably collected and added during the time of the scholar Ezra (Ezra 7:1–10). As with our modern hymnals, there are "collections within the collection," such as "The Songs of Degrees" (120–134), the writings of Asaph (Pss. 73–83), the psalms of the sons of Korah (42–49), and the "hallelujah psalms" (113–118, 146–150).

**Poetry.** Hebrew poetry is based on "thought lines" and not rhymes. If the second line repeats the first line in different words, as in Psalm 24:1–3, you have *synonymous parallelism*. If the second line contrasts with the first, as in Psalms 1:6 and 37:9, it is *antithetic parallelism*. When the second line explains and expands the first, the writer has used *synthetic parallelism* (Ps. 19:7–9), but when the second line completes the first, it is *climactic parallelism* (Ps. 29:1). With *iterative parallelism*, the second line repeats the thought of the first (Ps. 93), and in *alternate parallelism*, the alternate lines carry the same thought, as in Psalm 103:8–13. You don't bring these technical terms into the pulpit, but knowing what they mean can give you great help when you study. To interpret Psalm 103:3 as God's promise to heal every sickness is to ignore the synonymous parallelism of the verse: the forgiveness of sins is like the healing of disease (see Ps. 41:4).

Some of the psalms are laments to the Lord, written by people in dire circumstances. There are also messianic psalms that point forward to the Lord Jesus Christ. There are also psalms of praise and thanksgiving, royal psalms, wisdom psalms, psalms of affirmation and trust, penitential psalms, and even imprecatory psalms calling down God's wrath on the enemy. We will consider each of these categories as we meet them in our studies.

**Value.** There are over four hundred quotations or allusions to the Psalms in the New Testament. Jesus quoted from the book of Psalms (Matt. 5:5/Ps. 37:11; 5:36/Ps. 48:3; 6:26/Ps. 147:9; 7:23/Ps. 6:8; 27:46/Ps. 22:1; John 15:25/Ps. 69:4). The Lord gave guidance from the book of Psalms when the church in Jerusalem chose a new apostle (Acts 1:15ff; Pss. 69:25; 109:8). The early church also used the Psalms to buttress their preaching (Acts 2:31; Ps. 16:10) and to find encouragement in times of persecution (Acts 4:23–31; Ps. 2). Singing selected psalms was a part of their worship (Eph. 5:19; Col. 3:16; 1 Cor. 14:26) and should be a part of the church's worship today. It's helpful and interesting to study Bible history from the viewpoint of the psalmists: creation (8), the flood (29), the patriarchs (47:9, 105:9, 47:4), Joseph (105:17ff), The Exodus (114), the wilderness wanderings (68:7, 106:1ff), the captivity (85, 137).

But primarily, the psalms are about God and His relationship to His creation, the nations of the world, Israel, and His believing people. He is seen as a powerful God as well as a tenderhearted Father, a God who keeps His promises and lovingly cares for His people. The psalms also reveal the hearts of those who follow Him, their faith and doubts, their victories and failures, and their hopes for the glorious future God has promised. In this book, we meet all kinds of people in a variety of circumstances, crying out to God, praising Him, confessing their sins and seeking to worship Him in a deeper way. In the book of Psalms, you meet the God of creation and learn spiritual truths from birds and beasts, mountains and deserts, sunshine and storms, wheat and chaff, trees and flowers. You learn from creatures of all sorts—horses, mules, dogs, snails, locusts, bees, lions, snakes, sheep, and even worms. The psalms teach us to seek God with a whole heart, to tell Him the truth and tell Him everything, and to worship Him because of Who He is, not just because of what He gives. They show us how to accept trials and turn them into triumphs, and when we've failed, they show us how to repent and receive God's gracious forgiveness. The God described in the book of Psalms is both transcendent and immanent, far above us and yet personally with us in our pilgrim journey. He is "God Most High" and "Immanuel—God with us."

**Note:** In these expositions, references to verses in the psalms will not be marked Ps." (psalm) or "Pss." (psalms). References to verses in other Bible books will be identified in the usual manner. When referring to the book of Psalms, I will use "The Psalms."

# TWO

# Book IV

## Psalm 90

This is the oldest psalm in The Psalms and it was written by Moses, the man of God (Josh. 14:6; Ezra 3:2). It deals with themes that began with the fall of our first parents and will continue to be important and puzzling until the return of our Savior: eternal God and frail humans, a holy God and sinful man, life and death, and the meaning of life in a confused and difficult world. It's possible that Moses wrote this psalm after Israel's failure of faith at Kadesh Barnea (Num. 13–14), when the nation was condemned to journey in the wilderness for forty years until the older generation had died. That tragedy was followed by the death of Moses' sister Miriam (Num. 20:1) and his brother Aaron (Num. 20:22–29), and between those two deaths, Moses disobeyed the Lord and struck the rock (Num. 20:2–13). How did Moses manage to become a "man of God" after forty years in pagan Egypt that ended in failure, forty years in Midian as a humble shepherd, and forty more leading a funeral march through the wilderness? Life was not easy for Moses, but he triumphed, and in this psalm he shared his insights so that we, too, might have strength for the journey and end well.

*We Are Travelers and God Is Our Home (vv. 1–2)*

"For we are aliens and pilgrims before you, as were our fathers" said King David (1 Chron. 29:12 NKJV). For all mortals, life is a pilgrimage from birth to death, and for believers, it is a journey from earth to heaven, but the road is not an easy one. Jacob called the 130 years of his pilgrimage "few and evil" (Gen. 47:9), and he was a pilgrim to the very end, for he died leaning on the top of his staff (Heb. 11:21). For eighty years, Moses had lived a somewhat settled life, first in Egypt and then in Midian, but after that he spent forty years in the wilderness, leading a nation of complaining former slaves who didn't always want or appreciate his leadership. Numbers 33 names forty-two different places Israel camped during their journey, but no matter where Moses lived, God was always his home. He "lived in the Lord." He knew how to "abide in the Lord" and find strength, comfort, encouragement, and help for each day's demands. Moses pitched a special tent outside the camp where he went to meet the Lord (Ex. 33:7–11). This is the Old Testament equivalent of the New Testament admonition, "Abide in me" (see John 15:1–11). We must all make the Lord "our dwelling" (91:9).

Moses addressed God as "Elohim," the God of power and the God of creation. He described God "giving birth" to the mountains (v. 2; Job 15:7; 38:8, 28–29) and forming the world. To people in the ancient world, mountains symbolized that which was lasting and dependable, and to the Jews, mountains spoke of the everlasting God of Israel (93:1–2). There were six generations from Abraham to Moses—Abraham, Isaac, Jacob, Levi, Kohath, Amram, and Moses—and the same God had guided and blessed them! Those of us who have godly ancestors certainly have a rich heritage and ought to be thankful. In the midst of a changing world, living as we do in a "frail tent" (2 Cor. 5:1–4), it is good to hear Moses say, "The eternal God is your refuge and dwelling place, and underneath are the everlasting arms" (Deut. 33:27 AMP).

## We Are Learners and Life Is Our School (vv. 3–12)

Moses was "educated in all the learning of the Egyptians" (Acts 7:22 NASB), but the lessons he learned walking with God were far more important. In the school of life (v. 12), we need to learn two important lessons: life is brief and passes swiftly (vv. 4–6), so make the most of it; and life is difficult and at times seems futile (vv. 7–11), but this is the only way to mature. Were there no sin in the world, there would be no suffering and death; but people *made of dust* defy the God of the universe and try to repeal the inexorable law of sin and death, "For dust you are, and to dust you shall return" (Gen. 3:19 NKJV). While we all thank God for modern science and the ministry of skilled medical personnel, we cannot successfully deny the reality of death or delay it when our time comes. The school of life is preparation for an eternity with God, and without Him, we cannot learn our lessons, pass our tests, and make progress from kindergarten to graduate school!

The older we get, the better we understand that life is brief and moves past very swiftly. God dwells in eternity (Isa. 57:15) and is not limited by time. He can cram many years of experience and work into one person's lifetime or make the centuries flash past like the days of the week (2 Peter 3:8). Compared with eternity, even a long life is like yesterday when it is past or like the changing of the guards while we are sleeping (a "watch" was four hours). Only God is eternal, and we humans are like objects suddenly swept away by a flash flood (Matt. 7:24–27) or grass that comes and goes. In the east, the grass often grows on very thin soil and has no deep roots (Matt. 13:20–21). A field will be lush and green in the morning but become withered before nightfall because of the hot sun. (See 37:1–2; 92:7; 103:15; Isa. 40:6–7; and 1 Peter 1:24.) God is the one whose command "turns us back" (v. 3; see 104:29; 146:4; Job 34:15; Ecc. 3:20), and we need to fear and honor Him and use our lives for His glory. In the school of life, those students learn the most who realize that the dismissal bell rings when they least expect it!

In verses 7–11, Moses reflected on Israel's sad experience at

Kedesh Barnea (Num. 13–14), when the nation refused to obey God and enter the Promised Land. This foolish decision led to four decades of trials and testings in the wilderness while the older generation died off, except for Joshua and Caleb. God is "slow to anger" (Ex. 34:6), but the repeated complaints and rebellions of His people tested even His longsuffering. (See Ex. 32:10; Num. 11:11, 33; 12:9; 25:3; 32:10, 13; Deut. 4:24–25; 6:15; 9:7, 18–19.) God saw what Israel did and God knew what Israel *intended to do!* No secrets are hidden from Him. The twenty year olds would be close to sixty when the nation returned to Kadesh Barnea, and Moses saw eighty years as the limit for humans. He died at the age of 120 and Joshua at the age of 110, but King David was only seventy years old when he died. Sin takes its toll on the human race, and we no longer see lifespans recorded like those in Genesis 5. We don't like to think about the wrath of God, but every obituary in the newspaper is a reminder that "the wages of sin is death" (Rom. 6:23). We finish our years "like a sigh" (v. 9 NASB) and marvel that it all went by so fast! So, now is the time to ask God for wisdom to become better students and stewards of our time and opportunities (v. 12; Deut. 32:29). We number our years, not our days, but all of us have to live a day at a time, and we do not know how many days we have left. A successful life is composed of successful days that honor the Lord.

### We Are Believers and the Future Is Our Friend (vv. 13–17)

Yes, life is a difficult school, and God disciplines us if we fail to learn our lessons and submit to His will, but there is more to the story. In spite of the "black border" around this psalm, the emphasis is on *life* and not death. The past and present experiences of life prepare us for the future, and all of life prepares us for eternity. When you contrast verses 13–17 with verses. 7–12, you can see the difference. This closing prayer emphasizes God's compassion and unfailing love, His desire to give us joy and satisfaction, even in the midst of life's troubles, and His ability to make life count for eternity. When Jesus Christ is your Savior and Lord, the future is your friend.

"Return" (v. 13) carries the idea of "turn again—turn from your anger and show us the light of your countenance" (Ex. 32:12; Num. 6:23–26; Deut. 32:36). "How long?" is a question frequently asked; see 6:3. In verse 14, Moses may have been referring to the manna that fell each morning, six days a week, and met the physical needs of the people (Ex. 16:1–21). It was a picture of Jesus Christ, the bread of life. The manna sustained life for the Jewish people for nearly forty years, but Jesus gives life to the whole world for all eternity! When we begin the day with the Lord and feed on His Word (Deut. 8:3; Matt. 4:4), then we walk with Him throughout the day and enjoy His blessing. The nourishment of the Word enables us to be faithful pilgrims and successful learners.

There are compensations in life that we may not appreciate until we enter eternity. Moses prayed that God would give him and his people as much joy in the future as the sorrow they had experienced in the past. Paul may have had this in mind when he wrote Romans 8:18 and 2 Corinthians 1:5 and 4:16–18—except that God promises His children far more blessing than the burdens they carried! The glory to come far exceeds the suffering that we bear today. Moses lost his temper and could not enter Canaan (Num. 20:2–13), but he did get to the Promised Land with Jesus and share God's glory with Elijah and three of the disciples (Matt. 17:1–8).

Whatever the Lord doesn't compensate for here on earth will be compensated in heaven (1 Peter 5:10), and this includes our works for Him. At times, Moses must have felt that his work was futile, temporary, and not worth doing. Many times the people broke his heart and grieved his spirit. He sacrificed to serve them and they rarely appreciated him. But no work done for the Lord will ever go unrewarded, and those who do the will of God abide forever (1 John 2:17). Even a cup of cold water given in Jesus' name will receive its reward (Matt. 10:42; 25:31–46). The favor of the Lord does not desert us in our old age, in times of affliction, or when we come to die, and the blessings of our work and witness will go on. In verse 13, Moses addressed God as Jehovah, the God of the covenant who will never break His promises, and that is the God we love, worship, and serve.

Life is brief, so Moses prayed, "Teach us." Life is difficult, and he prayed, "Satisfy us." His work at times seemed futile, so he prayed, "Establish the work of our hands." God answered those prayers for Moses, and He will answer them for us. The future is your friend when Jesus is your Savior and Lord.

## Psalm 91

Psalm 90 focuses on dealing with the difficulties of life, but the emphasis in this psalm is on the dangers of life. The anonymous author (though some think Moses wrote it) warns about hidden traps, deadly plagues, terrors at night and arrows by day, stumbling over rocks, and facing lions and snakes! However, in view of terrorist attacks, snipers, reckless drivers, exotic new diseases, and Saturday night handgun specials, the contemporary scene may be as dangerous as the one described in the psalm. The saints who abide in Christ (vv. 1, 9) cannot avoid confronting unknown perils, but they can escape the evil consequences. Moses, David, and Paul, and a host of other servants of God, faced great danger in accomplishing God's will, and the Lord saw them through. However, Hebrews 11:36 cautions us that "others" were tortured and martyred, yet their faith was just as real. But generally speaking, walking with the Lord does help us to detect and avoid a great deal of trouble, and it is better to suffer in the will of God than to invite trouble by disobeying God's will (1 Peter 2:18–25). The psalmist described the elements involved in living the life of confidence and victory.

### Faith in God—the Hidden Life (vv. 1–4)

The most important part of a believer's life is the part that only God sees, the "hidden life" of communion and worship that is symbolized by the Holy of Holies in the Jewish sanctuary (Ex. 25:18–22; Heb. 10:19–25). God is our refuge and strength (46:1). He hides us that He might help us and then send us back to serve Him in the struggles of life. (See 27:5; 31:19–20; 32:7; 73:27–28;

94:22; 142:5; Deut. 32:37.) The author of the psalm had two "addresses": his tent (v. 10) and his Lord (vv. 1, 9). The safest place in the world is a shadow, if it is the shadow of the Almighty. Through Jesus Christ, we find safety and satisfaction under the wings of the cherubim in the Holy of Holies (36:7–8; 57:1; 61:4; 63:2, 6–7). Jesus pictured salvation by describing chicks hiding under the wings of the mother hen (Matt. 23:37; Luke 13:38), and the psalmist pictured communion as believers resting under the wings of the cherubim in the tabernacle.

The names of God used in these verses encourage us to trust Him. He is *the Most High* (Elyon; vv. 1, 9), a name found first in Genesis 14:18–20. He is higher than the kings of the earth and the false gods of the nations. He is also *the Almighty* (Shaddai), the all-sufficient God who is adequate for every situation. (See Gen. 17:1; 28:3; 35:11.) He is Lord (vv. 2, 9, 14), Jehovah, the covenant-making God who is faithful to His promises. He is God (Elohim, v. 2), the powerful God whose greatness and glory surpass anything we can imagine. *This is the God who invites us to fellowship with Him in the Holy of Holies!* This hidden life of worship and communion makes possible the public life of obedience and service. This God shelters us beneath the wings of the cherubim, but He also gives us the spiritual armor we need (v. 4; Eph. 6:10–18). His truth and faithfulness protect us as we claim His promises and obey Him. The shield is the large shield that covers the whole person. (See Gen. 15:1; Deut. 33:29; 2 Sam. 22:3.) Some translations give "bulwark" or "rampart" instead of "buckler." The Hebrew word means "to go around" and would describe a mound of earth around a fortress. But the message is clear: those who abide in the Lord are safe when they are doing His will. God's servants are immortal until their work is done (Rom. 8:28–39).

### Peace from God—the Protected Life (vv. 5–13)

When we practice "the hidden life," we are not alone for God is with us and compensates for our inadequacies. This paragraph emphasizes that we need not be afraid because the Lord and His angels watch over us. In the ancient Near East, travel was dangerous, unless you were protected by armed guards. (It is not much different in some large cities today.) "Terror by night" could mean simply "the fear of the dark" and of what can happen in the darkness. Contaminated water and food, plus an absence of sound health measures, made it easy to contract diseases by day or by night, although "the destruction that lays waste at noon" (v. 6 NASB) could refer to the effects of the burning rays of the sun.

Verses 7 and 8 read like the description of a battle and may have a direct relationship to the covenant promises God made with Israel (Lev. 26:8; Deut. 32:30). With their own eyes, Israel saw the grief of the Egyptians over their firstborn who died on Passover night (Ex. 12:29–30), and they also saw the Egyptian army dead on the shore of the Red Sea (Ex. 14:26–31), yet no harm came to the people of Israel. God's angel went before them to prepare the way and to lead the way (Ex. 23:20). Satan quoted part of verses 11–12 when he tempted Jesus in the wilderness (Matt. 4:6), and the Lord responded with Deuteronomy 6:16. If the Father had commanded Jesus to jump from the temple pinnacle, then the angels would have cared for Jesus, but to jump without the Father's command would have been presumption, not faith, and that would be tempting the Father. In Scripture, the lion and serpent (cobra) are images of Satan (1 Peter 5:8; Gen. 3; 2 Cor. 11:3; Rev. 12:9; 20:2; and see Luke 10:19 and Rom. 16:20). In the ancient Near East, both were dangerous enemies, especially for travelers walking along the narrow paths.

### Love for God—the Satisfied Life (vv. 14–16)

The Lord spoke and announced what He would do for those of His people who truly loved Him and acknowledged Him with obedient lives. The word translated "love" is not the usual word but one that means "to cling to, to cleave, to be passionate." It is used in Deuteronomy 7:7 and 10:15 for the love Jehovah has for His people Israel. (See John 14:21–24.) Among His blessings will be deliverance and protection ("set him on high"), answered prayer, companionship in times of trouble, honor, satisfaction, and a long life (see 21:4; Ex. 20:12; Deut. 30:20). The salvation mentioned at the end of the psalm may mean help and deliverance during life, as in 50:23, or the joy of beholding the glory of God after a long and satisfied life. To the Jewish people, living a long life and seeing one's children, grandchildren, and great-grandchildren, was the ultimate of blessing in this life. Like Abraham, they wanted to die in a good old age and "full of years" (Gen. 25:8), which means "a fulfilled life." It's one thing for doctors to add years to our life, but God adds life to our years and makes that life worthwhile.

## Psalm 92

The major theme is the sovereign rule of God, as stated in verse 8, which is the central verse of the psalm. It proclaims that God is most high (KJV), He is on high (NASB), and He is exalted forever (NIV). The covenant name Jehovah (LORD) is used seven times; Elyon (Most High) is found in verse 1 and Elohim in verse 13. The inscription relates the psalm to the Sabbath Day worship at the sanctuary. During the week, a lamb was sacrificed each morning and another in the evening, but on the Sabbath Day, those sacrifices were doubled (Ex. 29:38–46; Num. 28:1–10). Because our God reigns supremely, and always will, we can be the people of God that He wants us to be. The psalm describes the characteristics of believers who trust a sovereign God.

### A Worshiping People (vv. 1–5)

A part of Israel's covenant relationship with the Lord was their honoring of the weekly Sabbath. It was a special sign between Israel and the Lord (Ex. 20:8–11; 31:12–17; Neh. 9:13–15) and reminded them that God had delivered them from Egypt (Deut. 5:12–15). But the Sabbath also reminded them of God the Creator (Gen. 2:1–3; Ex. 20:8–11), and seven times in Genesis 1 we are told that what God made was "good." The psalmist added an eighth "good thing"—it is "good to give thanks [praise] unto the Lord." Believers today can praise the Lord for His generous creation gifts, His salvation through the blood of the Lamb, and

His gracious covenant with us because of what Jesus did on the cross. Worship ought to be the natural outflow of a heart that loves the Lord and appreciates who He is and what he has done for His people.

Whether we use voices alone or voices accompanied by instruments, we can express our praises to God and focus on His wonderful attributes. We can worship all day long, from morning to evening. We can begin the day assured of His love and end the day looking back on His faithfulness. We can look around and marvel at His works, including His providential care and leading in our own lives, and we can look into His Word and probe the depths of His great thoughts (Rom. 11:33–36). Whether we are stirred by the creation around us or the Scriptures before us, we have every reason to worship and praise God, for He is reigning above us! The prayer of 90:15–16 is answered in verse 4.

### An Overcoming People (vv. 6–11)

The psalmist shifts our attention to the enemies of the Lord who make life difficult for God's people. *The Authorized Version* calls them "brutish," which means "beastly, lacking values and discernment, savage, living only to satisfy the appetite." Other translations use "stupid, senseless, rude, uncultivated." The fool in Psalm 14 would qualify, and see also 49:10–12, 20, and 94:8–11. These people are like grass; they have no deep roots and their luxuriant growth passes quickly (90:5–6). God's faithful people, however, are like palm trees and cedars (v. 12). The "horn" is a symbol of power (v. 10), and God gives His people power to overcome their foes (75:4–5, 10; 89:17, 24; 1 Sam. 2:1, 10; Luke 1:69). Oil was used to anoint special people—kings, priests, and prophets—but the anonymous psalmist rejoiced because the Lord had anointed *him* with fresh oil. He may also have been speaking for all Israel and praising God for a special victory He had given them. God wants His people to be overcomers (Rom. 12:21; 1 John 2:13–14; 4:4; 5:4–5; Rev. 2:7, 11, 17, 26; 3:5, 12, 21; 21:7), and this comes when first we are worshipers.

*Flourishing People (vv. 12–15)*

The senseless brutish crowd is like grass (v. 7), but the righteous are like trees (see 1:3; 52:8; Prov. 11:30; Isa. 1:30; 61:3; Jer. 11:16; 17:8). The wicked may look like sturdy trees, but they don't last (37:35–36; 52:5). The word "flourish" in verse 7 means "to be conspicuous, to shine," while the word in verses 12–13 means "to be vigorous, to flourish richly." The stately date palm and cedar were highly valued by people in the Near East, the palm for its fruit and the cedar for its wood. Both were appreciated for their beauty, and both trees can survive for many years. Not all godly people live long; some, like Robert Murray M'Cheyne and David Brainerd, die very young. But generally speaking, those who obey God avoid a great deal of the danger and disease that can cause an early death. The promise in 91:16 is still true, and so is the picture in 92:13–14. To stay "fresh and green" in old age and not spend one's life complaining and demanding is a mark of God's special blessing. (See Ps. 71 for a description of an older saint who is fresh, fruitful and flourishing.) We change as we grow older, but the Lord never changes. He is our Rock (32:4, 15, 18, 30–31), and what He wills for us is perfect, so we will not complain.

# Psalm 93

Psalms 93 and 95–100 emphasize the sovereign rule of Jehovah, the King of Israel, in the affairs of the nations. (Ps. 94 focuses on God the Judge, which is an important aspect of His righteous rule.) Psalm 93 was perhaps written by one of the Levites who returned to Judah with the Jewish remnant after the Babylonian captivity. The Medes and Persians defeated Babylon in 539 B.C., and the next year Cyrus, the new king, gave the Jews permission to return to their own land, rebuild their temple, and restore their nation. It was an especially difficult time for the Jewish remnant (see Ezra and Haggai) and their work was interrupted, attacked, and neglected. The leaders and the people needed encouragement to continue the work, and this encouragement could come only from the Lord. This brief hymn magnifies the Lord by presenting three divine assurances.

## God Reigns Supremely (vv. 1–2)

It was God who allowed Nebuchadnezzar to attack and conquer the kingdom of Judah and to destroy the temple and the holy city. The Lord used Daniel in Babylon to teach this basic truth to Nebuchadnezzar (Dan. 1–4; see especially Dan. 4:17, 25, 32), but Nebuchadnezzar's successor, Belshazzar, learned it when it was too late (Dan. 5). The Medes and Persians attacked Babylon and killed Belshazzar the very night he was boasting of his kingdom and blaspheming the Lord. "Jehovah is king!" (See 92:8; 96:10; 97:1; 99:1; Ex. 15:18; Deut. 33:5.) He is enthroned in heaven, robed in the majestic robes of glory, and armed with all the power He needs to humble puny rulers. His eternal throne is majestic, strong and firmly established (65:6; 104:1), and the world He created is also firmly fixed (24:2; 78:69; 119:90). No matter what happens to human rulers on earth, the throne in heaven is safe and secure.

## God Is Greater Than Our Circumstances (vv. 3–4)

The raging seas and the pounding waves are often used as symbols of the rise and fall of the nations and the great noise that rulers make as they try to impress people. (See 46:1–3, 6; 60:5; 65:6–7; 74:13–14; Isa. 17:12–13; 51:15; 60:5; Jer. 31:5; 51:42; Dan. 7:1–3; Luke 21:25; Rev. 13:1; 17:15.) God used the Euphrates River to illustrate the Assyrians (Isa. 8:7–8), and He connected Egypt with the Nile River (Jer. 46:7–8). No matter how stormy the nations on earth may become, God is still on His throne and is not frustrated by the foolish words and deeds of "great leaders" who are only made of clay. Do not focus on the threats around you; focus on the throne above you (see 29; Isa. 6; Rev. 4–5).

## God Always Keeps His Word (v. 5)

When the tempest is around us, we look by faith to the throne of grace above us and the Word of God before us. The truth about what is going on in this world is not in the newspapers but in the Scriptures. The false prophets among the Jews in Babylon gave a message different from that of Jeremiah, the true prophet of the Lord (Jer. 29), but it was the messages of God's servants that finally proved true. "Your testimonies are very sure" (v. 5 NKJV). (See Jer. 25:12; 27:22; 29:10; 2 Chron. 36:22–23; Ezra 1:1; and Isa. 44:28–45:3.) False prophets, false teachers, and scoffers abound (2 Peter 2–3), but God's promises will all be fulfilled in their time, and God's children live by promises, not explanations. Satan has attacked God's Word since he lied to Eve in Genesis 3, but the Word still stands. "The counsel of the Lord stands forever, the plans of His heart to all generations" (33:11 NKJV).

Led by Zerubbabel the governor, Joshua the high priest, and the prophets Haggai and Zechariah, the Jewish remnant trusted God, labored, sacrificed, and completed the temple. We don't read that the glory of the Lord moved into the second temple, as it did the tabernacle (Ex. 40) and the first temple (1 Kings 8:10–11), but the Lord was with His people just the same and accomplishing His purposes. It is a holy people that makes the temple holy, and "the beauty of holiness" (29:2) is the greatest adornment for any structure dedicated to the Lord.

## Psalm 94

Along with 10, 14, 73, and 92, the writer deals with the seeming triumph of the wicked and the unjust treatment of the helpless. But it is not foreign conquerors who were guilty, but the leaders of the nation cooperating with the local judges. Even the king was abusing the people by issuing unjust edicts (v. 20). Perhaps the psalm came out of the sufferings of the godly during the reign of wicked King Manasseh (2 Kings 21), whom the Lord blamed for the destruction of Jerusalem (2 Kings 24:1–4). But why is this psalm included in the section that magnifies the kingship of the Lord (93–100)? Because few problems cause God's people to question His rule more than, "Why do the helpless and the godly suffer and the wicked get away with their crimes?" When it comes to dealing with the injustices in society, the psalm teaches us that the righteous have four responsibilities.

### Praying to the Lord for Justice (vv. 1–7)

God's requirement for His people is that they "do justly … love mercy, and … walk humbly with [their] God" (Mic. 6:8), for the Lord loves justice (33:5; 37:28) and hears the prayers of those who have been treated unjustly (Ex. 22:26–27; Deut. 24:14–15; James 5:1–4). The word "vengeance" is often misinterpreted to mean "revenge" or "being vindictive," as though God were having a temper tantrum, but "to avenge" means to uphold the law and give justice to those who have been wronged. Since the Lord is omniscient, He is able to judge motives as well as actions and deal with situations and people justly (Lev. 19:18; Deut. 32:35, 41; Rom. 12:17–21; Heb. 10:30–31). He is the Judge of all the earth (58:11; 82:8) and always does what is right (Gen. 18:25). "Shine forth," means "show yourself, reveal your power and glory" (50:2; 80:1; Deut. 33:2; Hab. 3:1–5).

We want the Lord to act immediately (v. 3; see 6:3), but He is gracious and longsuffering (Ex. 34:6–7) and we must walk by faith (Luke 18:1–8). The proud and arrogant "belch out" evil words and commit evil deeds (10:2–11), and the godly can do nothing to stop them. Orphans, widows, and aliens in the land were under the special care of the Lord (68:5–6; 146:9; Ex. 22:20–24; Deut. 10:18–19; 14:28–29; 24:17–18; 26:12–13; 27:19; Isa. 1:17; 7:6; 22:3). The helpless are God's covenant people and He is Jehovah—the LORD—a name used nine times in the psalm (vv. 1, 3, 5, 11, 14, 17, 18, 22, 23). The wicked convince themselves that God does not see their evil deeds (v. 7; 10:11; 59:7), but He does!

### Warning the Wicked of Their Danger (vv. 8–11)

After praying to the Lord, we must confront the wicked with the truth, as the Lord gives us opportunity. In verses 8–11, the psalmist speaks to the offenders and calls them "senseless people," the word "brutish" that we have met before (49:10; 92:6, KJV; and see 2 Peter 2:12 and Jude 10). These people were behaving like animals and not like humans made in the image of God. They had such a low view of God (v. 7) that they were unable to think logically. If God made the eye and ear, is He unable to see and hear? Is the creature greater than the Creator? If God is able to rule the nations by His providential decrees (Acts 17:24–28), is He unable to deal with a band of wicked officials who are breaking His law and exploiting His people? The Lord gave Israel His law and taught them what it meant, so is He not intelligent enough to apply that law? The word translated "thoughts" in verse 11 means "inventions, schemes, plans." The subversive plans and plots of these evil leaders cannot be hidden from the Lord, nor will they go unpunished. Paul quoted this verse in 1 Corinthians 3:20 to warn church leaders in Corinth not to try to guide the church using the world's wisdom, but to rely only on the wisdom of God found in Scripture—the gold, silver, and precious stones (3:12–15; Prov. 2:1–4; 3:13–15; 8:10–11, 18l–19).

*Accepting God's Discipline (vv. 12–15)*
The words "chasten" or "discipline" (v. 12) mean "teaching and instruction from God's law" (Deut. 8:5; Prov. 3:11–12). The psalmist recognized the fact that the difficulties of life could help him mature in his faith. If God immediately rescued His people from their personal difficulties, they would become "spoiled brats" and never grow in faith or character. "For whom the Lord loves He chastens" (Heb. 12:6). God uses personal difficulties to teach us new truths from His Word (Ps. 119:50; 75; 92–95). There is coming a time of judgment ("days of adversity"), but the Lord will spare His people from it. The longer the wicked persist in their sins, the deeper is the pit they are digging for themselves and the stronger the net that will trap them (9:15–16). God cannot reject His people who are bound to Him in His covenant (37:28–29; Deut. 32:9; Isa. 49:14–18; Jer. 10:16). The psalmist believed in the justice of God, the future judgment of the wicked, and the promise of a righteous kingdom for the upright in heart.

*Working with God for Justice (vv. 16–23)*
Even in Solomon's day, people who were abused and exploited had no redress and found no one to execute justice on their behalf (Eccl. 4:1), so it must have been much worse in the days

of Manasseh, just before the fall of Jerusalem. The question in verse 16 is rhetorical and the writer answered it himself in verse 17—"the LORD." The psalmist was experiencing the devious plots of the evil leaders and cried out to God for help. He knew that the judges were twisting the law to exploit the poor (v. 20), and he was slipping into a deep and dangerous situation. His heart was anxious within him, but the Lord held him up, pulled him out, and gave him peace within. He was grateful for other believers who stood with him and prayed with him, for "my God" in verse 22 became "our God" in verse 24. He trusted the Lord to bring about the judgment that the evil leaders deserved. Like Asaph in Psalm 73, he had been slipping in his faith and walk, but God showed him that the wicked were in slippery places and heading rapidly toward judgment (73:2–3, 18, 27–28).

In evil days, we give thanks that we have the Lord as our refuge and fortress. But we hide in Him, not that we may escape responsibility, but that we might be equipped to go forth and fight the enemy. As the salt of the earth and the light of the world (Matt. 5:13–16), God's people should do all they can to encourage justice in this world. As Edmund Burke said, "It is necessary only for the good man to do nothing for evil to triumph." But in the end, it is the Lord who knows the hearts of people and who will judge justly.

## Psalm 95

The annual Feast of Tabernacles was a joyful event as the people looked back on their ancestors' wilderness wanderings, looked around at the bountiful harvest, and looked up to give thanks to the Lord (Lev. 23:33–44). It has been conjectured that this psalm was written for this feast after the exiles returned to Judah from Babylon.[1] Certainly verses 8–11 would remind them of those wilderness years, but they are quoted in Hebrews 3:7–4:13 and applied to believers today. The church must take heed to what happened to Israel (see 1 Cor. 10:1–13). While 95 calls on Israel to worship, 96 calls all the nations of the earth to worship the God of Israel (96:1, 3, 7, 10, 13). As the psalmist calls God's people to celebrate the Lord, he gives us three admonitions to obey.

## Come and Praise the Lord (vv. 1–5)

He tells us *how* we should praise Him (vv. 1–2) and *why* we should praise Him (vv. 3–5). This is communal praise, not individual, although both are important. Our praise should be joyful and enthusiastic—he even commands us to shout (v. 1 NASB)—and wholly focused on the Lord. The verb "come" in verse 2 means "to go to meet God face-to-face, to be in His presence." Believers today do this through Jesus Christ (Heb. 10:19–25). We should be thankful in our praise as we extol the Lord for His great mercies. (On God the Rock, see 18:2.)

Why should we praise Him? Because He is great and above the false gods of this world (v. 3; 81:8; 92:8; 93:4; 96:4; Ex. 18:11). After His ascension to heaven, Jesus Christ was enthroned "far above all" (Acts 2:33; Eph. 1:19–23; Phil. 2:9–11; Col. 1:15–18), and nothing can separate us from His love (Rom. 8:37–39). He is our "great God and Savior" (Titus 2:13) and we should delight in praising Him. But our God is also the Creator of the universe and controls all things (vv. 4–5). The depths of the sea and the earth, and the heights of the mountains all belong to Him, and He knows what is going on in the waters as well as on the earth. The pagan nations had gods and goddesses for different parts of creation—the seas, the land, the mountain peaks, the sun, moon and stars, the storms, the crops—but our God is King over all. No wonder we praise Him!

## Bow Down and Worship the Lord (vv. 6–7a)

Praise means looking up, but worship means bowing down. Alas, some people who enjoy lifting their hands and shouting do not enjoy bowing their knees and submitting. True worship is much deeper than communal praise, for worship involves realizing the awesomeness of God and experiencing the fear of the Lord and a deeper love for Him. Too often, Christian "praise" is nothing but religious entertainment and it never moves into spiritual enrichment in the presence of the Lord. Our singing must give way to silence as we bow before the Lord. He alone is Jehovah, the LORD, the covenant-making and covenant-keeping

God. He is our Maker and our Shepherd. (See 23 and John 10.) Jubilation has its place only if it becomes adoration and we are prostrate before the Lord in total submission, "lost in wonder, love, and praise." What a remarkable miracle of grace that we sinners should be called "His people." He made us, He saved us, and He cares for us! Why should we hesitate to fall before Him in total surrender?

### Hear and Obey the Lord (vv. 7b–11)

The Word of God is a vital part of Christian worship, especially in this age when inventing clever new worship forms is a common practice and novelty is replacing theology. Hearing and heeding God's Word must be central if our worship, private or corporate, is to be truly Christian. It isn't enough for God to hear my voice; I must hear His voice as the Word of God is read, preached, and taught. The Scriptures written centuries ago have authority today, and we have no right to ignore them, change them, or disobey them. We are to respond to God's Word *now*, when we hear it, and not just later in the week when we review our sermon notes or listen to the message on cassette tape. How tragic when worshipers go home with full notebooks and empty hearts! (See Heb. 3:7—4:13 where this passage is applied to the church today, warning us not to harden our hearts against the Lord.) *The way we treat the Word of God is the way we treat the God of the Word.* Jesus admonishes us to take heed *that* we hear (Matt. 13:9), take heed *what* we hear (Mark 4:24), and take heed *how* we hear (Luke 8:18).

The writer reached back and cited two tragic events in the history of Israel—the nation's complaining at Rephidim (Ex. 17:1–7) and their unbelief and disobedience at Kadesh Barnea (Num. 13–14). The Jews had seen God's wonderful works in Egypt, especially His defeat of the Egyptian army when He opened and closed the Red Sea—but they refused to trust Him for their daily needs. No sooner were they liberated from Egypt than they complained that they were hungry, so He sent them the manna, the bread of heaven (Ex. 16). When they arrived at

Rephidim, the people complained again because they were thirsty (Ex. 17:1–7). Instead of trusting God, they blamed God and His servant Moses. God graciously gave them water out of the rock, but Moses commemorated the event with two new names for the site: Meribah means "strife, quarreling, contention" and Massah means "testing." (See also Num. 20:1–13.) Instead of trusting God, the people had contended with God and had even tempted Him by their arrogant attitude and words. He could have sent immediate judgment, and they dared Him to act.

Israel spent a year and two months at Sinai (Num. 10:11) and then departed for Kadesh Barnea, the gateway into Canaan (Num. 13–14). Here they refused to trust the Lord and obey His orders to enter the land and claim their inheritance. In spite of all they had seen Him do, the Israelites hardened their hearts and refused to do God's will. God judged His people at Kadesh Barnea and consigned them to thirty-eight years in the wilderness while the older generation died off. It was the world's longest funeral march. "They shall not enter into My rest" (v. 11; Num. 14:26–38). The writer of Hebrews used this event to warn Christians not to harden their hearts and thereby fail to claim what God had for them to do, to receive, and to enjoy. God has a perfect plan for each of His children (Eph. 2:10), and we claim that inheritance by faith in God's Word, the kind of faith that leads to obedience.

In Moses' day, God's "rest" was the land of Canaan, where the Jews would do no more wandering (Ex. 33:14; Deut. 12:9–10; Josh. 1:13, 15). But Hebrews 4 broadens the meaning of "rest" to include the salvation rest and inheritance we have in Christ (Matt. 11:28–30; Eph. 1:3, 11, 15–23) and the future eternal "Sabbath rest" in glory (Heb. 4:9; Rev. 14:13). Hebrews 1–4 is God's admonition to the church today to live by faith, and "faith comes by hearing, and hearing by the word of God" (Rom. 10:17 NKJV). Because the Jews refused to hear His Word but hardened their hearts instead, God was disgusted with His people, and all the people twenty years old and older died during that wilderness journey. We harden our hearts when we see what God can do but refuse to trust Him so He can do it for us. We fail to cultivate a godly heart that fears and honors the Lord. It is a grievous sin to ask for the gifts (food, water, etc.) but ignore the Giver, and the consequences are painful.

## Psalm 96

This psalm is found in another version in 1 Chronicles 16:23–33. The psalm in Chronicles is a combination of quotations from 96, 105 (1–15 = 16:8–22), and 106 (1, 47–48 = 16:35–36). The Jewish worship leaders, led by God's Spirit, felt free to excerpt and combine portions of existing psalms to construct songs for special occasions. Some students believe Psalm 96 was used in the dedication of the second temple when the Jews returned to Judah from their exile in Babylon. As you read the psalm, you can see how it would apply to the weak Jewish remnant surrounded by strong Gentile nations. The psalm also looks ahead to the kingdom age when Messiah shall reign and the Gentile nations will worship the God of Israel. The psalmist gives four commands to God's people and backs up each command with a reason for their obedience.

### Sing! The News Is Good! (vv. 1–3)

Three times we are commanded to sing to the Lord, and this parallels the three times in verses 7–8 that the psalmist commands us to "give" ("ascribe" NASB, NIV) glory to Him. (For "a new song," see 33:3.) A new experience of God's blessing, a new truth discovered in the Word, a new beginning after a crisis, a new open door for service—all of these can make an old song new or give us a new song from the Lord. This call to worship is not extended to Israel alone, but also to the Gentile nations (see also vv. 3, 7, 9, 11, 13). One day, when Jesus reigns on earth, all nations will come to Jerusalem to worship Him (Isa. 2:1–4). It will be a time when the glory of God will be revealed to all peoples (vv. 3, 7–8; Gen. 12:1–3; 22:18; Isa. 60:1–3). In the Greek translation of the Old Testament, "show forth" (v. 2; "proclaim" NASB, NIV) is the word used in the New Testament for "preaching the good news" and gives us the English word "evangelize." The good news of the victory of Jesus Christ gives us something to sing about, for He is the only Savior and will save all who trust Him (John 14:6; John 4:22; Acts 4:12; Rom. 10:1–15).

### Praise! Our God Is Great! (vv. 4–6)

The gods of the nations were "no-gods," for the word translated "idols" in verse 5 means "things that are nothing, things that are weak and worthless." "We know that an idol is nothing in the world" (1 Cor. 8:4 NKJV). It was Jehovah who created the universe, and His great glory rested in His sanctuary in Jerusalem (Ex. 40:34–38; 1 Kings 8:10–11; Rom. 9:4). The presence of this glory brought the divine splendor, majesty, and strength to the people. The ark of the covenant in the Holy of Holies was the throne of God, and He ruled over His people. (See 21:5; 45:3; 104:1.) Both in His sanctuary in heaven and His sanctuary on earth, God was enthroned in glory and power. How we ought to praise Him!

### Worship! The Lord Is Worthy! (vv. 7–9)

When praising the Lord, the Jews lifted their hands and voices and looked up, but in their worship, they reverently bowed down. (See 29:1–2.) The invitation went out to all nations to come to God's sanctuary, bring a sacrifice, and worship Him. (See 65:4; 84:2, 10; 92:13; 100:4; 116:19; 135:2.) "Fear before him" (v. 9) is translated "tremble before him" in the NIV and NASB (see 29:9; 97:4; 114:7). Just as the Jewish priests had to dress in the garments required by the Lord (Ex. 28), so God's people must worship with "clean hands and a pure heart" (24:4) and experience cleansing from the Lord before they worship Him (Heb. 10:19–25). The only beauty that God accepts is "the beauty of holiness," the righteousness of Christ imputed to us by faith (Rom. 4) and the righteousness we live as we obey Him in the power of the Spirit (Rom. 8:1–4). We approach God only through Christ's righteousness, but we please God when we are obedient children.

*Rejoice! The King Is Coming! (vv. 10–13)*

"The Lord reigns" (v. 10; see 93:1) can also be translated, "The Lord has become King" (see Rev. 11:17), referring to the day Jesus will sit on David's throne and rule over the nations (Luke 1:26–33; Rev. 19:11–16). Only then will there be true justice on the earth (Isa. 9:6–7; 32:1, 16; 42:1–4). Today, creation is in bondage to corruption and futility because of Adam's sin, but when the children of God are fully redeemed at Christ's return, creation will also be set free (Rom. 8:18–23). No wonder the psalmist described the joy of heaven and earth, the seas and the dry land, and even the trees of the earth as they welcome their Creator, and then there will be justice on the earth (7:6–8; 9:7–8; 98:7–9; Isa. 55:12). "The whole creation is on tiptoe to see the wonderful sight of the sons of God coming into their own" (Rom. 8:19 PH). Rejoice!

## Psalm 97

The psalmist picked up the theme in 96:13 and described the King coming to judge His enemies and reward His people. In 95, the emphasis was on God's people, and 96 focused our attention on the nations of the world. This psalm combines both themes and tells us that Jehovah is "the Lord Most High" in heaven (v. 9 NASB) who has all things under His control. Believers today see Jesus as God's exalted King (see Acts 2:32–33; 5:31; Eph. 1:17–23; Phil. 2:5–11; Heb. 1:3; 1 Peter 3:22; Rev. 3:21).

### The Lord Is Exalted on His Throne (vv. 1–2)

No matter what the circumstances around us or the feelings within us, "the Lord reigns" (93:1; 96:10; 99:1; 117:1), and He reigns over all the earth (vv. 1, 4, 5, 9; 96:1, 9, 11, 13; 98:3, 4, 9). His sovereign authority reaches beyond the land of Israel to the farthest islands and coastlands, places that the Jews had never visited. God's desire was that Israel be a light to the Gentiles (Gen. 12:1–3; Isa. 42:6; 49:6) to show them the truth of the one true and living God, just as the church today is to be a light to the world by sharing the gospel message (Luke 2:32; Acts 13:47). Knowing that "the Lord God omnipotent reigns" (Rev. 19:6) ought to bring joy to our hearts and our worship (vv. 1, 8, 11, 12; see 96:11). Though His throne is surrounded by clouds and darkness, and we do not fully understand the mysteries of His providence, we know that His throne rests on righteousness and justice and that "the Judge of all the earth [will] do right" (Gen. 18:25). The psalm begins with darkness (v. 1) but ends with light for the righteous (v. 11).

### The Lord Is Exalted over His Enemies (vv. 3–6)

The picture is that of a storm sweeping across the land and destroying everything in its path (see 18:9–12; 29; Hab. 3:3–15). The image of the storm takes us back to the exodus of Israel from Egypt (68:7–8; 77:15–20) as well as Israel's meeting with God at Sinai (Ex. 19:9, 16–19; 20:21; 24:15–16; Deut. 4:11; 5:22; Heb. 12:18–21). The storm also speaks of the future "day of the Lord" when God will judge the nations of the world (Isa. 2:10–21; 8:22; Joel 2:2; Amos 5:16–20; Zeph. 1:7–18). The fire and lightning remind us that God is a consuming fire (Deut. 4:24; 32:22; Heb. 12:29). His judgments bring Him glory and manifest His holiness to a godless world. The name "Lord of all the earth" (v. 5) is found in only four other places in the Old Testament: on the lips of Joshua before Israel crossed the Jordan River (Josh. 3:11, 13), and from the prophets Micah (4:13) and Zechariah (4:14; 6:5). (See also 50:12.) From the beginning of Israel's national history, the people knew that Jehovah was not a "tribal god" like the false gods of the neighboring nations, but the Lord of all the earth (Ex. 19:5; Deut. 10:14. Jesus used this title when speaking to His Father [Luke 10:21]).

### The Lord Is Exalted over the False Gods (vv. 7–9)

In the ancient Near East, when one nation conquered another, people interpreted the victory to mean that the gods of the conquering nation were greater than those of the defeated nation. But the Jews were taught that Jehovah was the God of all the earth and that the idols were nothing (see 95:3; 96:5). God allowed Babylon to defeat the Jews because the Jews had greatly sinned against the Lord, not because Babylon's gods were stronger than Jehovah. The defeat of Babylon by the Medes and Persians was the work of the Lord and not of their false gods, for the prophets predicted this event would occur (Isa. 45–47; Jer. 50–51; Dan. 2:36–38; 7:1–5). Israel's release from captivity was proof that Jehovah was in control (Jer. 25:1–14; 29:1–14). God's victories over the idolatrous nations put the idols and their worshipers to shame (v. 7; see Isa. 45:15–17). No wonder the people of Israel rejoiced, for God's victories were evidence that He alone is "Most High over all the earth" (v. 8 NASB; 83:18). People may not bow down before ugly man-made idols today, but there are certainly plenty of false gods for them to worship—money, power, possessions, sex, pleasures, recognition—for whatever people serve and sacrifice for, that is what they worship (Matt. 4:10).

### The Lord Is Exalted among His People (vv. 10–12)

God's people are those who love Him and do not turn to idols for help (91:14; 1 Cor. 8:1–3). But if we love Him who is holy, we will hate that which is unholy (34:14; 36:4; 37:27; 119:104; Prov. 8:13; Rom. 12:9). In this paragraph, God's people are called "saints" or "godly ones," "the righteous," "the upright in heart," and all of these names speak of a life devoted to God. We should love Him, obey Him ("hate evil"), rejoice in Him, and give thanks to Him for all His mercies. After all, He protects His people, delivers them, gives them light for their path, and puts gladness into their hearts. What more could they want?

The image in verse 11 is that of the sower; the Lord plants light like seeds so that His people will not always walk in darkness, and what He plants will eventually bear fruit. "Sowing" is a frequent metaphor in Scripture for the deeds of both God and people (112:4; Prov. 11:18; Hos. 8:7; 10:12; James 3:18). The psalm begins with a universal revelation of God's glory (vv. 2–6), with dramatic flashes of lightning, but it ends with His light quietly shining on the paths of His people. Some see the image as that of the dawn, with the morning light diffused along the ground as though the Lord were planting it like seed. But God also sows joy with that light, for when we walk in the light, we also have joy in the Lord (16:11; Isa. 60:1–5). God's people have their dark days when life is difficult, but there are always seeds of light and joy to accompany us along the way. Is there any reason why we should not be rejoicing *now*?

## Psalm 98

From this psalm. Isaac Watts found the inspiration for his popular hymn "Joy to the World," often classified as a Christmas carol but more accurately identified as a "kingdom hymn." Watts described Christ's *second* advent and not His first, the Messianic kingdom and not the manger. The parallels to 96 are obvious but the psalms are not identical. This psalm was written to praise the Lord for a great victory over Israel's enemies ("salvation," vv. 1–3), perhaps the victory of the Medes and Persians over Babylon (Dan. 5) that led to the return of the Jewish exiles to their land (Ezra 1). Some of the vocabulary in the psalm reflects the language of Isaiah the prophet, who in chapters 40–66 of his book wrote about the "exodus" of the Jews from Babylon (44:23; 49:13; 51:3; 52:9–10; 59:16; 63:5). But the psalm also speaks of a future judgment (vv. 7–9). The psalmist saw in the destruction of ancient Babylon a picture of God's judgment of end-time Babylon (Rev. 17–18).

### A Marvelous Salvation (vv. 1–3)

The focus in this section is on the Jewish people and the wonderful new demonstration of God's power they had seen. It was so great it demanded a new song from His people (see 33:3; 96:1). The picture of God as warrior disturbs those who seem to forget that a holy God cannot compromise with sin. (See 68:1–10; 77:16–19; and Ex. 15:1–2.) The cross declares not only that God loves sinners (Rom. 5:8), but also that God hates and opposes sin (Matt. 12:22–30; Col. 2:15). Since God is a spirit (John 4:24), He does not have a body, so the references to His hand and arm are metaphorical (17:7; 18:35; 20:6; 44:3; 60:5; 77:10; Ex. 15:6, 11–12; Isa. 52:10; 59:16; 63:5). What God did for Israel was a witness to the Gentile nations and a vivid demonstration of His faithfulness to His covenant and His love for His chosen people. But surely the writer was looking beyond a mere local victory, for he wrote about the witness of this event to the nations (v. 2), the earth (vv. 3, 4, 9), and the world (vv. 7, 9). It appears that the psalm points ahead to the return of Jesus Christ. (See Isa. 52:1–10.)

### A Joyous Celebration (vv. 4–6)

The command went out to all nations of the earth to shout joyfully in praise to the Lord for what He had done for Israel, and the emphasis is on the King (v. 6). Again we are reminded of what the prophet Isaiah wrote concerning the Jewish "exodus" from Babylon (Isa. 14:7; 44:23; 49:13; 52:9; 54:1; 55:12). But the shout was only the beginning, for singing and the playing of instruments followed. Loud music played and sung with enthusiasm was characteristics of Jewish worship (2 Chron. 5:11–14; Ezra 3:10–13; Neh. 12:27–43).

### A Glorious Expectation (vv. 7–9)

The psalmist has written of the Lord as Deliverer and King, and now he presents Him as the Judge who will one day come and deal with the world as He once dealt with the kingdom of Babylon. He had seen Israel delivered from bondage (vv. 1–3) and he had heard the nations of the world praising the Lord (vv. 4–6). Now he heard all creation eagerly anticipating the Lord's return, for the second advent of Jesus sets creation free from the bondage of sin caused by Adam's fall (Rom. 8:18–25). The lapping of the waves of the sea on the shore sounds to him like a prayer to the Lord and the flowing of the river like applause in response to the announcement, "The King is coming!" The play of the wind on the mountains sounded like a song of praise. (See Isa. 55:12.) All nature combined to sing, "Even so come, Lord Jesus" (Rev. 22:20). There will come a day when all wrongs will be righted and all sins will be judged, and the Judge will bring justice and equity to the earth.

# Psalm 99

This is the sixth of the "royal psalms" (93, 95–100), all of which magnify the sovereign rule of Jehovah the King. Like 93 and 97, it opens with "The Lord reigns," and it emphasizes that Jehovah is exalted above all the nations (v. 2) and not just Israel. The psalmist describes the throne of the Lord and encourages the people to exalt the Lord as they worship Him (vv. 5, 9).

### An Awesome Throne (vv. 1–3)

Jehovah sits upon the throne in heaven (9:11; 110:2; 146:10), but in the psalmist's day, He was also enthroned on the mercy seat in the Holy of Holies of the sanctuary on Mount Zion (see 80:1; 1 Sam. 4:4; 2 Sam. 6:2; 2 Kings 19:15 [Isa. 37:16]; 1 Chron. 13:6). It was there that God's glory rested, and from there God spoke to Moses and ruled the nation of Israel (Num. 7:89). God chose the Jews to be His vehicle for telling the Gentile nations about the true and living God, and God chose Mount Zion to be His dwelling place. The prophet Isaiah saw the heavenly throne (Isa. 6) and so did the prophet Ezekiel (Ezek. 1). The name LORD is used seven times in this psalm, for God made His covenant with Israel alone and they were His special people. "Salvation is of the Jews" (John 4:22). When the Gentiles beheld what God did for Israel, they should have trembled with awe and put their trust in Him (96:9; 114:7). God's throne is awesome because He is holy (Lev. 11:44–45; 1 Peter 1:15–16). "The Holy One of Israel" is a name found thirty times in the book of Isaiah. The word "holy" means "separate, set apart, totally different." God's nature is "wholly other," yet He was willing to dwell with His people and meet their needs. (Note the repetition of "he is holy" [vv. 3, 5, 9], and see Isa. 6:3.)

### A Just Throne (vv. 4–5)

The Lord ruled His people of Israel through the kings in the Davidic dynasty (Deut. 17:14–20). The Lord is perfectly righteous in His character and just in His actions, and He wanted the throne of Israel to be just. A leader who loves justice will have the strength to obey God's Word and will seek to please Him.

Romans 13 teaches us that civil authorities are the ministers of God, not just the employees of the government. In Scripture, the "footstool" (v. 5) could be the ark of the covenant (1 Chron. 28:2), the sanctuary of God (132:7; Isa. 60:13; Ezek. 43:7), the city of Jerusalem (Lam. 2:1), or even planet earth (Isa. 66:1; Matt. 5:35). Solomon's throne had a footstool of gold (2 Chron. 9:18), and visitors would kneel there in homage before him. The sanctuary on Mount Zion was God's chosen dwelling place, and the ark in the sanctuary was His appointed throne, so when the Jewish pilgrims came to Jerusalem, they were worshiping at His footstool. Note that verse 5 is the central verse of the psalm and emphasizes the three major themes of the psalm: God's holiness and our privilege and responsibility to worship Him and exalt Him (see vv. 3 and 9).

### A Gracious Throne (vv. 6–9)

You could not approach the throne of the king of Persia unless he held out his scepter and gave you permission (Est. 4:10–11), but access to God's throne is available to His children through Jesus Christ (Heb. 10:19–25). Under the old covenant, God provided priests who ministered at the altar and were mediators between His needy people and their Lord, but today Jesus Christ is the Mediator (1 Tim. 2:5) who constantly intercedes for us (Rom. 8:34; Heb. 7:25). To the lost sinner, God's throne is a throne of judgment, but to the believer, it is a throne of grace (Heb. 4:14–16), and we can come to Him with our worship and praise as well as our burdens and needs.

Often Moses, Aaron, and Samuel had to intercede for the disobedient people of Israel, and the Lord heard them and answered (Ex. 17:1; 32–33; Num. 14:11–38; 16:48; 1 Sam. 7, 12). God named Moses and Samuel as great men of prayer (Jer. 15:1). God's gracious ministry to His old covenant people is still available to His new covenant family: He speaks to us from His Word (Ex. 33:9; Num. 12:5–6; 1 Sam. 3:3), hears our prayers and answers, disciplines us when we sin, and forgives us when we confess (1 John 1:9). How many times the Lord forgave Israel and gave them another opportunity to serve Him! (103:13–18). The throne and the altar were not far apart in the sanctuary (see Isa. 6:1–7).

How should we respond to this kind of a God who sits on this kind of a throne? We must worship Him (vv. 5, 9), praise and exalt Him (vv. 3, 5, 9), and remember that He is holy (vv. 3, 5, 9). We must pray to Him and seek to glorify His name by our obedience and service. The next psalm describes all of this and climaxes the "royal psalm" series.

## Psalm 100

For centuries, Christian congregations have sung William Kethe's paraphrase of this psalm, wedded to the beloved tune "Old Hundredth." First published in 1561, the words summarize the message of the psalm and help the worshipers give thanks to the Lord. Sometimes the traditional "Doxology" ("Praise God from whom all blessings flow") by Thomas Ken is sung as the last verse. The psalm is a fitting climax to the collection of "royal psalms" (93, 95–100) and sums up their emphasis on God's sovereign rule, His goodness to His people, the responsibility of all nations to acknowledge Him, and the importance of God's people exalting and worshiping Him. (See 95:1–2, 6–7.)

We are admonished in Ephesians 5:18 to be filled with the Spirit of God, and the evidence of this fullness is that we are joyful (5:19), thankful (5:20), and submissive (5:21–6:9). In Colossians 3:16–25, we are instructed to be filled with the Word of God, and when we are, we will be joyful (3:16), thankful (3:17), and submissive (3:20–25). These three characteristics of the believer controlled by God's Spirit and God's Word—and they go together—are presented in this wonderful psalm of thanksgiving.

### Joyful (vv. 1–2)

We can easily understand the people of Israel shouting joyfully in praise to their great God (vv. 3, 5), but the psalmist calls for all the nations of the earth to praise Him. This is a recurring theme in the "royal psalms" (97:1, 6; 98:2–4, 7; 99:1–2), for it was Israel's responsibility to introduce the Gentiles to the true and living God. The church has been commissioned to take the good news into all the world (Matt. 28:18–20; Mark 16:15), and it will be a glorious day when God's people gather at His throne from "all nations, tribes, peoples and tongues" (Rev. 7:9). But our shouting ought to lead to serving Him, for He is the only true God (Deut. 6:13; 10:12; Josh. 24:15–24). Worship leads to service, and true service is worship. If we sing in the Spirit and with understanding, our songs are received in heaven as sacrifices to the Lord (Heb. 13:15).

### Submissive (v. 3)

The verb "know" means "to know by experience." It also carries the meaning of "acknowledge." What we have experienced in our hearts we openly confess to others and bear witness of our glorious God. (See 1 Kings 18:39.) The phrase "made us" means much more than "He created us," for He also created the nations that do not know Him. It means "Jehovah constituted us as a nation, His chosen people." (See 95:6–7; 149:2; Deut. 32:6, 15; Isa. 29:23; 60:21.) The phrase "not we ourselves" can also be translated "and we are his." This connects with the next statement, "We are his people ..." (see Isa. 43:1). The image of God's people as a flock of sheep is frequently found in Scripture (74:1; 77:20; 78:52; 79:13; 80:1; 95:7; Gen. 48:15; 49:24; Num. 27:17; Isa. 40:11; John 10; 21:16–17; Heb. 13:20–21; 1 Peter 2:25; 5:1–4). This verse is a simple statement of faith: Jehovah is God, Creator, Redeemer and Shepherd, and we are submitted to Him. If the sheep do not submit to their shepherd, they will stray into danger.

### Thankful (vv. 4–5)

The procession of worshipers has now reached the gates of the sanctuary, and they burst out in songs of praise. Why? Because of the Lord's goodness, mercy (lovingkindness), and faithfulness. (See parallels in 106:1, 107:1, 118:1, and 136:1–3; and see also 1 Chron. 16:34 and 2 Chron. 5:13.) "O, taste and see that the Lord is good" (37:8), and He gives that which is good (85:12; Rom. 8:28). The word "truth" is a form of the Hebrew word *amen* and refers to God's faithfulness and reliability. It is the same word used in Exodus 17:12 to describe Moses's hands "staying steady," and in Genesis 15:6 it is translated "believed" ("relied on," literally "said amen to the Lord"). (See Deut. 7:9 and 32:4.) From generation to generation, the Lord can be trusted (90:1; Ex. 34:5–7). It is significant that the fathers' and mothers' worship today will have an important influence on their children tomorrow.

If we are controlled by the Holy Spirit of God and the holy Word of God, we will reveal it in the way we worship God. Instead of imitating the world, we will be led by the Word and the Spirit to be joyful in the Lord, submissive to the Lord, and thankful to the Lord, and the world will see the difference. Finally, note that a spirit of thanksgiving helps us overcome some of the "sins in good standing" that too often invade our lives: complaining (v. 1), idolatry (v. 2), pride (v. 3), and ingratitude (v. 4). It was when our first parents became "unthankful" that the human race began that terrible descent into sin and judgment (Rom. 1:18–32; note v. 21). Instead of being thankful for what they had, Adam and Eve believed Satan's lie that the Lord was holding out on them (Gen. 3:1—"every tree"), and this led to their sin. A thankful spirit is a triumphant spirit.

## Psalm 101

When David became king, first in Hebron and then at Jerusalem, he inherited a divided land and a discouraged people whose spiritual life was at low ebb. Asaph described the situation in 78:56–72 and named David as God's answer to Israel's problems. Everything rises and falls with leadership, but many of King Saul's officers were fawning flattering "toadies" who were unable to work with a man like David. Once David was established on the throne in Jerusalem, he had a consuming desire to bring the ark of God back to the sanctuary so that God's throne might near his throne. His question in verse 2, "When will you come to me?" reflects this desire. The ark had been in the house of Abinidab for many years (1 Sam. 6:1–7:2) and then in the house of Obed-Edom after David's aborted attempt to relocate it (2 Sam.

6:1–11). This psalm of dedication was probably written early in his reign in Jerusalem. We could accurately call this psalm "Leadership 101" because in it David spells out the essentials for successful leadership in the work of God.

### Devotion to God (vv. 1–2)

The king of Israel was God's representative on earth and was expected to rule the way God commanded. (Deut. 17:14–20, and see 2 Kings 23:1–3.) The emphasis here is on the heart, for the heart of leadership is the leader's devotion to the Lord. This devotion results in a life lived blamelessly to the glory of the Lord. David was determined to be that kind of leader, and he opened the psalm with "I will" and repeated this promise eight more times. He made it clear that there must be no separation between the leader's personal life and his or her official life, the private and the public. David wanted his reign to be characterized by lovingkindness (mercy) and justice, for this is the way God rules the world (89:14; Isa. 16:5).

"Blameless" does not mean "sinless," for David was a sinner like the rest of us. However, unlike David, we have not seen the account of our sins written down for all the world to read! "Blameless" is another word for integrity, cultivating wholeness of heart and singleness of mind, instead of a double heart and a double mind (15:2; 18:23, 25; 26:1, 11; 78:70–72; 86:11; Gen. 6:9; 17:1). Believers today should have integrity whether we are leaders or not (119:1; Matt. 5:8; Eph. 1:4; Phil. 1:10; 2:15). Faith is living without scheming, and the way of faith is "the blameless way" (v. 2 NASB). David vowed to live a godly life in his "house" (palace) and have an administration characterized by mercy, justice, and integrity.

### Discernment (vv. 3–5)

David moved from the heart of the leader to the hearts of the sinners (vv. 4–5) and turned the emphasis to the leader's eyes and what he saw (vv. 3, 5, 6, 7 ["tarry in my sight" KJV]). The heart and the eyes work together, for what the heart loves, the eyes will seek and find (Eccl. 2:10; Jer. 22:17). This section

42

parallels Psalm 15 where David described the ideal worshiper whom God welcomes to His dwelling. David did not want anyone in his official family who was not walking with the Lord. "I will set no worthless thing before my eyes" (v. 3a NASB) means more than beholding vile things "the lust of the eyes" (1 John 2:16). It also means setting worthless goals and seeking to reach them. Leaders must set the best goals, guided by God's will, for outlook determines outcome. The spiritual leader not only sets the best goals but he or she also uses the best methods for achieving those goals (v. 3b). "Faithless" people are apostates, people who have abandoned God's way for their own way and the world's way. David had his eyes on the faithful, not the faithless (v. 6). A "perverse heart" is a twisted heart, one that does not conform to God's will (Prov. 3:32; 6:16–19; 11:20), and a twisted heart produces a deceitful tongue (v. 7; Matt. 12:34–35; see Prov. 17:20). The word translated "proud" in verse 5 means "wide, expanded" and describes people who are inflated with their own importance. It is important that leaders cultivate humility and lead by being servants, not dictators.

### Decision (vv. 6–8)

We have moved from the leader's heart to the leader's eyes, and now we look at the leader's will. The repeated "I will" statements in the psalm give evidence of David's determination to serve God and God's people successfully and be a man of decision. He would not make excuses and he would not delay making decisions. But some of those decisions would be difficult to make and perhaps more difficult to implement. He wanted associates who were not defiled by sin, whose walk was blameless, and who would treat people with fairness. He knew that no king could build a lasting government on lies (31:5; 43:3; 57:10). Deception is the devil's tool, and Satan goes to work whenever a lie moves in (2 Cor. 11:1–3). Eastern kings often administered justice in the mornings at the city gate (2 Sam. 15:1–2; Jer. 21:12), so David promised to hear these cases patiently, consider them carefully, and render judgment wisely. He vowed to God that he would punish offenders according to God's law, silencing the liars and expelling the evildoers. Jerusalem was known as "the city of God," (46:4; 48:1) "the city of the great King," (48:2) and the city God loved the most (87:1–3), and David did not want to blemish that reputation.

Was David successful in maintaining the high standard of this declaration? No, not completely; but what leader besides Jesus Christ has ever maintained an unblemished record? David failed in his own family. His sin with Bathsheba set a bad example for his sons and daughters (2 Sam. 11–12), and David failed to discipline Amnon and Absalom for their sins (2 Sam. 13–15). He had problems with his generals Joab and Abishai, and his trusted counselor Ahithophel betrayed him. But David reigned for forty years, during which time he expanded the borders of the kingdom, defeated Israel's enemies, gathered the wealth used to build the temple, wrote the psalms, and established the dynasty that eventually brought Jesus Christ into the world. Like us, he had his weaknesses and failings, but over all, he sought to honor the Lord and be a good leader. Jerusalem is known as "the city of David" and Jesus as "the Son of David." Could any compliment be higher than that?

## Psalm 102

This is both a penitential psalm (see 6) and a Messianic psalm (vv. 25–27 = Heb. 1:10–12). The anonymous author probably wrote it long after the destruction of Jerusalem (vv. 8, 14, 16), about the time he thought Jeremiah's prophecy of the seventy-year captivity was about to be fulfilled (v. 13; Jer. 25:11–12; 29:10; see Dan. 9:2). According to the title, the psalmist was afflicted and faint (61:2; 77:3; 142:3; 143:4) and burdened to present his complaint ("lament" NIV) to the Lord. He was groaning in distress (vv. 2, 5) and weeping over the ruins of Jerusalem (v. 9). His opening prayer in verses 1–2 draws from a number of other psalms, giving us an example of what it means to pray the Word of God. (See 18:16; 27:9; 31:2; 37:20; 59:16; 69:17; 88:2.)

As believers face and deal with the painful crises that come to us, if we are to overcome and glorify God, we must keep three assurances before us.

### The Changing Circumstances of Life (vv. 1–11)

The longer we live, the more evidence we see that *things will change*. The Greek philosopher Heraclitus wrote, "There is nothing permanent except change," a statement that John F. Kennedy paraphrased as, "Everything changes but change itself." There are the normal changes of life, from birth to maturity to death, but there are also providential changes that God sends for our good and His glory. Many Jewish leaders in the days of Jeremiah the prophet thought that God would never allow Judah to be captured and Jerusalem and the temple destroyed (Jer. 7), but the Babylonian army did all three. They also took prisoners to Babylon and left only the poorest of the people to care for the land. Because of their rebellion against the law of God, Israel was left without a king, priesthood, temple, or sacrifice. Instead of the Lord's face shining upon them with blessing (Num. 6:25), His face was turned away from them in judgment (27:9; 59:17; Gen. 43:3, 5; Deut. 31:17–18).

Whether we are suffering because of our sins, or because we stand up for the Lord, or simply because we need to be better equipped for service, these changes are not pleasant. The psalmist recorded his personal plight in a series of vivid pictures. With his days as flimsy and temporary as drifting smoke, and his frame burning with fever (31:10; 32:3; 42:10), he was like a man in a furnace. His heart was like the cut and withered grass (vv. 4, 9; 90:4–5; Job 19:20; Lam. 4:8), paining him so much that he forgot to eat. When he did eat, the food tasted like ashes and his drink like tears (v. 9; 42:3; 80:5; Lam. 3:16). Therefore, he became a living skeleton that could only groan because of his wretched situation (v. 5). He compared himself to the unclean birds (Lev. 11:17–18) that lived solitary lives amid the ruins of the city. He was awake all night, a lonely man, like a sparrow bereft of his mate and chirping his lament on the roof. The enemy officers showed no sympathy but used his name in their curses (v. 8). It was as though God's hand picked him up and threw him on the trash heap, like a piece of discarded junk (v. 10; 51:11; 71:9; 147;17; Isa. 22:17–18). Like the evening shadows as the sun goes down, his life kept changing, *but his days had no substance.* Then the darkness fell and the long hard night lay before him. (See Deut. 28:66–67.)

One of the first steps toward personal peace and victory is to accept the fact that there will be changes in life, and how we respond will determine what these changes do to us and for us. The psalmist responded by turning to the Lord for help.

### The Unchanged Covenant of God (vv. 12–22)

"But you, O Lord" marked a change in the psalmist's outlook as he turned from himself and his problems to behold by faith the Lord enthroned in heaven (see 93:2; 97:2; 99:1; 113:5; Lam. 5:19). The throne of David was gone and would not be claimed until the Son of David came to earth (Luke 1:30–33), but the throne of God in heaven was secure. Judah and Jerusalem were experiencing shame, but God's "memorial name" of great renown would not change. One day the nations would respect that name (v. 15) and praise that name in a new Jerusalem (v. 21). From generation to generation, His people had known and revered that name and the Lord had not failed them, but they failed the Lord. He had made a wonderful covenant with His people (Lev. 25–26; Deut. 28–30) and had not changed it. If His people obeyed His law, He would bless them, but if they disobeyed and turned to idols, He would chasten them. Either way, He would show His love and faithfulness.

The writer was confident that God would arise and rescue Zion, for it was time for His promises to be fulfilled (Jer. 25:11–12; 29:10). Even more, The Lord loved Zion more than the Jewish people did, and they revered her very dust and stones! (see 46:4; 48; 69:35–36; 87:1–5; 132:13; 137). Even more, the restoration of Zion means the glory of the Lord (vv. 15–16, 21–22), and this involves the salvation of the Gentile nations.

When the Jewish exiles were released from captivity in Babylon and allowed to return to Judah, this was a witness to the surrounding nations that Jehovah was on the throne and guiding in the destiny of His people. And what about the future generations in Israel? The Lord made His covenant with them as well, and He will fulfill it (vv. 18, 28). God's compassion, God's covenant, God's glory, and God's people are all a part of the future of Jerusalem! As Alexander Maclaren wrote, "Zion cannot die while Zion's God lives." Surely the Lord will keep His promises and His glory will return to Zion (Ezek. 40–48). He hears the prayers of His people and will one day answer them. Israel and the Gentile nations will assemble and worship the Lord together (vv. 21–22; Isa. 2:1–4).

*The Changeless Character of God (vv. 23–28)*
The psalmist was afraid he would die in mid-life and never see the restoration of Judah, Jerusalem, and the temple. (See Isa. 38:10.) The eternal God would remain forever, but frail humans have only a brief time on earth (90:1–12). This passage (vv. 25–27) is quoted in Hebrews 1:10–12 and applied to Jesus Christ, which reminds us that it is in Him that these promises will be fulfilled. He is God and He is the same from generation to generation (Heb. 13:5–8). Leaders come and go, cities and buildings appear and vanish, but the Lord is the same and never abdicates His throne. God's eternality reminds us of our own frailty and the transitory nature of our lives, but it also reminds us that His promises and purposes will be fulfilled. The psalmist closed his prayer by remembering the future generations, for though he did not see his prayer answered in his day, he knew that the answer would come. May we today be concerned about God's work on earth and the future generations who will serve Him after we are gone! May the future not weep because we have not been faithful!

# Psalm 103
The four psalms that close Book Four of the book of Psalms (90–106) emphasize praise to the Lord for several reasons: His

benefits to His people (103), His care of His creation (104), His wonderful acts on behalf of Israel (105), and His longsuffering with His people's rebellion (106). There are no requests in this psalm; it is only praise to the Lord. In studying this psalm, we must remember that God's blessings on Israel depended on their obedience to His covenant (vv. 17–18), and believers today must also be obedient to God's will if they would enjoy God's best (2 Cor. 6:14–7:1). The psalm also admonishes us not to *forget* the blessings after we have received them and enjoyed them. "In everything give thanks; for this is the will of God in Christ Jesus for you" (1 Thess. 5:18 NKJV). David started with individual and personal praise (vv. 1–6), then moved to national praise (6–19), and concluded with universal praise (vv. 20–22).

### Personal Praise to the Lord (vv. 1–6)

To "bless the Lord" means to delight His heart by expressing love and gratitude for all He is and all He does. Parents are pleased when their children simply thank them and love them, without asking for anything. True praise comes from a grateful heart that sincerely wants to glorify and please the Lord. "All that is within me" means that all of our inner being is focused on the Lord—heart, soul, mind, and strength (Mark 12:28–31). It also means that we are prepared to obey His will after our praise has ended. The word "all" is found at least nine times in the psalm (1–3, 6, 19, 21–22), for the psalm is a call for total commitment to God. We give thanks to the Lord before we receive our food, and this is right, but the Jewish people were also to give thanks *after* they had eaten and to remember that the Lord had given them their food (Deut. 8:7–20). My immigrant Swedish relatives used to follow this practice. At least fourteen times in the book of Deuteronomy, Moses admonished the people to remember the Lord and what He did for them, and nine times he cautioned them not to forget. (See Deut. 32:18.) It was when the third generation of Jews came on the scene and forgot the Lord that the nation began to decay (Judg. 2:7–3:7).

David listed six special blessings from the hand of the Lord (vv.

3–5): forgiveness, healing, redemption, love, satisfaction, and renewal. The word translated "forgives" is used in Scripture only of God's forgiveness of sinners (see vv. 10–12). The word for "iniquity" pictures sin as something twisted and distorted. Those who have trusted Christ have experienced God's forgiveness (Eph. 1:7; Col. 1:14 and 2:13). When you read 32 and 51, you learn that David knew something about God's gracious forgiveness (and see vv. 10–12). God is able to heal every disease (Matt. 9:35), but He is not obligated to do so. Paul was not able to heal two of his friends (Phil. 2:25–30; 2 Tim. 4:20), and David's own baby son died in spite of his fasting and praying (2 Sam. 12:15–23). The believer's body will not be completely delivered from weakness and disease until it is redeemed and glorified at the return of Jesus Christ (Rom. 8:18–23). In Scripture, sickness is sometimes used as a picture of sin and healing as a picture of salvation (41:4; 147:3; Isa. 53:10; Luke 5:18–32; 1 Peter 2:23–24).

The word "redeem" (v. 4) would remind the Jewish people of their deliverance from the bondage of Egypt at the Exodus (Ex. 12–15). The statement describes God rescuing someone about to fall into a pit, and "the pit" is a symbol of sheol (6:5; 16:10; 28:1), the world of the dead. David himself was often very near to death, so perhaps he had premature death in mind. David also knew something about crowns, but no crown he ever wore compared with God's lovingkindness and compassion (tender mercies). These attributes also appear in verses 8, 11, 13, and 17. Believers should "reign in life through the One, Jesus Christ" (Rom. 5:17 NKJV; and see Rev. 1:1:6). We are seated with Christ in the heavenlies (Eph. 2:1–7), and He helps us to "reign in life."

There is no satisfaction in this world, but we have satisfaction in Christ who is the Bread of Life (John 6:33–40) and the Good Shepherd who leads us into green pastures (23:2). (See 107:9 and 145:16.) The word translated "mouth" is a bit of a puzzle since it is usually translated "ornaments" or "jewelry," words that hardly fit this context. Some students interpret the word to mean "duration" or "years" (see NASB). No matter how old we become, God can satisfy the needs of our lives and the spiritual desires of our hearts. The legend about the physical renewal of the eagle is not what David had in mind in verse 5. Like most birds, eagles do molt and have what seems to be a new lease on life. But the picture here is that of the believer being strengthened by the Lord even in old age and able to "soar" like the eagle (Isa. 40:31). (See 71:17–18; 92:14; 2 Cor. 4:16–18.)

### National Praise to the Lord (vv. 6–18)

The nation of Israel was certainly blessed of the Lord and therefore obligated to express their praise and thanksgiving to Him. Jehovah was their righteous Deliverer (v. 6), not only when He rescued them from Egypt, but all during their history. He gave David many great victories on the battlefield. The Lord also gave His people guidance (v. 7), leading them by His glory cloud, His Word, and His prophets. The people know God's acts, *what* He was doing, but Moses knew God's ways, *why* He was doing it. Moses was intimate with the Lord and understood His will. Jehovah was also the merciful and compassionate Savior who forgave His people when they sinned. In verses 8–12, we have a summary of what Moses learned about God while on Sinai (see Ex. 33:12–13; 34:5–9; and see Num. 14:18). Being a holy God, He did get angry at sin, and the Israelites were prone to rebel against Him, but in His compassion, He forgave them. This was possible because one day His Son would die for those sins on a cross. (See 86:15; Isa. 57:6.) The picture in verses 8–12 is that of a courtroom in which God is both judge and prosecuting attorney. He has all the evidence He needs to condemn us, but He does not prolong the trial. When the judge is your Father, and when Jesus has died for your sins, there is full and free forgiveness available to all who will ask for it. If God gave us the punishment we deserved, we would be without hope (Ezra 9:13). The punishment that we deserve was given to Jesus (Isa. 53:4–6).

David looked up to the heavens and said that God's love reached that high and higher. David remembered the ceremony on the annual Day of Atonement (Lev. 16) when the goat was released in the wilderness, symbolically bearing Israel's sins far away (see John 1:29). (For other descriptions of God's forgiveness of sin, see Isa. 1:18; 38:17; 43:25; Jer. 31:34.) But we must remember that it is not God's love or pity that saves us, but God's grace (Eph. 2:8–10), for grace is love that has paid a price. Were it not for the death of Christ on the cross, there could be no forgiveness of our sins. Yes, God is like a tender Father, but His pity is not a shallow sentimental feeling. A holy God demands that His law be satisfied, and only His perfect Son could provide that satisfaction (Rom. 3:19–31). Is the human race worth saving? We are only grass that grows up and then fades away and dies (vv. 15–16; see 37:2, 10, 36; 40:6–8; 90:6–8). But the Lord knows our "formation" (frame) because He formed us from the dust (Gen. 2:7) and even kept watch on us in the womb (139:13–16). He is the eternal God and wants to share His eternal home with us. What grace! He promised His people that He would bless them and their descendants if they feared Him and kept His precepts. (See Deut. 6:1–15.) Believers today have already been blessed "with every spiritual blessing … in Christ" (Eph. 1:4), and as we trust Him and obey His will, He meets our every need.

### Universal Praise to the Lord (vv. 19–22)

When we worship the Lord God, we worship the King of the universe. The "Lord of Hosts" is sovereign over all things He has created, including the stars and planets (33:6; Isa. 40:26) and the angels (91:11; 2 Kings 6:17–20), who are servants to the saints (Heb. 1:14). As a youth, David confronted the giant Goliath with, "I come to you in the name of the Lord of hosts, the God of the armies of Israel" (1 Sam. 17:45 NKJV). The apostle John heard the vast choir of all creation praise the Lord (Rev. 5:13), and one day, we shall join in that anthem. But the final shout of praise in the psalm comes, not from the angels, but from David the psalmist: "Bless the Lord, O my soul." After all, redeemed men and women have more to praise the Lord for than do all the angels in heaven and all the galaxies in the universe.

Nobody in hell blesses the Lord, but every creature in heaven does nothing else but bless the Lord. We who are in this world can enjoy "heaven on earth" as we join them in expressing thanksgiving and blessing to our great God. "Bless the Lord, O my soul!"

## Psalm 104

This is a magnificent hymn celebrating the glory of the Creator and the incredible greatness of His creation. Paul may have had this psalm in mind when he spoke to the Athenian philosophers (Acts 17:22–34, especially vv. 24–28), for it presents a God who created and now sustains a beautiful and bountiful world that reflects His glory (v. 31). The writer of the psalm certainly had Genesis 1 in mind when he wrote, even though he did not follow all six days of creation in detail, nor did he include the creation of man and woman (see vv. 14, 23). He began with light (v. 2; Gen. 1:1–5) and continued with the separation of the upper and lower waters (vv. 2–4; Gen. 1:6–8) and the separation of land and water (vv. 5–9; Gen. 1:9–10). The provision of vegetation is mentioned (vv. 14–17; Gen. 1:11–13), as well as the placing of the sun and moon (vv. 19–23; Gen. 1:14–19), and the creation of land and sea creatures (vv. 24–25; Gen. 1:20–28). The psalm declares that our God is very great (v. 1), very wise (v. 24), and very generous (v. 27). In spite of the fact that creation is in bondage to sin since the fall of man (Rom. 8:18–23), we still live in an amazing universe run by divinely ordained laws that are so remarkable we can send people to the moon and bring them back! Whether the scientist uses the telescope, the microscope, or the x-ray, he beholds the wonders of God's creation.

### The Greatness of Our God (vv. 1–9)

The psalm opens with the description of a King so great (95:3; Hab. 3:4) that He wears light for a robe (93:1; Isa. 59:17; 1 John 1:5; 1 Tim. 6:16) and has a palace in heaven above the waters (Gen. 1:7). He uses the clouds for His chariot and the winds to move them (18:7–15; 68:4; 77:16–19). His servants (the angels, 148:8; Heb. 1:7) serve as quickly and invisibly as the wind and possess awesome power like flames of fire. This King is so great that creating the heavens was as easy as putting up a tent (19:4; Isa. 40:22). Though He hung the earth on nothing (Job 26:7), it remains firmly fixed as if resting on a foundation that cannot be moved (Job 38:6). When He made the earth, it was "wearing" deep waters like a garment (Gen. 1:2, 6–10), but one command from the King and those waters "were frightened away." They settled where they belonged on the planet and dared not go beyond the established boundaries (Job 38:8–11; Jer. 5:22). In all this creative activity, the Lord has revealed Himself in His power and glory. "The heavens are telling of the glory of God; and their expanse is declaring the work of His hands" (19:1 NASB). Day and night, the visible things of creation shout aloud to the inhabitants of the earth that there is a God, that He is powerful and wise, and that all people are accountable to Him (Rom. 1:18–32). Are the people paying attention?

### The Generosity of Our God (vv. 10–23, 27–30)

God did not wind up the clock of creation and then let it run down, for the tenses of the verbs indicate that God is constantly at work, meeting the needs of His creatures. Note the emphasis on water, both the springs (v. 10) and the rain (v. 13), for water is a precious commodity in the Near East. The "mountains" (v. 13) refer to the upland regions where the grain grows (76:16; Deut. 11:10–12). God supplies not only water for vegetation but also food for the birds and animals (vv. 14, 21, 27–28), and the plants and animals provide food for the people. God uses the cooperation of the farmers and herdsmen to provide this food (v. 14; Gen. 2:8–15; Ex. 20:9), but ultimately He is the giver. Wine, oil, and bread were basics in the life of the people in biblical days. The wine was diluted with water and drunkenness was not acceptable (Judg. 9:13 and Eccl. 10:19). Wine, oil, and water are symbols of the Holy Spirit (Eph. 5:18; John 7:37–39; Zech. 4:1–7; ), and bread speaks of the nourishing Word of God (Matt. 4:4). God has written spiritual truths into the very world of nature.

But without the days, nights, and seasons, there could not be fruitfulness on earth, and therefore he praises God for the sun and moon (see Gen. 1:14–19). The Hebrew religious calendar was built around the seasons (Lev. 23), and there were special monthly celebrations as well (Ex. 12:2; Num. 10:10; 28:14; 1 Chron. 23:31). Without the cycle of day and night and of the seasons, life would come to a halt. "To everything there is a season, a time for every purpose under heaven" (Eccl. 3:1 NKJV). All of creation looks expectantly to the Lord to provide what it needs (vv. 27–30), and He does so generously. However, people made in the image of God think they can "make it" alone. Yet God provides the very breath in our nostrils, and when He turns it off, we die (Gen. 2:7; Eccl. 12:7). On the first day of creation, the Holy Spirit brooded over the waters (Gen. 1:1–2), and that same Spirit gives new life to creation when the winter season ends (v. 30). The Spirit also provides life and power to the church, God's "new creation." Mankind has learned to control a great deal of nature, but the issues of life and death are still in the hands of God. How generous He is to a world that ignores Him, rebels against Him, and rarely gives thanks for His generous gifts! (Ponder Job 34:14–15; Acts 17:25–28; Col. 1:17.)

### The Wisdom of Our God (vv. 24–35)

Whether we study invisible microscopic life, visible plant and animal life, human life, or the myriad of things that have no life, the diversity in creation is amazing. God could have made a drab colorless world, one season everywhere, only one variety of each plant and animal, cookie-cutter humans, no musical sounds, and a few minimal kinds of food—but He did not, and how grateful we are! Only a wise God could have planned so many different things, and only a powerful God could have brought them into being. "The earth is full of thy riches" (v. 24 KJV). The word translated "riches" means "possessions, property," reminding us that God made it all, God owns it all, and God has the right to tell us how to use it all. God wants us to enjoy His creation (1 Tim. 6:17) and employ it wisely. When we exploit our wonderful world, we sin and forget that we are stewards, not owners, and that one day we must give an account of how we have used these precious and irreplaceable gifts. The sea monsters (whales? Gen. 1:21) frolic and play in the ocean and God enjoys them! But God does not enjoy seeing us ruin His handiwork just to make money. Creation is glad for what the Lord has done (v. 26), mankind ought to be glad (v. 15). God's people especially should be glad (v. 34)—and the Lord Himself rejoices over His works! (v. 31).

Knowing all this about God and His creation, we have some serious responsibilities to fulfill, and the first is *glorifying the Lord* (*vv. 31–32*). Beginning with our own bodies and minds, our abilities and possessions, we must gratefully accept all He has graciously given us and use it to glorify Him, not to please ourselves (Rom. 12:1–2; 1 Cor. 4:7). Second, *we must praise the Lord, the Creator.* What a marvelous gift is His creation! We need to get back to singing the great hymns and paraphrases of the psalms that exalt God the Creator. The more we thank God, the less we will exploit His gifts. Third, *we should think about His creation and rejoice in it (v. 34).* The study of natural science is but "thinking God's thoughts after Him." If earth and sky are declaring the glory of God (19:1), we who have been saved by His grace ought to be glorifying Him even more! Finally, *we must pray for Christ's return (v. 35),* for only then will the curse of sin be lifted from creation (Rom. 8:18–25). We must share the gospel with sinners so that they might be able to sing with us, "This is my Father's world."

## Psalm 105

Psalm 104 magnifies the God of creation and 106, the God who chastens His people and forgives them, but this psalm focuses on the God of the covenant (vv. 8–10) who works out His divine purposes in human history. "Make known his deeds" (vv. 1–2, 5) is the major thrust, referring, of course, to God's mighty acts on behalf of Israel. (See also 78, and note that 105:1–15 is adapted in 1 Chron. 16:8–22.) The psalm does not go beyond the conquest of Canaan (v. 44) or mention the Davidic dynasty, which suggests that it may have been written after the Babylonian exile, possibly by one of the Levites who returned to Judah with the Jewish remnant. The psalmist saw the hand of God in the events of Jewish history, and this was the kind of encouragement the struggling remnant needed. He reminded them that they were God's chosen people and that God worked according to His schedule. Beginning with Egypt, the Lord had already revealed His power over the Gentile nations, and He will always keep His promises. Remembering these truths can bring God's people encouragement at any time in history! (v. 5).

### The Patriarchs—God's Gracious Election (vv. 1–15)

As in 32:1–2, the joyful praise recorded in verses 1–5 is the worshipers' response to the wonderful truths stated in the psalm. The name "Jehovah—LORD" is used five times (vv. 1, 3, 4, 7, 19) and is the covenant name of God, the "holy name" that Israel was to call on (v. 1) and glory in (v. 3) as they worshiped. Israel was a chosen people; Jehovah had made no covenant with any other nation (147:20; Rom. 9:1–5). There are ten commandments in verses 1–5 ("seek" is found twice), climaxing with "remember" (v. 5). Their thanksgiving, praying, and singing were a witness to the nations around them and a testimony to the power and glory of the Lord. An obedient Israel was to be God's "exhibit A" to the nations so that they would want to know the true and living God of the Jewish people.

In His sovereign grace, the Lord chose Abraham (vv. 6, 9, 42) and made His covenant with him (Gen. 12:1–5; 15:9–21; Acts 7:1–8), a covenant that would apply to all of Abraham's physical descendants as well as to believers today as Abraham's spiritual children (Luke 1:68–79; Gal. 3:1–9, 29). One of the covenant promises was the gift of the land of Canaan to the people of Israel (vv. 11, 42–44), and this promise was repeated to Abraham's son Isaac (Gen. 26:1–6) and to his grandson Jacob (Gen. 28:13–17). We see here the electing grace of God, for He chose Isaac, not Ishmael, and Jacob, not Esau (Rom. 9:6–18). This covenant will endure forever (vv. 8–11; Deut. 7:9). Again, this was an act of grace on the part of the Lord, for none of the patriarchs had any claim to upon God nor did He owe them anything. They were homeless nomads—pilgrims and strangers (Heb. 11:8–16)—who depended on the Lord to protect and guide them (Gen. 34:30; Deut. 7:6–11; 26:5). Even when they erred, the Lord protected them and even reproved kings on their behalf (Gen. 12:10ff; 20; 26; 32–33). God is sovereign, and though He does not turn men and women into robots, He does rule and overrule when they disobey. His will shall be done and His plans shall be fulfilled (vv. 8–11; 19; 42; 33:11).

### Joseph—God's Wise Preparation (vv. 16–25)

According to verse 6, the Jewish people are the descendants of Abraham, who believed God and received the covenant, and also the sons of Jacob, whose sons built the nation of Israel. In Joseph's dreams, God had promised him that his brothers would bow before him one day, but He did not explain how this would occur. Envy and a family quarrel took Joseph to Egypt where he prepared the way for his relatives and kept them alive during the famine (Gen. 45:55–57; 50:20). But before he became the second ruler of Egypt, Joseph experienced great suffering in prison, for in God's economy, suffering precedes glory (1 Peter 5:10), and being a servant precedes being a ruler (Matt. 25:21). But the Word that God gave Joseph came true, and Jacob and his family moved from Canaan to Egypt (Gen. 46, the land of Ham; vv. 23, 27; 78:51; 106:22; Gen. 10:6). It was there that God, in His grace, turned Jacob's family of seventy persons into a nation so large and powerful that it threatened the security of Egypt. No matter how dark the day, God always sends His servant ahead to prepare the way. God permitted the Egyptians to persecute His people, for suffering is one of the secrets of fruitfulness. God did not force the Egyptians to hate the Jews nor did He force Pharaoh to harden his heart. The Lord arranged the circumstances so that Pharaoh and his officers could either obey or disobey His Word, and their repeated disobedience hardened their hearts more. The record in Exodus reports that Pharaoh hardened his heart (Ex. 7:13–14, 22; 8:15, 19, 32; 9:7,

34–35; 13:15) but also that God hardened it (4:21; 7:3; 9:12; 10:1, 20, 27; 11:10; 14:4, 8, 17). God sent the plagues, but Pharaoh would not obey. The same sun that melts the ice will harden the clay.

### Moses—God's Awesome Judgments (vv. 26–41)

Again, God had His servants prepared to take Israel through another crisis. The ten plagues were both a demonstration of the power of the God of Israel and a condemnation of the gods of Egypt (Ex. 12:12; 18:11; Num. 33:4). Egypt worshiped the sun, so God sent three days of darkness. The Nile River was a god, so God turned the water to blood. The Egyptians worshiped over eighty different gods and goddesses, all of whom were helpless to deliver the land from the onslaught of the plagues, the judgments that God pronounced (v. 5). Jehovah proved that they were false gods who could do nothing.

The psalmist began his list with the plague of darkness (v. 28), which was actually the ninth plague. After mentioning this plague, the writer stayed with the original sequence: water turned to blood, and the invasions of frogs, flies, and gnats. He omits the fifth and six plagues—the death of the livestock and the boils— and moves on to the hail, locusts, and the death of the firstborn on Passover night. What a demonstration of the awesome power of Jehovah! This led to the triumphant exodus of the Jewish people from Egypt, like a victorious army carrying the spoils of battle (v. 37; Ex. 3:21–22; 11:1–3; 12:36–37; Gen. 15:14). This wealth was payment for the slave labor that the Jews had provided for many years. God went before His people, led them by a cloud (78:14; Ex. 13:21–22; 14:19–20), opened the sea for them to pass through, and then closed the waters and drowned the Egyptian army. It was "a night of solemn observance to the Lord" (Ex. 12:42 NKJV).

But the Lord did not abandon His people after He delivered them, for He had brought them out that He might bring them into the Promised Land (Deut. 4:37–38). He led them in the wilderness, sheltered them from the sun, fed them bread (manna) and meat, and provided water to drink. (See Ex. 16 and 17 and Num. 20.) "The Lord is my shepherd; I shall not want" (23:1). Remembering God's deliverance and His care of His people would give courage to the Jewish remnant as they returned to Judah to reestablish the nation. God remembers His covenant (v. 8), and God's people must remember the Lord and what He has done.

### All Believers—God's Dependable Promise (vv. 42–45)

The psalmist moved immediately from the Exodus to the conquest of Canaan. He wrote nothing about Israel's failures at Sinai (the golden calf), in the wilderness (repeated complaining), and at Kadesh Barnea (refusing to enter the land). After all, the purpose of the psalm was to magnify God's great works, not to expose man's great failures. God kept the promise He made to Abraham and gave his descendants the land, helping Joshua and his army defeat the enemy on every side. The people of Israel claimed their inheritance, including the wealth they took from the former inhabitants, another payment for their service in Egypt. "Not a word failed of any good thing which the Lord had spoken to the house of Israel. All came to pass" (Josh. 21:45, and see 23:14; 1 Kings 8:56; Neh. 9:8).

God's people live on promises, not explanations, and it is "through faith and patience" that we see these promises fulfilled (Heb. 6:12). But God's keeping His promise meant much more for Israel than victory over the enemy and the acquisition of riches. *It meant accepting the responsibility of obeying the God who had been so faithful to them.* Before his death, Joshua reminded the people what the Lord had done for them and admonished them to serve the Lord and not turn to idols (Josh. 24:1–28). When we consider all that the Lord has done for us, we find we have the same obligation.

## Psalm 106

After reading this psalm, we might be tempted to say, "Those Israelites were certainly a sorry band of sinners!" Instead, we ought to be commending the psalmist for telling the truth about his own people. Most historians present their nations in the best possible light and blame other nations rather than their own, but our anonymous psalmist told the truth. "History will bear me out," said Sir Winston Churchill, "particularly as I shall write that history myself." But the writer is also to be commended for identifying himself with his struggling people and saying "*We* have sinned" and "Save *us*" (vv. 6 and 47, italics mine). We noted that 105 said nothing about Israel's failings, but that deficiency is remedied by 106. However, the purpose of the psalm is not to condemn Israel but to extol the Lord for His longsuffering and mercy toward His people. In order to glorify God, the writer had to place God's mercies against the dark background of Israel's repeated disobedience. The psalm was probably written after the Babylonian captivity, when the Jewish people were scattered and a remnant had returned to the land to rebuild the temple and restore the nation (vv. 44–47). After expressing his praise to the Lord (vv. 1–6), the writer pointed out nine serious offenses the nation had committed. He began with the Exodus and closed with the Babylonian captivity, and at the heart of the list he placed Israel's rebellion at Kadesh Barnea. He did not arrange these selected events in order of their occurrence, for his purpose was to teach us theology and not chronology.

### Joyful Faith (vv. 1–6)

The psalm begins on a high note of worship and praise. Before he looked back on the failures of his people, or looked around at the ruins of the kingdom, the psalmist looked up and gave thanks to God for His goodness and mercy (vv. 1–3). Jehovah had been merciful in all that He had done, and the writer accepted God's will as just and right. Then the psalmist turned from praise to prayer and asked God to include him in the blessings of the promised restoration of the nation (vv. 4–5). The prophets had promised that the captivity would end and the people would return and rebuild, and he believed those promises. But his prayer was not selfish, for he wanted the whole nation to prosper, to rejoice in the Lord, and to give praise to His name. His prayer climaxed with penitence as he confessed his sins and the sins of his people (v. 6). "We have sinned with our fathers" is better than "Our fathers sinned." (See Neh. 1:6, Dan. 9:5, 8, 11, and 15; and Lam. 5:16.) The psalmist claimed the promise that King Solomon asked God to honor when he dedicated the temple (1 Kings 8:46–53). As we study this psalm, it may be like witnessing an autopsy, but we will benefit from it if, like the psalmist, we keep our eyes on the Lord of glory and see His kindness and faithfulness to His sinful people.

### Triumphant Beginnings (vv. 7–12)

The reference here is to Israel's fear and unbelief at the Exodus, when they were caught between the Egyptian army behind them and the Red Sea before them (Ex. 14:10–31). They had witnessed the mighty power of God as He had devastated Egypt with plagues, but Israel did not believe that the Lord could successfully deliver them from the Egyptians. They were looking back instead of looking up and were walking by sight and not by faith. They preferred the security of slavery to the challenges of liberty. "Let us go back to Egypt!" was frequently their response when they found themselves in a situation that demanded faith. In that desperate hour, they did not remember God's kindness or His promises, and they panicked. But God led them through the sea on dry land and utterly destroyed the enemy army that tried to follow them. "Then they believed His words; they sang His praise" (v. 12 NASB; see Ex. 15). This one miracle should have assured them for all the trials to come, but they did not take it to heart or understand God's ways (78:42–51; 95:10; 103:7). For Moses, this was an experience of faith that glorified God, but for the people, it was just another spectacular event. They were spectators at a performance, not participants in a miracle. But are God's people any different today?

### Dangerous Decline (vv. 13–23)

The seeds of unbelief buried in the hearts of the Jewish people took root and bore bitter fruit in the years to come. As George Morrison wrote, "The Lord took Israel out of Egypt in one night, but it took Him forty years to take Egypt out of Israel." The people were slow to remember God's past deeds but quick to rush ahead and ignore His desires. However, they did not hesitate to make known their own desires, for they craved water (Ex. 15:22–27), food (Ex. 16), and meat (Num. 11:4–15, 31–35). "What shall we eat? What shall we drink?" (See Matt. 6:25ff.) God provided daily manna ("angels' food"—78:12), water at an oasis and then from the rock (Ex. 17), and enough fowl to give meat to the whole nation. People who grumble and complain are people not walking by faith in the promises of God (Phil. 2:14–15). We must resist the temptation to yield to our fleshly cravings (1 Cor. 10:1–13).

The rebellion of Korah (Num. 16–17) followed soon after Israel's apostasy at Kadesh Barnea when the nation refused to enter the Promised Land. Korah enlisted his 250 fellow rebels because of this crisis; all he had to do was blame Moses and claim that the nation needed new leadership. (Political candidates have been doing this ever since.) Korah was a Levite in the family of Kohath whose privilege it was to carry the tabernacle furnishings. But Kohath was not satisfied with that task; he wanted to function at the altar as a priest (Num. 14:8–10). Pride and selfish ambition have always brought trouble to God's people (Phil. 2:1–11; James 4:1–10). These rebels were opposing the will of God, for it was the Lord who chose Moses and Aaron to lead the nation, and so the Lord destroyed Korah and his followers. Respect for God's leaders is important to the success of the Lord's work (Heb. 13:7, 17).

The first failure involved the lusts of the flesh and the second involved the pride of life (see 1 John 2:15–17). The third failure, the worship of the golden calf (Ex. 32; Deut. 9:8–29), involved the lust of the eyes. For forty days, Moses had been on Sinai with the Lord, and the Jewish people were nervous without their leader. (When he was with them, they opposed him and criticized him!) In spite of what the Lord had taught them at Sinai, they wanted a god they could see (Deut. 4:12–19). Aaron collected gold jewelry and molded a calf for the people to see and worship, and Moses had to intercede with the Lord to turn away His wrath. They rejected the eternal God ("their Glory"—Rom. 1:26) for a man-made piece of gold that could not see, hear, speak, or act! Once again, Israel forgot what the Lord had done for them. The phrase "stood in the breach" (v. 23) describes a soldier standing at a break in the city walls and preventing the enemy from entering. What a picture of intercessory prayer! (Ezek. 22:30).

### Tragic Failure (vv. 24–27)

Israel had been out of Egypt about two years when the Lord brought them to Kadesh Barnea on the border of the Promised Land (Num. 13–14). Instead of trusting God to give them the land, the people asked Moses to appoint a committee to survey the land. (God had already done this for them—Ezek. 20:6). But Israel did not need more facts; they needed more faith. It was a "pleasant [beautiful] land" (v. 24; Jer. 3:19; 12:10) and a "good land" (Deut. 8:7–9), but ten of the twelve spies reported that Canaan was a dangerous land filled with giants, high-walled cities, and formidable armies. The people reverted to their usual crisis mode of weeping, complaining, and planning to return to Egypt (Num. 14:1–10). The Lord announced that the generation twenty years and older would all die in the wilderness during the next thirty-eight years, and then He sent a plague that killed the ten unbelieving spies. What should have been a triumphant victory march became a tragic funeral march. That is what happens when we want our own way and refuse to trust the Lord and obey Him.

### Costly Disobedience (vv. 28–33)

These two events occurred toward the end of Israel's march through the wilderness, and both of them illustrate the high cost of willful disobedience to the Lord. The failure at Baal Peor is described in Numbers 25, but read Numbers 22–24 to get the background. The king of Moab hired the prophet Baalam to curse the nation of Israel, but God turned his curses into blessings (Deut. 23:5; Neh. 13:2; see 109:28). But Baalam knew how to trap Israel: he suggested that the king act like a good neighbor and invite the Jewish tribal leaders to share a feast with the Moabites. This would be a religious feast, of course, which meant eating meat dedicated to demons and dead people and cohabiting with cult prostitutes. Once more, the people of God yielded to their fleshly desires and tasted the wrath of God, and 24,000 people died (Num. 25:9). The plague would have claimed more lives, but Phinehas, the son of the high priest, killed a Jewish man and his Moabite partner as they arrogantly sinned in the camp of Israel. "The wages of sin is death" (Rom. 6:23). (On v. 30, see Gen. 15:6 and Rom. 4.)

The second demonstration of carnality was seen in Moses, not a sin of the flesh but of the spirit: he became proud and angry and took for himself the glory that belonged only to the Lord (Num. 20:1–13). Provoked by the people, the "pride of life" possessed Moses and he lost his temper and spoke rash words that offended the Lord (78:40; Isa. 63:10; 1 John 2:15–17). This sin cost Moses the privilege of leading the people into the Promised Land (Deut. 3:23–29). "Meribah" means "quarreling" (see Ex. 17:1–7).

### Repeated Rebellion (vv. 34–46)

God, in His grace, took His people into Canaan and gave them victory over the nations living there. The twelve tribes claimed their inheritance and settled down to enjoy the land and serve the Lord. They were faithful all during the leadership of Joshua and the elders that he selected and trained, but when the third generation came along, they compromised and began to serve the false gods of their defeated enemies (Judg. 2:7–23). The people knew the terms of the covenant that Moses had given them (Lev. 26; Deut. 28–30), but they disobeyed it. Instead of destroying the godless society of the nations in Canaan as God commanded (Num. 33:50–56; Deut. 7:12–26; 20:16–18), the Israelites gradually compromised with them and then imitated them, including the inhumane practices that defiled the land God gave them (Lev. 18:24–28; Num. 35:30–34; Deut. 21:22–23; Jer. 3:1–10). They had been "married" to Jehovah at Sinai, but now they prostituted themselves to idols and grieved the Lord, inviting His chastening. The Lord brought six nations against Israel and for over one hundred years, punished His people right in their own land. When they cried out to Him for mercy, He heard them and raised up judges to deliver them from their enemies; but then the nation lapsed into idolatry again, and the cycle was repeated. In His mercy, the Lord heard their cries and forgave them (Judg. 3:9, 15; 4:3; 6:6–7; 10:10; Lev. 26:40–42), but this could not go on forever.

### *Final Discipline (v. 47)*

In His covenant, the Lord warned that if Israel continued to resist and disobey, even after experiencing His chastening, He would take them out of their land and scatter them (Lev. 26:27–39; Deut. 28:48–68). First, the kingdom was divided between the ten tribes of Israel (the northern kingdom) and the two tribes of Benjamin and Judah (the southern kingdom). In 722 B.C., the Assyrians captured Israel and absorbed the ten tribes into their own empire. In 606–586 B.C., the Babylonians invaded Judah, destroyed Jerusalem and the temple, and took the best of the people captive to Babylon. The Jewish people were rooted out of their own "beautiful land" and scattered among the nations. The Medes and Persians conquered Babylon in 539 B.C. and the next year Cyrus decreed that the Jews could return to their land. However, the Davidic dynasty was not restored in their kingdom. The psalmist closed with a prayer that the scattered children of Abraham, Isaac, and Jacob would one day be gathered together so that they might worship Jehovah and give glory to His name.

The last verse, written by an ancient editor, brings to a close the Fourth Book of the Psalms.

# THREE

# Book V

## Psalm 107

The emphasis in 105 is on Israel's exodus from Egypt and in 106 on God's longsuffering care of His people. This psalm focuses on the Lord's redemption of the nation from captivity in Babylon (vv. 2–3). While the circumstances described in the psalm could be experienced by almost anyone, they especially apply to what Israel had to endure while in captivity. The word "redeemed" is often used in Isaiah to describe this great deliverance (Isa. 35:9; 43:1; 44:22–23; 48:20; 62:12). Note the words describing their plight: adversity (v. 2), trouble and distress (vv. 6, 13, 19, 28), misery (vv. 10, 26, 39), labor (v. 12), affliction (vv. 17, 41), destruction (v. 20), oppression (v. 39), and sorrow (v. 39). The psalmist begins by urging us to give thanks to the Lord for His goodness and mercy (lovingkindness), and he closes by exhorting us to be wise and learn from the mistakes of other people (v. 47). The people described in this psalm needed God's help, either because of their own folly or because of circumstances beyond their control, and they called on the Lord and He delivered them. Five specific situations are described involving people who lose something valuable.

### When You Lose Your Way (vv. 4–9)

It was a long way from Babylon to Judah and the dangers were many, but the Lord brought His people safely home (Ezra 1–2; Isa. 41:14–20; 43:1–21). In their need, they cried out to Him (vv. 6, 13, 19, 28) and He brought them out, led them through the wilderness, and brought them to their own land where they found cities to live in. During their journey, He provided food and drink for them (see Luke 1:53; Jer. 31:25). Surely they would want to give thanks to Him for all that He did for them (vv. 8, 15, 21, 31).

### When You Lose Your Freedom (vv. 10–16)

These people were in prison (vv. 10, 14, 17) because they had rebelled against the Lord, a good description of the Jewish people exiled in Babylon (2 Chron. 36:15–23). They violated their covenant with the Lord, and He had to discipline them (Lev. 26:33; Deut. 28:47–48). God used Cyrus, a pagan king, to set His people free (Isa. 45:1–7, and note 45:2 and 107:16). Anyone who rejects God's message of life in Christ is imprisoned in sin, and only Jesus can set him or her free (Luke 1:79; 4:18ff).

### When You Lose Your Health (vv. 17–22)

Again we meet rebellious fools who deliberately disobeyed God's law and suffered for their folly. The "gates of death" (v. 18) led into sheol, the land of the dead (9:13; Job 17:16; 38:17; Isa. 38:10). The Lord heard their cries and stopped them at the very gates and permitted them to live. They did not deserve this blessing, but such is the mercy of the Lord. In Scripture, sickness is often used as a picture of sin and its painful consequences, but not all sickness is the result of sin (John 9:1–3; 2 Cor. 12:7–10). Because the Lord healed these repentant rebels, they should praise Him, sing to Him, and bring thank offerings to Him. In verse 20, the Word of God is compared to medicine that God sends for their healing. This reminds us of the three people Jesus healed *from a distance*: the centurion's servant (Matt. 8:5–13), the demonized girl (Matt. 15:21–28), and the nobleman's son (John 4:46–54).

### When You Lose Your Hope (vv. 23–32)

Being away from home and living as captives in Babylon was to the exiles like being on a boat in a terrible storm (see Isa. 54:11). The Jews were not a seafaring people like the Phoenicians, but Solomon did carry on a lucrative trading business (1 Kings 9:26–27). In the previous two pictures (vv. 10–22), the people were in trouble because they sinned against the Lord, but these sailors didn't cause the storm that almost drowned them. This is one of the most powerful descriptions of a storm at sea to be found anywhere in literature. The crew had used every device they knew to save the ship, but to no avail, so they called on the Lord for His help. Not only did He still the storm (see Luke 8:22–25), but He guided them to the right port (John 6:21). This wonderful deliverance should motivate the sailors to give thanks to the Lord personally, to exalt Him in the sanctuary worship, and to bear witness to the leaders of the people. The thanksgiving continues to expand! There are no hopeless situations in God's sight, for He can do the impossible. Nobody but the crew and the Lord saw the miracle, so it was up to the grateful crew to spread the word and give glory to the Lord.

### When You Lose Your Home (vv. 33–43)

The approach changes and the focus of attention is not on the people in trouble but on the Lord. He can turn the garden into a desert and the desert into a garden (Isa. 35; 41:18; Deut. 28:1–5). God can judge the land because of the wickedness of the people who live there (v. 34; see Gen. 19:24–28), and He can also heal the land and bless it because of the faith and obedience of the people. This is a part of His covenant relationship with Israel (Deut. 28:15, 22–24, 58–59, 62–63). If necessary, the Lord can summon foreign armies like Babylon to invade the land and use them to chasten the leaders (vv. 39–40; Job 12:21, 24). However, His purpose is not to destroy but to cleanse, and He will restore the blessing to the land and the people (vv. 41–42). This closing paragraph (vv. 39–42) reminds us of Mary's song in Luke 1:46–55.

And what should we learn from these five pictures that depict God's power and mercy in action? To be wise and heed the Word of God (v. 43; Hos. 14:9). Yes, God shows His love and mercy to the disobedient who repent and call on His name, but our Father would rather share that love with *obedient* children who would enjoy it more (2 Cor. 6:14–7:1).

## Psalm 108

The worship leader took the first five verses from 57:7–11 and the last eight from 60:5–12 and made a new psalm. (For commentary, see those psalms.) God's truth is adaptable to new situations and old songs become "new songs" when new challenges are matched with changeless theology. The writer opened with praise to the Lord (vv. 1–5) and then reminded Him of His promises to conquer Israel's enemies and give them the land (vv. 6–9). He closed with prayer for God's help and an expression of confidence in the power of the Lord (vv. 10–13). Praise, prayer, and promises form a combination found often in the psalms, a pattern that we ought to imitate in our own daily lives.

## Psalm 109

This is the last of the "imprecatory psalms," and some consider it to be the most vehement. (See Ps. 5.) The psalm is ascribed to David (Acts 1:20), but it must have been written before he took the throne, for no king would be obligated to put up with this kind of treatment from an officer (v. 8) in his own court. The man was outwardly religious (v. 7) but hated David (vv. 3, 5) and falsely accused him (vv. 1–2, 4; see Ex. 23:6–8; Deut, 19:15–21) and cursed him (vv. 17–19). David's attempts to return good for evil failed (vv. 4–5), and the man showed him no mercy (v. 16). This unknown opponent may have been King Saul himself, whose life David spared on at least two occasions, or perhaps one of Saul's important officers who wanted to please his master. Had we been in this situation with David, we might have prayed as he did! There was terrible injustice in the land,

and only God could remove Saul and put the rightful king on the throne. David did not avenge himself but put the matter in the hands of the Lord (Rom. 12:17–21). The psalm is built around three major requests.

### Lord, Do Something! (vv. 1–5)

The silence of God indicated that the Lord was not answering prayer and working on David's behalf (28:1; 35:22–24; 50:3; 83:1). Often, we cry out to Him but nothing seems to happen. David reminded the Lord that he did not pray only when he needed help, for he praised the Lord often and thanked Him for His mercies ("God of my praise"; see v. 30; 22:25; Deut. 10:21; Jer. 17:14). In fact, in the Hebrew text, "O God of my praise" opens the psalm. God was silent but the enemy was vocal, speaking hateful lying words and accusing David of crimes he had never committed. The word translated "adversaries" or "accusers" (vv. 4, 6, 20, 29) gives us the English word "Satan," one of the names of the Devil (see 38:20; 71:13; Job 1–2; Zech. 3). Satan is the accuser (Rev. 12:10) and the adversary of believers (1 Peter 5:8), and he uses people to accomplish this work. Like our Savior who was falsely accused, David was innocent of the charges (v. 3; 35:7, 19–20; 69:4; Jer. 18:18; 20:10). God's people return good for evil, most people return good for good and evil for evil, but Satan's crowd returns evil for good (v. 5; 35:12; 38:20; Jer. 18:20). David responded to God's silence and to the enemy's attacks by praying to the Lord. His faith did not waver.

### Lord, Judge the Enemy! (vv. 6–20)

Some students try to take the barbs out of David's prayer by making verses 6–20 the words of the enemy about David, but the approach will not work. Does verse 18 apply to David? And what about verse 20? Years later, the prophet Jeremiah prayed a similar prayer against the enemies that wanted to kill him (Jer. 18:18–23), and the Lord did not rebuke him. It has also been suggested that the tenses of the verbs should read as futures and not as requests: "His days will be few ... His children will be beggars," and so on. Knowing God's covenant, David was predicting what would happen because of the sins his enemy had committed. (See Lev. 26:14–39.)

David was willing for the court to solve the problem, for that is the image found in verses 6–7. Note that the pronouns shift from *they* and *them* to *he, him* and *his*. David focused his prayer on the leader of the evil band that was attacking him, and he asked God to appoint a judge or prosecuting attorney as wicked as the defendant himself! After all, the way we judge others is the way we ourselves will be judged (Matt. 7:1–2). Or perhaps he wanted Satan himself to be there (Zech. 3:1ff). David expected the Lord to stand at his right hand to defend him (v. 31; 16:8). Our Savior is enthroned at the right hand of God and intercedes for us (110:1; Acts 2:25, 34; Rom. 8:34).

David prayed that God's judgment would be thorough and would include the family of his enemy (vv. 9–13). Certainly he knew what the law said about this (Deut. 24:16), so the family must have participated in the father's sins. Every Jewish man wanted many descendants so that his name would be perpetuated, along with much wealth and a long life, but David prayed that none of these blessings would come to his enemy. Even more, he asked that his enemy's parents' sins would never be forgiven. (This must have been a very wicked family.) This would mean perpetual judgment on the family until it died out (Ex. 20:5; 34:7; Lev. 26:39). Peter quoted verses 8 and 69:25 in Acts 1:20 when the church elected a new apostle to replace Judas. In verses 16–20, David focused on his enemy's sins of omission: he did not show kindness to the poor and he did not seek to be a blessing to others (see Ex. 22:22–24; Deut. 10:18; 14:29; 16:11–14; 24:17–21). All of this would come right back on his own head and penetrate his very being, for sinners hurt themselves far more than they hurt their victims.

### Lord, Help Me! (vv. 21–31)

As a faithful son of the covenant, David had a right to ask God for the help he needed. His desire was that God might be glorified by showing mercy to His servant (vv. 21, 27). He wanted

God to do some wonderful thing that only He could do, and this would tell his enemies that Jehovah was fighting David's battles. "Magnify your mercy!" was David's cry (vv. 21, 26). He wanted the Lord to be mindful of his needs, for he was "poor and needy" (vv. 22–25; 70:5; 86:1). He had a broken heart and he felt as if his life was fading away like the shadows of evening. As the sun sets, the shadows grow longer and longer and then vanish. Like a locust hanging on clothing, his grip on life was feeble and he could be shaken off at any minute. Imagine the future king of Israel comparing himself to a fragile insect! David asked the Lord to send him a blessing every time his enemy cursed him and to bring shame to the enemy but joy to His servant. Finally, David promised to praise the Lord and give glory to Him when all these trials were ended, and he did. After David had been made king over all Israel, he brought the ark of the covenant to Jerusalem and sought to honor the Lord (2 Sam. 5–6). God did help David, in His own time and His own way, and so He will do for us.

## Psalm 110

Jesus and Peter both stated that David wrote this psalm (Matt. 22:43; Mark 12:36; Luke 20:42; Acts 2:33–35), and, since David was a prophet, he wrote it about the Messiah (Acts 2:30; 2 Sam. 23:2). He certainly did not write about any of his own descendants, for no Jewish king was ever a priest, let alone a priest forever (v. 4; 2 Chron. 26:16–23). Also, no Jewish king ever conquered all the rulers of the whole earth (v. 6). The psalm is quoted or alluded to in the New Testament more than any other psalm, verse 1 at least twenty-five times and verse 4 another five times. Ten of these quotations or allusions are in the book of Hebrews alone. Jesus used verse 1 to prove His deity and silence the Pharisees (Matt. 22:41–46) and also to answer the high priest during His trial (Matt. 26:64). The psalm presents two pictures of Messiah from the past—His exaltation as King (vv. 1–3) and His consecration as Priest (v. 4)—and a third picture from the future, His victory over the enemies of God (vv. 5–7).

## Exaltation: Jesus is King (vv. 1–3)

"Jehovah says to my *Adonai*" is the way the psalm opens, and since David was the highest ruler in the kingdom, his *Adonai* had to be the Lord Himself. It was this fact that Jesus presented to the Pharisees (Matt. 22:41–46), asking them how David's Lord could also be David's son (Messiah). The only answer is *by incarnation*: the eternal Son of God had to come to earth as a human born into the family of David (Luke 1:26–38). As eternal God, Jesus is the "root [originator] of David" and as man He is "the offspring of David" (Rev. 22:16; 5:5). Had the Pharisees honestly faced this truth, they would have had to confess that Jesus is indeed the Son of God come in the flesh, but they refused to do so.

To sit at a ruler's right hand was a great honor (1 Kings 2:19; Matt. 20:21). When Jesus ascended to heaven, the Father honored Him by placing Him at His own right hand, a statement repeated frequently in the New Testament. (See Acts 2:33–34; 5:31; Rom. 8:34; Eph. 1:20; Col. 3:1; Heb. 1:3, 13; 8:1; 10:12; 12:2; 1 Peter 3:22). Jesus is "far above all" (Eph. 1:21; 4:10; Col. 2:10; see Phil. 2:9–11). When the Son was exalted and enthroned at His ascension, the Father made three promises to him: that He would defeat His enemies (v. 1), extend His kingdom (v. 2), and give Him a victorious army (v. 3). Note that in verses 1–3, the key phrase is "I will," the Father speaking to the Son, but in verses 5–7, the key phrase is "he will," the psalmist speaking about the Son. To use the enemy soldiers as footstools meant to defeat and humiliate them (Josh. 10:24; see 1 Cor. 15:24–25 and Eph. 1:22), and this victory is described in verses 5–7. (See also the Messianic promises in Psalm 2.) Both David and Solomon extended the borders of the kingdom of Israel, but when Messiah establishes His kingdom, with Jerusalem as the center (2:6), the whole earth will share in the glory and the blessing (72:1–11; Isa. 2:1–4; Mic. 4:1–3). Today, the Lord has enemies who oppose Him, but He is sovereign and rules from His throne even though they refuse to submit. When our Lord was here on earth, the powerful ministry of the apostles brought defeat to the devil (Luke. 10:17–20), and today His church has victory through Him as we pray, share the Word, and depend on the Spirit.

The third promise is that Messiah would have a great army assist Him in the final battle against the enemies of the Lord (v. 3). This army is remarkable in three ways: it is made up of willing volunteers; they are dressed in holy garments like priests (Rev. 19:14); and they are a great multitude, like the dew that falls in the early morning (2 Sam. 23:4). Just as the dawn gives birth to the sparkling dew, so the Lord will "give birth" to this vast holy army. You expect *kings* to be warriors—David is a good example—but you don't expect *priests* to be warriors. However, Benaiah was a priest (1 Chron. 27:5) who was also a soldier. He was one of David's mighty men (2 Sam. 23:20–23), became captain over the king's bodyguard (1 Chron. 18:17), and eventually was made general over King Solomon's army (1 Kings 2:35). Imagine a huge army of men like Benaiah! The book of Revelation indicates that there will be great battles fought in the end times (see 14:14–20; 16:12–16; 19:11–21; 20:7–10) and that Jesus Christ will defeat the enemy.

### Consecration: The King Is a Priest (v. 4)

This central verse of the psalm announces that Messiah will also be a priest, something unheard of in Old Testament history. This verse is important to the message of the book of Hebrews (Heb. 5:6, 10; 6:20; 7:17, 21; see Rom. 8:34) because the present high priestly ministry of Christ in heaven is described in that book. If Jesus were on earth, He could not minister as a priest because He was from the tribe of Judah and not from Levi. But because His priesthood is after the order of Melchizedek, who was both a king and priest (Gen. 14:18–24), He can minister in heaven today. Melchizedek was not an appearance of Jesus Christ on earth; he is only a type of Jesus in His present priestly ministry. (See Heb. 5:1–11; 7–8; Zech. 6:12.) No Aaronic priest was "a priest forever" because each high priest died and was replaced by his eldest son. Being a mere human, Melchizedek died, *but there is no record of either his birth or death in the Scriptures*. This makes him a type of Jesus Christ, the eternal Son of God and the High Priest forever. In Jesus Christ, David has a throne forever (2 Sam. 7:13, 16, 25, 29; Luke 1:30–33) and a priest forever, and all who have trusted Christ share in those blessings. Jesus Christ is our glorified King-Priest in heaven, interceding for us (Rom. 8:34). His throne is a throne of grace to which we may come at any time to find the help we need (Heb. 4:14–16).

### Vindication: The King-Priest Is a Conqueror (vv. 5–7)

All of the "royal psalms" contain predictions about battles and victories for God's King (2:7–9, 12; 18:16–19, 31–34, 37–42; 20:1–2, 7–8; 21:8–12; 45:3–5; 61:3; 72:8–9; 89:22–23; 132:18). Today is the Lord's "day of salvation" (2 Cor. 6:1–2) when He is calling sinners to be reconciled to God (2 Cor. 5:18–21). But there will come a day of wrath, "the day of the Lord," when Jesus, the Lamb of God, will begin to "roar" as the Lion of the tribe of Judah (Rev. 5:5–6), and judgment will fall on the world. This is the victory the Father promised in verse 1 and also in 2:5, 9. The psalmist describes stacks of corpses on the battlefield with nobody to bury them. Even allowing for poetic license, the picture is not a pretty one—but consider what John (the apostle of love) wrote in Revelation 14:17–20 and 19:11–19 (and see Isa. 66:24). The word in verse 6 translated "heads" (KJV) or "chief men, rulers" (NASB, NIV) is singular in the Hebrew. It could be a collective noun or it may refer to the last great world ruler, the Antichrist or Beast (Rev. 13:1–10) whom Jesus Christ will destroy at His coming (2 Thess. 2:1–2; Rev. 19:17–21).

The image in verse 7 is difficult to decipher. The NIV margin reads, "The One who grants succession will set him in authority," meaning that Christ will win the victory and receive the promised throne. But it is necessary to alter the Hebrew text to get this meaning. The picture is obviously not to be taken literally, for a King riding out of heaven on a horse doesn't need a drink of water to keep going. The warrior David, who knew something about battles, is saying, "Nothing will detain Him, detour Him, or discourage Him as He attacks the enemy. Like every good soldier, He will linger only long enough to get a sip of water, and then He will raise His head and continue the chase." We remember that before His crucifixion, Jesus refused to receive the narcotic drink, but tasted death to the full on the cross (Matt. 27:34). Gideon and his men also come to mind (Judg. 7:4–7), for their fitness for the battle was tested by the way they drank at the river.

Jesus Christ is exalted and enthroned in heaven! One day He will come and conquer the devil and his armies and establish His kingdom on earth! Hallelujah, what a Savior!

# Psalm 111

Life was not easy for the Jewish remnant that returned to Jerusalem after their exile in Babylon. Their neighbors were often hostile, the Persian officials were not always cooperative, and the economic situation was difficult. Ezra the scribe, and the prophet Haggai describe some of these problems in their books and point out that the Jewish people were not always faithful to the Lord or generous to each other. This was why God withheld His blessing. This psalm may have been written by one of the Levites to remind the people to put the Lord first and trust Him to meet every need. The next psalm describes the blessings God will give to those who truly fear Him and do His will. Both psalms are acrostics with each line beginning with a successive letter of the Hebrew alphabet. Other acrostic psalms are 9, 10, 24, 34, 37, 119, and 145. This was a special style of writing and perhaps the arrangement helped the people to memorize God's Word. The writer gives us four instructions to follow if we would enjoy the help and blessing of the Lord in the difficult situations of life.

### Begin with Worship and Praise (v. 1)

Psalms 111 and 112, along with 115–117, are "hallelujah" psalms that either begin or end with "Praise the Lord!" If we cannot rejoice in our circumstances, we can always rejoice in the Lord (Phil. 4:4). This opening verse is actually a vow; the writer is determined to praise God no matter what happens. Sometimes we simply need to get ourselves by the nape of the neck and decide to do what is right no matter how we feel! But he does not stay at home and worship in private, as important as that is; he goes to the sanctuary and joins in with others, for we encourage one another as we praise God together. The "company [assembly, council] of the upright" is a smaller group of the psalmist's friends who, like him, are a part of the larger "congregation." All of us have people in church who are very special to us, and as long as we do not form an exclusive clique, there is nothing wrong with worshiping God with your close friends. The "growth group" movement in the church today has proven very helpful, especially in larger congregations. But the important thing is that we are wholehearted in our worship, giving God our very best.

### Remember God's Great Works (vv. 2–6)

God's people do not live in the past, but they know how to use the past to give them encouragement in the present and hope for the future. The celebrating of special days and weeks as commanded in Leviticus 23 was one way the Lord helped His people recall His great deeds on their behalf. But even more, His works reveal His attributes, for like Him they are great (v. 2), glorious, majestic and righteous (v. 3), wonderful, gracious and compassionate (v. 4), powerful (v. 6), faithful, just and trustworthy (v. 7), and holy and awesome (v. 9). Who could not trust a God with that kind of character!

In reviewing the kinds of works God did, the psalmist also reminded us of what some of those works were. He provided food for His people after they left Egypt and gave them His covenant at Sinai (v. 5). He helped them conquer the nations in Canaan (v. 6; Deut. 4:35–40) and delivered them from bondage in Babylon (v. 9). As A. T. Pierson used to say, "History is His story," and we should read it with that in mind. We should delight in pondering the record of God's works and learn more about the Lord from our study, but we should also review how He has worked in our own lives. The word "remembered" in verse 4 is "memorial." We may read it, "He has caused His wonders to be a memorial." In fact, Israel itself is a memorial to the power and grace of God. As Abraham went from place to place, he left behind altars and wells as memorials that God had brought him that way, and the Jewish nation left "memorial stones" after they entered Canaan (Josh. 4:1–7) and during their passage through the land. Jewish parents were commanded to teach their children the meaning of the special days and the memorial stones (Ex. 13:3–10; Deut. 6:4–9; Josh. 4:4–7). There are no "sacred places" where God dwells in some unique way, but there are special places where God can bring edifying memories to mind that will help us remember His greatness and grace.

### Rely on God's Word (vv. 7–9)

From the works of God it was an easy transition to the Word of God, for it is God's Word that brought all things into being and that keeps things together (33:6–11). God gave His law to His people so that they might enjoy His blessings. His righteousness is forever (v. 3), but so are His covenants (vv. 5, 9) and His precepts (v. 8). God's Word is trustworthy and we can rely on it. His precepts are given in love and His promises never fail. As for the covenant He made with Israel, He has been faithful to keep it even when Israel was not faithful to obey it. If we obey His Word, He is faithful to bless; if we disobey, He is just to chasten us in love. As the people of God, we bear His name and want to glorify His name in all that we say and do. "Reverend is his name," says the KJV (v. 9), meaning "His name should be revered and held in honor." The word "reverend" is usually applied to the clergy, but there is no biblical basis for this. Both the NIV and NASB use "awesome." To the Jewish people, God's name was so awesome that they would not speak the name "Jehovah" but substituted "Adonai" lest they would inadvertently blaspheme His holy name. Would that God's people today had such reverence for the name of the Lord!

### Obey His Will (v. 10)

The awesomeness of God's name leads to the importance of fearing the Lord and obeying His will. The fear of the Lord is a topic mentioned frequently in Scripture, especially in the book of Proverbs. It is not the slavish fear of a criminal before a judge, but the loving and reverential fear of a child for his or her parents. *If we want to understand God's works and God's Word, we must maintain this reverential fear of the Lord, for this attitude is the basis for receiving spiritual wisdom and understanding.* (See Job 28:28; Prov. 1:7 and 9:10.) The word "beginning" means "the principal part," and without this, we are unprepared to learn God's truth. But fearing the Lord leads to obeying the Lord, and obedience is important to spiritual understanding (John 7:17). How all of this works out in our practical daily life is explained in the next psalm.

## Psalm 112

In the previous psalm, the writer extolled the Lord for His great and marvelous works, and he ended by admonishing us to fear the Lord and obey His precepts (111:10). The blessings of obeying that admonition are described in 112 (note v. 1). Like 111, this psalm is an acrostic, and you will find the vocabulary of 112 similar to that of 111. Both psalms use delight (111:2; 112:1), righteousness (111:3; 112:3–4, 6, 9), established (111:8; 112:8), grace and compassion (111:4; 112:4), and just (111:7; 112:5). Both psalms must be read in light of God's covenant with Israel in which He promises to bless them if they fear Him and obey His Word (Lev. 26:1–13; Deut. 28:1–14). Nothing is said about the wife and mother in this home, but surely a man of such godly character would have a wife like the one described in Proverbs 31. We must not conclude that, on the basis of this psalm, all believers today can claim health, wealth, success, and happiness if they faithfully obey the Lord, for this promise is not found in the new covenant. For that matter, the believer described in this psalm had times of darkness (v. 4), occasionally received bad news (v. 7), had his enemies (vv. 8, 10), and had to consider the justice of his decisions (v. 5). We who live under the new covenant have in Jesus Christ every spiritual blessing that we will ever need (Eph. 1:3; 2 Peter 1:3–4), and we have the promise that our God will meet our needs (Phil. 4:19). The attributes of God given in 111 become the character qualities of the godly believer in 112, for becoming more and more like Jesus Christ is the greatest reward of a faithful life of obedience (Rom. 8:29; 2 Cor. 3:18). We want more than the blessing; we want to be like the One who gives the blessing. The psalmist describes the faithful believer in various relationships of life.

### Our Relationship to the Lord (v. 1)

The psalmist wrote about fear of bad news (v. 7) and fear of the enemy (v. 8), but the first and most important fear is the fear of the Lord. This verse takes us back to 111:10, for if we fear God, we need fear nothing else. Solomon came to the same conclusion: "Fear God and keep His commandments, for this is the whole duty of man" (Eccl. 12:13 NKJV). Of itself, fear is not an evil thing. We teach children to fear danger when they cross the street, use sharp objects, or are approached by strangers, but those are rational fears that energize us and protect us. The psalmist is writing about fears that can paralyze us and make life miserable. To overcome these fears, we cultivate a right relationship with the Lord: we fear Him, learn His will from His Word, and obey what He commands. Learning His will and doing it is not a burdensome thing, because we delight in His Word (1:2; 119:16, 35, 47–48, 70, 97, 143). Fear and delight can live together in the same heart because they are tied together by love (2:11; 119:19–20; 1 John 4:16–19). Because we love the Lord, His commands are not burdensome to us (1 John 5:3).

The person described in this psalm praises the Lord in worship, stands in awe of the Lord, delights in fellowship with the Lord, and seeks to obey the Lord. This kind of life brings blessing to the entire family (34:8–14; 37:25; 127:3–5; 128:3). If our life doesn't make an impact at home, among people we know and love, it is not going to make much of a difference out in the marketplace where people blaspheme the name of the Lord. The person also is a blessing to "the generation of the upright" (v. 2), the people of God who frequent the sanctuary (33:1; 37:37; 111:1; 140:13).

The Scriptures know nothing of an isolated believer who ignores other believers. We all need each other, and our united worship and witness can accomplish more than anything we can do by ourselves. Once again, we must not use verse 1 as a "charm" to ward off the troubles of life, for Job had the qualities listed in verse 1 (Job 1:8) and still greatly suffered. This kind of godly character does not protect us from pain and trials, but it does enable us to use those trials to glorify the Lord and to grow in grace (1 Peter 3:13–17; 4:12–19; 5:10).

### Our Relationship to Material Wealth (vv. 3–5, 9)

Under the old covenant, material wealth was one of the evidences of the Lord's blessing on His people as they moved into the Promised Land (Deut. 7:12ff; 28:1–14). This explains why the apostles were shocked when Jesus said that it was difficult for rich people to enter God's kingdom (Matt. 19:16–30). If rich people could not be saved, then who could? To Job's three friends, the fact that Job had lost everything was proof that God was punishing him for his sins. It was faulty logic, but they tenaciously held to it. The person described in this psalm was righteous before the Lord (vv. 3, 4, 6, 9) and did not acquire his wealth in some unlawful manner. He was generous in his use of the wealth the Lord gave him, sharing it with the poor and lending it freely without interest (Deut. 23:19–20). He was certainly not miserly or covetous, and he was obedient to the Lord's admonition to care for the poor and needy (Ex. 23:11; Lev. 25:35–38; Deut. 15:7, 11). When he quoted verse 9 in 2 Corinthians 9:9, the apostle Paul used him as an example for believers today to follow. (See also Prov. 11:24.) The word "horn" in verse 9 is an image of power and dignity (75:5; 132:17; Luke 1:69). Because of this man's generosity, the Lord allowed him to be lifted up in the eyes of his peers. As you see this man's faith in the Lord and love for those in need, you cannot help but think of the promise in Matthew 6:33.

### Our Relationship to Circumstances (vv. 6–8)

A believing heart is a steadfast heart, one that is not easily shaken by bad news or difficult circumstances. The person described was confident that the Lord could handle any problem that might come to him. A double-minded person has no stability (119:113; James 1:8; 4:8) and therefore, no ability to face the demands of life. (See 57:7; 108:1; and Isa. 26:3.) Believers with a confident heart and a clear conscience have nothing to fear when they receive bad news because they know the Lord is in control. If there is darkness around them, they wait for the Lord to send the light (v. 4). This is what encouraged Joseph during thirteen years of waiting and suffering in Egypt. "Wait on the Lord; be of good courage, and He shall strengthen your heart; wait, I say, on the Lord" (27:14 NKJV).

### Our Relationship to the Wicked (v. 10)
God rewards the delight of the righteous (v. 1) but ignores the desires of the wicked (v. 10; see 35:16; 37:12). Those who walk with the Lord and live godly lives are opposed and hated by the wicked, because the good works of the godly are like lights that reveal the evil in the world (Matt. 5:14–16; Eph. 5:1–14). The fact that the wicked oppose the godly is a good sign that the godly are living as they should. The witness of one dedicated life is a witness in the darkness of this world. Having seen and heard the witness of the godly, the wicked will have no excuse when they face the Lord (John 15:22).

## Psalm 113
It was traditional for the Jewish people to sing 113–114 before they ate their Passover meal, and they closed the meal by singing 115–118 (Matt. 26:30; Mark 14:26). These psalms were also sung in celebration of Pentecost, Tabernacles, the new moon festivals, and the Feast of Dedication. Because of the emphasis in 114, this small collection of psalms was called "The Egyptian Hallel." The psalm opens and closes with "hallelujah" ("praise Jehovah") and gives us three wonderful reasons for praising the Lord.

### God's Name Is the Greatest (vv. 1–3)
Four times you find the word "praise" (vv. 1, 3), but who are

the "servants" that the writer admonished to sing God's praises? Perhaps the temple choir in the newly restored temple, for this is a post-exilic psalm, but most likely he addressed the entire nation of Israel, which is often called "God's servant" (34:22; 69:36; 136:22; Isa. 41:8–9; 54:17). They had the privilege and responsibility of sharing the true and living God with their Gentile neighbors (Isa. 42:6), and Paul applied that verse to his own ministry and to the ministry of the church (Acts 13:47; 26:26; and see Luke 2:32). The word "name" is used three times in these verses and refers to the character of God and the revelation of who He is and what He does. God has a "good name" and that name should be magnified among those who have never trusted Him. To "glorify God" means to make God look good to those who ignore Him, oppose Him, or do not know Him. This kind of praise pays no attention to time ("forever more") or space (from east to west). The prophet Malachi foresaw the day when the Gentiles would honor the name of the Lord (Mal. 1:11). God's name is attached to His covenant with Israel (Deut. 28:1–14, note v. 10), and both His name and His covenant can be trusted.

### God's Throne Is the Highest (vv. 4–6)

Earthly kings are concerned about the splendor and prominence of their thrones (2 Kings 25:27–30), but the Lord's throne is exalted above the nations and even above the heavens (57:5, 11; 99:2). Jesus Christ, the King of Kings (Rev. 19:16), is today exalted "far above all" (Eph. 4:10; Phil. 2:9–11). The question in verses 5–6 remind us of Exodus 15:11 (and see 35:10; Deut. 3:24; Isa. 40:18 and 25; and Mic. 7:18). It is not our Lord's transcendence that captivates the psalmist but His willingness to "stoop down" and pay attention to mere mortals who do not always honor Him. Most ancient kings were inaccessible to their people, but our God sees us and knows our every need (138:6; Isa. 57:15). For the believer, God's throne is not only a throne of glory and authority, but it is also a throne of grace, a topic the psalmist explained in the next three verses.

*God's Love Is the Kindest (vv. 7–9)*

The Lord in His grace not only sees us but He cares for us and helps us. He "stoops down" and condescends to work on our behalf (138:6–8). The picture in verses 7–8 comes from verses 7 and 8 of the song of Hannah (1 Sam. 2:2:1–10), part of which was borrowed by Mary in her song of praise to God (Luke 1:46–55). Hannah was a barren wife to whom God gave a son, Samuel the judge and prophet. The history of Israel contains the stories of several barren women to whom God gave sons. It begins with Abraham's wife Sarah, who gave birth to Isaac (Gen. 17:15–19), and then Isaac's wife Rebekah became the mother of Jacob, who fathered the twelve tribes of Israel (Gen. 25:19–23). Jacob's favorite wife Rachel gave birth to Joseph (Gen. 29:31; 30:22–24), the man who protected the sons of Israel in Egypt. Hannah gave birth to Samuel (1 Sam. 1:1–2:11), and Elizabeth gave birth to John the Baptist (Luke 1:13–15), the forerunner of Jesus Christ.

The ash heap was the gathering place of the outcasts of the city, the unwanted poor, and the diseased (Job 2:8). The sun would warm the ashes during the day and the ashes would keep the people warm at night. It was the one place that people avoided going near, but our God visits rejected people and changes their lives! If this is a post-exilic psalm, as many believe it is, this truth must have been a great encouragement to the Jewish remnant struggling to rebuild their nation and their lives. The love of God and the grace of God made our God stoop to our level, especially when He sent Jesus Christ to become one of us and die for us on the cross (Phil. 2:1–11). In John 8:6 and 8 and 13:1–11, Jesus stooped to forgive a sinful woman and to wash His disciples' feet. But His greatest demonstration of grace was when He died for us on the cross. He condescended to become like us that we might become like Him (1 Cor. 1:26–29; Eph. 2:1–10). There can be no greater love (John 15:13). Only Jesus Christ can lift sinners out of the ash heap and put them on the throne! (Eph. 2:1–10). One day the Lord will visit "barren Israel" and bless the nation with many children (Isa. 54:1–3; 66:8–11).

No matter how dark the day or impossible the circumstances, our God is able to do the impossible (Eph. 3:19–20).

## Psalm 114

In beautiful poetic language, this psalm describes Israel's exodus from Egypt, God's provision for their wilderness journey, their entrance into the Promised Land, and their conquest of their enemies. The psalmist used striking poetic metaphors to teach history and theology, and this approach reaches the imagination and stirs the heart. When Jewish families sing this psalm at Passover, it must be very meaningful to them. But the psalm is about God and reveals His gracious relationship to His own people.

### God Is for Us (v. 1)

The Exodus is mentioned frequently in the psalms (74:13; 77:17–20; 78:12–16, 52–53; 106:9–12; 136:10–15) because Israel's deliverance from Egypt was their "national birthday." The people were now set free to serve God and accomplish the important tasks He had assigned to them: bearing witness of the true and living God, writing the Scriptures, and bringing the Savior into the world. In terms of "biblical geography," Egypt represents the world and the bondage of the sinner to its evil forces (Eph. 2:1–3). It was the blood of the lamb applied to the doors that protected the Jewish firstborn from death, just as the blood of Christ, God's Lamb, saves us from sin and death. God's power in opening the Red Sea liberated Israel and separated them from their cruel taskmasters. This is a picture of the resurrection of Christ and the believer's participation in it (Eph. 2:4–10; Col. 3:1ff). In the centuries that followed, each annual celebration of Passover reminded the Jewish people that Jehovah was their God and that He was for them. "If God be for us, who can be against us?" (Rom. 8:31). The prophet Isaiah saw the Jewish exiles' deliverance from Babylonian captivity as a "second exodus" (Isa. 43:14–21). What an encouragement it was to that struggling Jewish remnant to know that Jehovah God was for them!

### God Is with Us (v. 2a)

The Lord not only separated Israel *from* Egypt, but He also separated Israel *unto* Himself. They were His people, His treasure and His inheritance. "Judah" and "Israel" refer to the whole nation and not to the two kingdoms that formed after the death of Solomon. After the tribes conquered the land of Canaan, the sanctuary of God was placed in Judah (Ex. 15:17) and that was where Solomon built the temple. The nations around Israel had their temples, but they were empty. God's glorious presence dwelt in the tabernacle (Ex. 40) and later in the temple (1 Kings 8:1–11). Today, God does not dwell in man-made houses (Acts 7:48–50), but He does dwell with His people, for our bodies are His temples and the church is His sanctuary (1 Cor. 3:16–17; 6:19–20; 2 Cor. 6:14–18; Eph. 2:19–22). Jesus is "Immanuel, God with us" (Matt. 1:23; 28:19–20). What a privilege it is to be in the family of God!

### God Is over Us (v. 2b)

Not only was God's sanctuary in Judah but so was His throne (Ex. 19:6). David and his descendants were God's chosen rulers, but they represented the Lord God and had to obey His law. God made a covenant with David in which He promised him a throne forever and an heir forever on that throne (2 Sam. 7). David's throne is gone (Hos. 3:4–5), but that covenant is fulfilled in Jesus Christ (Luke 1:30–33, 68–73). One day He will sit on David's throne and rule over His kingdom. Had the people of Israel obeyed the Lord and allowed Him to exercise dominion over them, they would have been a great witness to the Gentile nations around them. Instead, they followed the ways of these nations and worshiped false gods instead of the true and living God.

### God Is before Us (vv. 3–8)

Most of the psalm is devoted to describing the miracles God performed for Israel as they left Egypt and headed for Canaan. The key thought is that God went before His people, and everything in nature trembled at His presence and obeyed His will (v. 7). The Red Sea opened and Israel marched through on dry land. Forty years later, the Jordan River opened and the people of Israel marched into the Promised Land. During their long march, God gave them bread and meat to eat and water to drink. Two different Hebrew words are used for "rock" in verse 8; the first refers to Exodus 17:1–7 and the second ("flint cliff") refers to Numbers 20:1–13, one at the beginning of their journey and the other near the end. It is likely that the mountains and hills mentioned in verses 4 and 6 were in Canaan, and the picture is that of God removing all obstacles from before Joshua and the victorious Jewish army. God goes before His people and takes them through the hopeless places (Red Sea, Jordan River) and the hard places (mountains, hills), and He even provides water out of rocks! (He can also provide honey, see 81:16. Sweetness out of hardness!)

The Lord is not mentioned by name until verse 7, and then the psalmist calls upon the whole world to tremble at His presence! The Exodus may have been past history, but the presence of the God of Jacob is a present reality to those who trust Christ and allow Him to lead (John 10:4). Remember that the Jews used this psalm in those difficult post-exilic days when the work was hard and the dangers were many. This vivid picture of God going before His people must have helped them grow in their faith and trust Him for their needs. It can also help us today. "If God be for us—and with us—and over us—and before us—who can be against us?"

## Psalm 115

The Lord had given His people a great victory, and they wanted to acknowledge it before their pagan neighbors and give God the glory. If their neighbors had visited the returned exiles and seen their rebuilt temple, they would have asked, "Where is your god?" There were no idols in the temple or in the city. (See Acts 17:16 for contrast.) The question gave the Jews the opportunity to contrast the false gods of their neighbors with the true and living God of Israel. This psalm was written as a litany, with the leader opening in verse 1. The people then responded in verses 2–8, the choir in verses 9–11, and the people again in verses 12–13. The priests or the choir spoke in verses 14–15, and the people closed the litany in verses 16–18. The psalm may have been used at the dedication of the second temple (Ezra 6:16). It not only tells where the God of Israel is, but what kind of a God He is.

### The Reigning God (vv. 1–3)

Where is the God of Israel? In heaven on His glorious throne, reigning as the sovereign God of the universe! His throne is founded on mercy and truth (love and faithfulness), which reminds us of His covenant with Israel. Because He loved them, He chose them (Deut. 7:7–11) and gave them His covenant, which He faithfully kept. All of God's people can shout, "Alleluia! For the Lord God omnipotent reigns!" (Rev. 19:6 NKJV).

### The Living God (vv. 4–8)

Idolatry had always been Israel's most habitual and costly sin (Judg. 2:11–3:6), and even though their prophets ridiculed these man-made gods (1 Kings 18:27; Isa. 44:9–20; Jer. 10:1–16) and the Lord often chastened Israel, the people persisted in breaking God's laws. Israel did not seem to learn its lesson until Babylon carried the people away captive after destroying Jerusalem and the temple. In the great city of Babylon, two or three generations of Jews saw idolatry firsthand and the kind of society it produced. This cured them. They needed to remember that they were the servants of the living God (42:2; 84:2; Deut. 5:26; Josh. 3:10; 1 Sam. 17:26, 36; 2 Kings 19:4, 16), and the church today also needs to keep this truth in mind (Acts 14:15; 1 Thess. 1:9; 1 Tim. 3:15; 4:10; 6:17).

God is a Spirit and does not have a body (John 4:24), so when writers in Scripture speak about His eyes, ears, hands, and feet and so on, they are using what theologians call "anthropomorphisms" (*anthropo* = human; *morphos* = form, shape). This is a literary device which uses human characteristics to describe divine attributes. God uses the known to teach us the unknown and the unknowable. This section is repeated in 135:15–18.

Because the dead idols lacked the attributes of the living God, they were unable to do either good or evil, yet the people worshiped them!

> **No mouths**—They cannot speak to their people, make covenants, give promises, guidance, or encouragement. Our God speaks to us!
>
> **No eyes**—They offer their followers no protection or oversight. Our God's eyes are upon us (32:8; 1 Peter 3:12) and we can trust Him.
>
> **No ears**—No matter how much the idolaters pray, their gods cannot hear them! Remember Elijah on Mt. Carmel (1 Kings 18:20ff). Our God's eyes are upon us and His ears open to our cries (34:15).
>
> **No noses**—This speaks of God receiving our worship (Gen. 8:21) and being pleased with what we bring Him. (See John 12:1–8; Eph. 5:2; Phil. 4:18.)
>
> **No hands**—The workers whose hands made the idols have more power than the idols they call "gods." Our God is able to work for us as we seek to serve Him. His fingers made the universe (8:3) and His arm brought salvation (Isa. 53:1). (See also Isa. 41:10 and 46:1–7.)
>
> **No feet**—The people had to carry their idols (Isa. 46:1–7; Jer. 10: 1–10), but our God carries us and walks with us. (See Isa. 41:10, 13.)

But the greatest tragedy is not what the idols cannot do but what they *can do* to the people who worship them. *We become like the God we worship.* As we worship the true and living God, He transforms our ears to hear His truth and the cries of those in need. He gives us eyes to see His Word and His world and the path He wants us to walk. Our "spiritual senses" develop and we become more mature in Jesus Christ (Heb. 5:10–14). But those who worship false gods lose the use of their spiritual senses and become blind to the light and deaf to God's voice.

### The Giving God (vv. 9–15)

"Trust the Lord and He will give His blessing" is the theme of this section, and how the discouraged remnant needed that assurance! They needed His blessing on their crops, and they wanted their number to increase (v. 14). Of course, the Lord had stated this in His covenant with Israel (Lev. 26:1–13; Deut. 28:1–14), and all they needed was His reminder. In verses 11 and 13, "those who fear God" were not the Gentile "God fearers" that we meet in the New Testament (Acts 13:16, 26; 16:14; 17:17; 18:7), but the devoted Jewish believers in the nation of Israel (22:23; 111:10). We find similar threefold lists in 118:1–4 and 135:19–21. Both Ezra 6:21 and Nehemiah 10:28 indicate that the returned remnant was not too hospitable to the "strangers" in the land. God had been Abraham's "help and shield" (Gen. 15:1), and He will also protect us and provide for us (3:3; 28:7; 33:20; Deut. 33:29). Because Jehovah God is the "Maker of heaven and earth" (v. 15; 121:2; 124:8; 134:3; 146:6; Isa. 40:12–26; Jer. 10:11), we should worship Him and not what He has created *or what we manufacture ourselves*.

### The God Who Deserves Our Praise (vv. 16–18)

The word "bless" is used five times in verses 12–15, and we cannot live without His blessing, but it is also good for us to bless the Lord (v. 18). To "bless the Lord" means to ascribe all glory and praise to Him, to delight His heart with our joyful and willing thanksgiving and obedience. (See 16:7; 26:12; 34:1; 100:4; 103:1; 134:2.) He made the earth and gave it to men and women to meet their needs and give them work to do, cooperating with Him in the development of His abundant resources (Gen. 2:8–25). The people who worship dead idols are also dead, but we are alive in Jesus Christ and ought to extol the Lord! After all, if we expect to praise Him forevermore, we had better start now and be ready when we see Him!

## Psalm 116

At a time when the psalmist was "at rest" (v. 7), unscrupulous men whom he had trusted lied about him (v. 11) and created trouble for him. In fact, their deception almost cost him his life (vv. 3–4), but he called on the Lord and was saved from death (vv. 1–2). The psalm is very personal, with "I," "my," and "me" used over thirty times. In expressing his praise to the Lord, the writer borrowed from other psalms, especially 18, 27, 31, and 56, and it appears that he knew the texts of King Hezekiah's prayer (Isa. 37) and his psalm of thanksgiving (Isa. 38). As the psalmist reflected on his life-threatening experience, he discovered several reasons why the Lord God delivers people from danger and death.

### God Answers His Children's Prayers (vv. 1–4)

The writer could not trust in himself for deliverance (v. 3), nor could he trust the people around him, some of whom were liars (v. 11), but he knew he could trust in the Lord and call on Him for help (vv. 2, 13, 17). To "incline" one's ear is to pay attention and concentrate on what is being said (113:5–6; 17:6). Only a God as great as Jehovah can hear the voices of millions of His children who are praying to Him at the same time. The writer was in deep trouble and sorrow, like a man drowning who is so entangled in a net that death seems inevitable (vv. 3, 8, 15; see 18:4–6). The name of the Lord represents all that God is and does, and to call on His name is to trust Him to work on our behalf. (See vv. 4, 13, 17.) Like Peter sinking in the sea during the storm, he prayed, "Lord, save me!" (Matt. 14:29–31) and the Lord rescued him. When, through no fault of our own, we find ourselves in great danger, we can call on the Lord for His help. Peter referred to verse 3 in his sermon at Pentecost (Acts 2:24, "loosed the pains of death") and applied it to the resurrection of Jesus Christ.

### God Is Merciful and Gracious (vv. 5–11)

God's name represents God's character, and He is gracious, righteous, compassionate, and powerful. The Lord loved the psalmist and saved him, and the psalmist then loved Him even more (vv. 1, 5; see 1 John 4:19). Note the phrase "our God" in verse 5, which indicates that the writer was giving his testimony to a group of people, probably at the sanctuary (vv. 14, 18–19).

"Simplehearted" does not refer to ignorant or superstitious people but to childlike believers with sincerity and integrity, people who dare to believe that God means what He says.

But the Lord did even more than deliver him from death. He also "dealt bountifully" with him (v. 7), and some of this "bounty" is described in verses 8–9. God wiped away his tears, He held him up and prevented him from stumbling (Jude 24), and He walked with him to protect him from his enemies. And He did all of this in spite of the ambivalence of the psalmist's faith, one minute dismayed at the lies of so-called friends, the next minute affirming his faith in the Lord (vv. 10–11). In the pressure of danger and pain, we often say things we really do not mean, but the Lord sees our hearts and knows what we really believe. The psalmist held to his faith even though he said what he did, and the Lord ignored what he said with his lips and responded to what he was saying in his heart. Paul quoted verse 10 in 2 Corinthians 4:13.

### God Holds His Children Precious (vv. 12–15)

After he had been delivered, the psalmist wanted to express his gratitude to the Lord, and he did so in four ways. First, he brought a thank offering to the Lord at the sanctuary (v. 17; Lev. 3; 7:11–21). Second, part of this sacrifice, the priest would pour out a portion of wine on the altar as a symbol of the worshiper's life poured out to serve the Lord. This was indeed a "cup of salvation" for the psalmist whose life could have been destroyed by the enemy. Third, the priest kept back part of the offering for a feast held after the sacrifice, and there the worshiper shared his food and his joy with his family and friends. At that feast, the psalmist called on the Lord and publicly thanked Him for His mercies. Fourth, following the ceremony and feast, the psalmist began to keep the promises he had made to the Lord during his time of great suffering and danger (vv. 14, 18). We must not consider these vows to be "holy bribes" given in payment for God's help, for the psalmist surely knew that God's will cannot be influenced by man's gifts. (See Job 41:11, quoted in Rom. 11:35.) "Or who has first given to Him and it shall be repaid to him?" (NKJV).

God's Son is precious to the Father and to all believers (1 Peter 2:4–7), and the Father loves us so much that He gave Jesus Christ to die on the cross in our place (Rom. 5:8). If our Father loves us that much, then He must be concerned not only with how we live, but also how and when we die. For believers, death is not an accident but an appointment (Ps. 139:16, and see 39:4–6 and 92:12). If the Father pays attention to the death of every sparrow, surely He will be concerned about the death of His saints (Matt. 10:29–31; John 11:1–16). Just as the blood of Christ is precious (1 Peter 1:19), so our blood is precious to God (72:12–14). *God's servants are immortal until their work on earth is done.* They can be foolish and hasten the day of their death, but they cannot go beyond their appointed time. That is in God's hands (48:14; Job 14:5 NIV; Luke 2:26).

### God Is Faithful to His Covenant (vv. 16–19)

The phrase "I am your servant" is equivalent to "I am a son of the covenant." John's father and mother had brought him to the priest eight days after his birth, and there he received the sign of the covenant and the name his parents had selected for him (Lev. 12:3; Luke 1:57–63; 2:21). If he kept the covenant and obeyed the Lord, he had the right to come to the Lord with his needs and ask Him for help. Believers today belong to God's new covenant family in Christ, but this does not guarantee protection from pain and trials. However, it does mean that God is in control and will work all things for our good and His glory, even our death (Rom. 8:28; John 21:17–19; 2 Peter 1:12–15). Even our Lord lived on a divine timetable and they could not crucify Him until the chosen hour had come (John 2:4; 7:30; 8:20; 12:23; 13:1; 17:1). May the Lord help us to end well and be faithful to Him (2 Tim. 4:6–8).

# Psalm 117

An anonymous writer composed the shortest psalm and in three brief sentences encompassed the whole world. The psalm is an invitation to people everywhere to turn to the Lord and join with believers everywhere in praising Him. A proper understanding of this psalm will help us appreciate at least four privileges that belong to God's people.

### Worshiping God (v. 1a)

The psalm opens and closes with "praise the Lord," for praising the Lord ought to be a mark of every believer today as it was of the new Christians in the early church (Acts 2:47). The first "praise" translates the familiar Hebrew word *hallel* which gives us "hallelujah—praise the Lord." The second "praise" is *shavah*, which means "to boast, to extol and laud." When we praise the Lord, we not only tell Him of His greatness, but we also "brag on Him" to those who hear our songs. Worship and praise are the highest occupations to which we can dedicate our voices, the activities that will occupy us for all eternity!

### Sharing the Gospel (v. 1b)

The word translated "nations" is often translated "Gentiles," that is, all people who are not of Semitic origin. The Hebrew word translated "peoples" refers to the diverse nationalities in the world (Rev. 7:9). You find the phrases "all the earth" and "all peoples" frequently in the book of Psalms (47:1; 66:1; 96:1; 98:4, 7; 100:1). The Jewish people were supposed to be *separated* from the Gentiles but not *isolated* from them, for God called Abraham to found a nation that would bring blessing to all the earth (Gen. 12:1–3; Rom. 4:17–18; Gal. 3:8). However, Israel failed and became guilty of imitating the Gentiles instead of illuminating the Gentiles with the light of God's truth (Isa. 42:6; 49:6). "Salvation is of the Jews" (John 4:22; Luke 2:32), for God chose the Jewish people to give the world the knowledge of the true God, the Scriptures, and the Savior.

The church today needs to carry the light of the Gospel to the whole world (Acts 13:47). Paul quoted this verse in Romans 15:11 as part of his explanation of the relationship of the church to Israel. The apostles and other early Jewish Christians praised the Lord *among* both Jews and Gentiles (Rom. 15:9) as recorded in the book of Acts. Through this expanding witness, many Gentiles trusted Christ and praised God *with* the Jewish believers

(Rom. 15:10), for believing Jews and Gentiles were one body in Christ (Eph. 2:11–22).

If we are a worshiping people, praising the Lord, then we will be a witnessing people, telling others how wonderful He is. Like the lepers outside the gates of Samaria, believers today must confess, "We are not doing right. This is a day of good news, but we are keeping silent" (2 Kings 7:9 NASB). May we imitate the apostles who said, "For we cannot but speak the things which we have seen and heard" (Acts 4:20 NKJV).

### Depending on God's Great Love (v. 2a)

Have we forgotten that "it is of the Lord's mercies that we are not consumed" (Lam. 3:22)? We have been saved by grace, not by our good works (Eph. 2:8–9), and were it not for God's merciful lovingkindness, we would still be in darkness and death. How unfortunate that some of the Jewish leaders became proud of being God's chosen people and began to look down upon others. They even called the Gentiles "dogs." But God's people today are guilty of the same sin. "His lovingkindness is great toward us" (v. 2a NASB) so we have nothing to boast about. "Not of works, lest anyone should boast" (Eph. 2:9). If we are humble before the Lord, He can use us to reach others, but if we are proud, He will reject us. "God resists the proud, but gives grace to the humble" (1 Peter 5:5). We are saved by grace and we live by grace, depending wholly on the Lord's generosity in Jesus Christ. A proud church is a weak church. To enjoy the praise of men is to lose the blessing of God.

### Resting on Divine Assurance (v. 2b)

Yes, God's people are saved by faith and live by faith, but our faith would mean nothing were it not for His faithfulness that "endures forever." The word translated "truth" or "faithfulness" means in Hebrew "to be firm, to be unshakable." God's character cannot change and His promises will not change, so why are we fretting about the feelings within us and the circumstances around us? Why do we hesitate to obey Him when He abounds in faithfulness (Ex. 34:6)? If God calls us to do something, He is faithful to help us do it (1 Thess. 5:24). To rely on our faith is to put faith in faith, but to rely on God's faithfulness is to put faith in the Lord. Our assurance is in the Word of God and the God of the Word.

## Psalm 118

Sandwiched between the shortest psalm and the longest, this is the last song in the Egyptian Hallel. The background is probably the dedication of the restored walls and gates of Jerusalem during the Feast of Tabernacles in 444 B.C., in the time of Ezra and Nehemiah. The Jews in the city were surrounded by enemies who first ridiculed them and then threatened to attack them and stop the work (vv. 10–14; Neh. 2:19–20; 4:1–9; 6:1–9). The rebuilding project took fifty-two days, and the report of this remarkable accomplishment astounded the nations (vv. 15–16, 23–24; Neh. 6:15–16). The psalm mentions gates (vv. 19–20) and building (vv. 22) and certainly expresses the joy the people experienced as they beheld what the Lord had done. The repeated phrases in verses 2–4, 10–12, and 15–16 suggest that the psalm was written for public worship. The pronouns "I" and "me" in verses 5–21 refer to the nation of Israel and not to the psalmist. But the psalm speaks to all believers in every age and gives them four practical instructions.

### Give Thanks to the Lord at All Times (vv. 1–4)

The psalm is bracketed by thanksgiving (vv. 1–4, 28–29), for this is one of the purposes of the "hallelujah" psalms, and we have met the threefold address before (115:9–11). The human situation may change many times, but God's merciful lovingkindness endures forever. The nation of Israel certainly ought to praise God for all the blessings and privileges God has bestowed on her (Rom. 9:1–5). The house of Aaron ought to thank God for the great privilege of serving in the sanctuary and at the altar. "Those who fear the Lord" would include all of God's faithful people, Jews and Gentiles—"the upright in heart"—who faithfully obeyed His Word and feared His name. God's people today have every spiritual blessing in Jesus Christ (Eph. 1:3) and certainly ought to praise His name.

### Trust the Lord in Every Crisis (vv. 5–14)

"The Lord" is mentioned in every verse in this paragraph because He was the one who protected Israel from their enemies and enabled the people to complete the work in difficult times. In 537 B.C., Israel had been set free from captivity (v. 5), and about 50,000 Jews returned to Jerusalem under the leadership of Zerubbabel the governor and Joshua the high priest. (See Ezra 3–6.) The Jews laid the foundation of the temple in 536 B.C., but local officials interfered and the work stopped from 536 to 520 B.C. The nations around the city did not want a restored Jewish state in the neighborhood, so they opposed both the rebuilding of the temple and the fortifying of the city. The work was resumed in 520 B.C. and the temple was completed and dedicated in 515 B.C. The people learned to trust, not in kings and princes, but in the Lord alone (vv. 8–9). They also learned that, though the enemy might attack them like bees, the Lord would give them victory (vv. 10–12). This was also true when Nehemiah came to Jerusalem in 444 B.C. and directed the work of rebuilding the walls and restoring the gates. Knowing that the nation of Israel was God's chosen instrument for bringing blessing to the world, Satan opposed the work and sought to destroy both the people and their city, but faith and courage carried Israel through to victory (vv. 5–7; Heb. 13:6). The statement in verse 14 is significant. The Jews sang it when they were delivered from Egypt (Ex. 15:2) and when God enabled them to rebuild their temple and the city walls (118:14). They will sing it in the future when Messiah redeems them and establishes His kingdom (Isa. 12:2, see context). Just as "all nations" attacked Israel in the past, they will do so again in the future (Isa. 29:2–7; Zech. 12:9; 14:1–5; Joel 3:1–2), and the Lord will again rescue them. God's people must learn to trust Him in every crisis of life.

[Note: For what it is worth, vv. 8 and 9 are the central verses of the Bible. Of course, the verse divisions of the Bible are not inspired.]

### Glorify the Lord after Every Victory (vv. 15–21)

When the wall was dedicated, the joyful shouts of the people were heard afar off (Neh. 12:43), and the psalmist mentions this (vv. 15–16). The "tents of the righteous" are the homes of the people of Israel as well as their temporary dwellings during the Feast of Tabernacles (Lev. 23:33–44). The people were careful to give the Lord all the glory for what Israel had done in the restoring of the city. Israel has been sorely chastened, but Israel will not die (vv. 17–18). A festive procession came to the gates of the city (see Ps. 24), or perhaps to the temple courts (see v. 27), for the celebration would involve sacrifices offered at the temple. One of the best ways to "seal" God's blessing to our hearts and make sure He gets the glory is to publicly praise Him—and keep on praising Him!

### See the Lord in Every Experience (vv. 22–29)

Under Zerubbabel and Ezra, the Jewish people had been rebuilding the temple, and under the leadership of Nehemiah, they had rebuilt the walls of Jerusalem and restored the gates. During these activities, did they find among the ruins a large stone that they rejected, only to discover it was the most important stone of all? The Gentile nations had despised and rejected Israel (Neh. 2:18–20; 4:1ff), but God had spared them to finish the work He gave them to do.

In Scripture, the stone is a familiar image of the Lord God (18:2, 31, 46; Gen. 49:24; Deut. 32:4, 15, 18, 30–31; 2 Sam. 22:2–3, 32, 47; Isa. 17:10; 26:4; 30:29; 33:6). It particularly points to the Messiah (Isa. 8:14; 28:16; Dan. 2:34–35, 45; Matt. 21:42–44; Mark 12:10; Luke 20:17–18; Acts 4:11; Rom. 9:32–33; 1 Cor. 10:4; 1 Peter 2:6–8). Peter made it clear that the Jewish leaders ("builders") had rejected their Messiah, the Stone (Acts 4:11), and He became to them a stone of stumbling (Isa. 28:16; Rom. 9:32–33). But in His death, resurrection, and ascension, Jesus Christ has become the chief cornerstone of the church, God's temple, binding Jews and Gentiles together in one sanctuary (Eph. 2:19–22). One day Jesus will return as the

Stone of judgment and crush the arrogant kingdoms of this world (Dan. 2:34, 44–45). Every Christian believer can use verses 22–24 to praise the Lord for the salvation provided in Jesus Christ. "Save now" (v. 25) is the word "hosanna" which the people shouted when Jesus rode into Jerusalem (Matt. 21:9; Mark 11:9–10), and note the words, "Blessed is he who comes in the name of the Lord."

The blood of a sacrifice was applied to the horns of the altar (v. 27; Lev. 4:7), but there is no evidence that the sacrifices were tied to the altar before they were slain. The altar was considered so holy that it was not likely it would be used for tethering animals. The *New International Version* marginal reading suggests that the bound sacrifices were brought *up to the altar* where the priests cut the animals' throats, caught the blood, and offered both the animals and the blood on the altar to the Lord. Of course, each sacrifice was a picture of the death of Jesus Christ, the Savior of the world. On each of the seven days of the Feast of Tabernacles, the priests led a procession once around the altar and then offered one burnt offering, but on the eighth day, the procession marched seven times around the altar and seven sacrifices were offered.

Jesus Christ is seen in this psalm—His triumphal entry (vv. 25–26), His rejection (v. 27), His death and resurrection (v. 17), and His exaltation as God's chosen Stone (vv. 22–23). Perhaps verse 24 hints at the Lord's Day, the day of resurrection, as "the new day" of the new creation made possible by His atoning work. It is important that we see Jesus Christ in every experience of life, for then these experiences will help us grow in grace and become more like the Savior.

## Psalm 119

The emphasis in this, the longest psalm, is on the vital ministry of the Word of God in the inner spiritual life of God's children. It describes how the Word enables us to grow in holiness and handle the persecutions and pressures that always accompany an obedient walk of faith. The psalm is an acrostic with eight lines in each section, and the successive sections follow the letters of the Hebrew alphabet. Each of the eight lines of 1–8 begins with the Hebrew letter *aleph*, the lines in 9–16 begin with *beth*, in 17–24 with *gimel*, and so on. The unknown author used eight different words for the Scriptures: law (*torah*), testimony, precept, statute, commandment, judgment (in the sense of "a rule for living"), word (of God), and promise. All eight are found in 33–40, 41–48, 57–64, 73–80, 81–88, and 129–136. Students disagree on this, but it appears that every verse contains a *direct* mention of God's Word except seven: verses 3, 37, 84, 90, 121, 122, and 132. If you count "ways" as a synonym for God's Word, then you can eliminate verses 3 and 37. (The NIV has "your word" in v. 37, but most Hebrew texts read "your ways.") The writer may have been meditating on Psalm 19 where David listed six names for the Scriptures, five of which are found in 119—law, testimony, precept, commandment, and judgment. Some of the vocabulary of 19 is also found in 119, including perfect or blameless (13/119:1, 80); pure (8/119:9, 140); righteous and righteousness (9; 119:7, 40, 62, 75, 106, etc.); and meditate or meditation (14/119:21, 51, 69, 78, 85, 122). Both compare the Word of God to gold (10/119:72, 127) and honey (10/119:103), and in both there is an emphasis on keeping or obeying God's Word (11/119:4, 5, 8, 9, 17, 34, 44, 55, 57, 60, 63, 67, 88, 101, 106, 134, 136, 146, 158, 167, 168).

### The Writer and His Times

Since we do not know who wrote the psalm, we cannot know for certain when it was written, but our ignorance need not hinder us from learning from this magnificent psalm. Some attribute the psalm to Moses, which is unlikely, and others to a priest or Levite who served in the second temple after the Babylonian captivity. Whoever the author was, he is a good example for us to follow, for he had an intense hunger for holiness and a passionate desire to understand God's Word in a deeper way. In all but fourteen verses, he addresses his words to the Lord personally, so this psalm is basically a combination of worship, prayer, praise, and admonition. The writer must have been a high profile person because he mentioned the opposition of rulers (vv. 23, 161; "princes" in KJV and NASB), a word that can refer to Gentile rulers or local Jewish tribal leaders (Neh. 3), and he also spoke to kings (v. 46). In the psalm, there are no references to a sanctuary, to sacrifices, or to a priestly ministry. The cast of characters includes the Lord God, a remnant of godly people in the nation (vv. 63, 74, 79, 120, etc.), the psalmist, and the ungodly people who despised him (v. 141), persecuted him (vv. 84–85, 98, 107, 109, 115, 121–122, etc.), and wanted to destroy him (v. 95). The psalmist referred to them as "the proud" or "the arrogant" (vv. 21, 51, 69, 78, 85, 122). They were people who were born into the covenant but did not value the spiritual riches of that relationship. They disdained the law and openly disobeyed it. The writer was reproached by them (vv. 22–23, 39, 42) and suffered greatly from their false accusations (vv. 50–51, 61, 67, 69–71, 75, 78).

Whether right or wrong, I have often thought that the prophet Jeremiah might have been the author of Psalm 119 and that he wrote it to teach and encourage his young disciples (v. 9) after the destruction of the temple. Many of the statements in the psalm could be applied to Jeremiah. He spoke with kings, five of them in fact (Jer. 1:2), and bore reproach because he faithfully served the Lord (Jer. 15:15; 20:8). He was surrounded by critics and enemies who did not seek God's law (Jer. 11:19) but wanted to get rid of the prophet (Jer. 18:23). Jeremiah was definitely the prophet of "God's Word in the heart" (Jer. 31:31–34), and this is an emphasis in 119 (vv. 11, 32, 39, 80, 111). The writer wept over the plight of his people (vv. 28 NASB, 136; Jer. 9:1, 18; 13:17; 14:17; Lam. 1:16; 2:18; 3:48). However, in the midst of catastrophe and danger, Jeremiah rejoiced in God's Word and nourished himself in it (v. 111; Jer. 15:16). In both vocabulary and message, this psalm is rooted in the book of Deuteronomy ("second law"), which is Moses's second declaration of the law. However, unlike Exodus, Deuteronomy emphasizes love and obedience from the heart, not just a "ritual" following of God's rules. Jeremiah was a priest as well as a prophet and had a working knowledge of Deuteronomy.

## The Theme

The basic theme of Psalm 119 is the practical use of the Word of God in the life of the believer. When you consider that the writer probably did not have a complete Old Testament, let alone a complete Bible, this emphasis is both remarkable and important. Christian believers today own complete Bibles, yet how many of them say that they love God's Word and get up at night or early in the morning to read it and meditate on it (vv. 55, 62, 147–148)? How many Christian believers ignore the Old Testament Scriptures or read the Old Testament in a careless and cursory manner? Yet here was a man who rejoiced in the Old Testament Scriptures—which was the only Word of God he had—and considered God's Word his food (v. 103) and his greatest wealth! (vv. 14, 72, 127, 162). His love for the Word of God puts today's believers to shame. If the psalmist with his limited knowledge and resources could live a godly and victorious life feeding on the Old Testament, how much more ought Christians today live for the Lord. After all, we have the entire Bible before us and two millennia of church history behind us!

When the psalmist used the word "law" (*torah*), or any of the seven other words for the Scriptures, he was referring to much more than the Ten Commandments and the ceremonial instructions that have now been fulfilled in Christ. He was referring to the entire revelation of God as found in the Old Testament Scriptures. Until the books in our New Testament were written and distributed in the first century, *the Old Testament Scriptures were the only Word of God possessed by the early church!* Yet with the Old Testament and the help of the Holy Spirit, the first Christians were able to minister and win the lost in a dynamic way. Peter used Psalms 69:25 and 109:8 to receive guidance in choosing a new disciple (Acts 1:15–26). He quoted Joel 2:28–32 at Pentecost to explain the advent of the Holy Spirit and Psalms 16:8–11 and 110:1 to prove the resurrection of Jesus Christ (Acts 2:14–39). In his defense before the council (Acts 7), Stephen opened with Genesis 12:1 and closed with Isaiah 66:1–2, and between those two referred to Exodus, Deuteronomy, and Amos.

Philip led a man to faith in Christ by using only Isaiah 53 (Acts 8:26–40). Paul found in Isaiah 49:6 a mandate to continue ministering to the Gentiles (Acts 13:47), and James concluded the Jerusalem conference by quoting Amos 9:11–15 (Acts 15:13–21). Paul even quoted an Old Testament verse about oxen to encourage churches to support their spiritual leaders (Deut. 25:4; 1 Cor. 9:9; 1 Tim. 5:18). (Hab. 2:4 is quoted as a key verse in Rom. 1:17, Gal. 3:11, and Heb. 10:37–38). In their theology, decisions, and ministry, the first Christians depended on guidance from the Old Testament Scriptures.

Many believers today stand guilty of ignoring the Old Testament, except for reading "favorite psalms," and therefore many are ignorant of what God's law teaches. "The law is a yoke," they exclaim, and point to Acts 15:10 and Galatians 5:1, but the psalmist found freedom through the law (vv. 45, 133). "To pay attention to the law is to move into the shadows!" they argue, referring to Colossians 2:16–17 and Hebrews 10:1, but the writer of Psalm 119 found the law to be his light (vv. 105, 130). "By the law is the knowledge of sin" (Rom. 3:20), but the psalmist used the law to get victory over sin (vv. 9–11). "The law kills!" (Rom. 7:9–11), but the law brought the psalmist new life when he was down in the dust (see NASB vv. 25, 40, 88, 107, 149, etc.). "Law and grace are in opposition!" many declare, but the psalmist testified that law and grace worked together in his life (vv. 29 and 58). God used Moses to liberate the people from Egypt, but then God gave Moses the law to give to Israel at Sinai. The German philosopher Goethe wrote, "Whatever liberates our spirit without giving us self-control is disastrous." Law and grace are not enemies, for law sets the standard and grace enables us to meet it (Rom. 8:1–3).

The writer of Psalm 119 *delighted* in God's law (vv. 16, 24, 35, 47, 70, 77, 92, 43; and see 1:1 and 19:8 and 10), and this joy was echoed by Paul (Rom. 7:22). Paul did not annul God's law and set it aside; rather, he said that the law was "holy, just and good" and even "spiritual" (Rom. 7:12–14). Though we are carnal (fleshly), there is a lawful use of the law in our inner person. The law of God is spiritual and can be used by the Spirit to minister to our spirit. To be sure, nobody is saved or sanctified by striving to obey the law. But for the dedicated Christian believer, there is a deeper meaning to the law, a writing of the Word upon our hearts (Deut. 4:9, 29, 39; 6:5; 10:12; etc.), because of the new covenant in Jesus Christ (Jer. 31:31–34; Heb. 8:8–12; 10:16–17; 2 Cor. 3).

To unsaved sinners, the law is *an enemy* because it announces their condemnation and cannot save them. To legalistic believers, the law is *a master* that robs them of their freedom. But to spiritually minded believers, the law is *a servant* that helps them see the character of God and the work of Christ. The Old Testament believer who wrote Psalm 119 was not satisfied with having the law in his home, his head, or his hand; he wanted the law in his heart where it could help him love what was holy and do what was right (v. 11). It was this approach that Jesus took in the Sermon on the Mount. The attributes of God as revealed in the Old Testament parallel the characteristics of the Word of God as seen in Psalm 119. Both are gracious (vv. 29, 58; 86:15), true and the truth (vv. 30, 43, 160; Ex. 34:6), righteous (vv. 106, 123, 137–138, 143, 151), good (vv. 39, 68), trustworthy (vv. 9, 73, 86, 90, 138), eternal (vv. 89, 152, 160; Deut. 33:27), and light (v. 107; 27:1). The way we treat the Word of God is the way we treat the God of the Word.

The Word of God performs many wonderful ministries in the life of the devoted believer. It keeps us clean (v. 9), gives us joy (vv. 14, 111, 162), guides us (vv. 24, 33–35, 105), and establishes our values (vv. 11, 37, 72, 103, 127, 148, 162). The Word helps us to pray effectively (v. 58) and gives us hope (v. 49) and peace (v. 165) and freedom (vv. 45, 133). Loving the Word will bring the best friends into our life (vv. 63, 74, 79), help us find and fulfill God's purposes (v. 73), and strengthen us to witness (vv. 41–43). When we think we are "down and out," the Word will revive us and get us back on our feet (vv. 25, 37, 40, 88, 107, 149, 154, 156, 159). If we delight in His Word, learn it, treasure it within, and obey what it says, the Lord will work in us and through us to accomplish great things for His glory! As you read and study Psalm 119, you will see the writer in a variety of experiences, but His devotion to the Lord and His Word will not change. Circumstances may change, but God and His Word remain the same.

### Aleph (vv. 1–8)—Blessed and Blameless

The opening word of the psalm—"blessed"—is repeated in verse 2 but found nowhere else this psalm. How can we receive God's blessing? By being blameless before the Lord, obedient to His law, and wholehearted in our relationship to Him. But some of the words that follow—law, precepts, statutes, decrees, commands—have a way of frightening us and almost paralyzing us with despair. When we think of law, we usually think of "cursing" and not "blessing" (see Deut. 27:1–28:68; Josh 9:30–35), but we must remember that Jesus bore the curse of the law for us on the cross (Gal. 3:10–13). The law is not a weapon in the hands of an angry judge, but a tool in the hands of a loving Father, used by the Spirit to make us more like Jesus Christ. The Word enables us to know God better and draw closer to Him. "Blameless" does not mean sinless but wholehearted devotion to the Lord, sincerity, and integrity. Only Jesus Christ was totally blameless in His relationship to God and His law, but because believers are "in Christ," we are "holy and without blame before Him" (Eph. 1:4)). His love is in our hearts (Rom. 5:5) and His Spirit enables us (Gal. 5:16–26), so His law is not a heavy yoke that crushes us, for "His commandments are not burdensome" (1 John 5:3 NKJV).

Seeking God means much more than reading the Bible or even studying the Bible. It means hearing God's voice in His Word, loving Him more, and wanting to delight His heart and please Him. It means wholehearted surrender to him (vv. 2, 10, 34, 58, 69, 145) and an unwillingness to permit any rival love to enter. All of the psalms make it clear that this kind of life is not without its dangers and disappointments, for we often fail. The writer of this psalm found himself in the dust and had to cry out for "reviving" (vv. 25, 37, 40, 50, 88, 93, 107, 149, 154, 156,

159). Once he had done that, he confessed his sins, got up and started walking with God again. *The victorious Christian life is a series of new beginnings.* As we cultivate an appetite for the Word (vv. 10, 20, 40, 81, 131) and feed upon it, we give the Spirit something to work with in our hearts, and He enables us to walk in God's paths. If we feel ashamed when we read the Word (v. 6; see v. 80), then we have to stop and find out why and then confess it to the Lord. If we are ashamed because of our disobedience, then we cannot witness to others (v. 46) and we will be ashamed of our hope (v. 116). Better to be ashamed now and confess it than to be ashamed when we meet the Lord (1 John 2:28).

Praise is good preparation for learning about God and His Word (v. 7). It is so important that he repeated it in verses 12 and 171. Our ways (v. 5) may not yet be God's ways (v. 3), but as we press on by faith, He will help us and not forsake us (v. 8; Heb. 13:5). Jacob was far from being a spiritual man when he ran away from home, but the Lord promised not to forsake him, and Jacob believed that promise and became a godly man (Gen. 28:10–22). God even deigns to be called "the God of Jacob."

### Beth (vv. 9–16)—Take Time to Be Holy

The writer closed the first section determined to keep the law of the Lord (v. 8), a promise he repeated in verse 145. He began this section like a true Jewish teacher by asking a question of the young men he was instructing: "How can we fulfill this promise?" He also promised to meditate on the Word (vv. 15, 48, 78), to delight in the Word and not forget it (vv. 16, 47, 93), and to run in the way of the Lord (v. 32). But he knew that it is easier to make promises than to keep them, a lesson Paul learned when he tried in his own strength to obey God's law (Rom. 7:14–25). Paul learned, as we must also learn, that the indwelling Holy Spirit enables the child of God to fulfill God's righteousness in daily life (Rom. 8:1–11). We must live according to God's Word, which means cultivating a heart for God. Paul called this "seeking the things that are above" (Col. 3:1).

We need a heart that seeks God, for if our heart is seeking

God, our feet will not stray from God (v. 10; Prov. 4:23). Such a heart will see Him in all of life, learn more about Him, fellowship with Him, and glorify Him in all that is said and done. Again, the Holy Spirit enables us to do this as we yield to Him. But we must also spend time in the Word and treasure it in our hearts (v. 11; Job 23:12; Prov. 2:1; 7:1). It is not our promises to the Lord but His promises to us that will give us victory over sin. We also need a thankful heart and a teachable spirit that will enable us to learn from the Lord (vv. 12, 108, 171). A. W. Tozer used to warn against being "man taught" instead of "God taught" (v. 102). The Lord has given teachers to His church and we should heed them. But unless the truth we hear moves from the head (and the note-book) into the heart, written there by the Spirit (2 Cor. 3:1–3), and then to the will, we have not really learned the Word or been blessed by it. The blessing comes, not in hearing the Word but in doing it (James 1:22–25). We should also speak with others about the Word (v. 13) and seek to enrich them with spiritual treasures. The heart is a treasury from which we draw spiritual wealth to encourage and help ourselves and others (Matt. 12:35; 13:51–52). The Scriptures as riches is a repeated theme in 119 (vv. 14, 72, 127, 162; see 19:10). To treasure any possession above the Word of God is idolatry and leads to trouble. Consider Lot (Gen. 13, 18–19), Achan (Josh. 6–7), King Saul (1 Sam. 15), and Ananias and Sapphira (Acts 5). On the positive side, consider Abraham (Gen. 14:18–24), Moses (Heb. 11:24–27), Mary of Bethany (Mark 14:3–9), and Paul (Phil. 3:1–11).

Whatever delights will capture our attention and we will think about it and meditate on it. This is true of God's Word. In this psalm, delighting in the Word, loving the Word, and meditating on the Word are found together (vv. 15–16, 23–24, 47–48, 77–78, 97–99), and they should be found together in our hearts and lives. We must take time to be holy.

### Gimel (vv. 17–24)—We Need God's Word!

If ever we feel we can ignore our daily time with God in His Word, then this is the Scripture to read. We need the Word because we are *servants* (vv. 17, 23, 38, 49, 65, 76, 84, 122, 124, 125, 135, 140, 176), and in His Word, our Master gives us directions for the work He wants us to do. Eli the priest was wrong in many things, but he was right when he taught young Samuel to pray, "Speak, Lord, for your servant is listening" (1 Sam. 3:9 NASB). As God's faithful servant, the anonymous writer of this psalm is ranked along with Moses, Joshua, David, Daniel, James, Paul, and Timothy, all of whom carried that title. But each child of God can serve the Lord and bear that same title (113:1; 134:1; 2 Tim. 2:24; 1 Peter 2:16). Everything in creation serves the Lord (v. 91), and we who are His redeemed people ought to join them. He always deals bountifully with His servants and provides for them adequately (13:6; 116:7; 142:7; Luke 22:35; Phil 4:19).

Not only are we servants, but we are also *students* (v. 18), and our basic manual is the Word of God. However, unless God opens our eyes, we will never see the wonderful things hidden in its pages (Eph. 1:17–18). God's Word is wonderful (v. 129), His works are wonderful (107:8, 15, 21, 24, 31), and His love is wonderful (31:21 NIV), and we must meditate on the wonder of His Person, His truth, and His mighty works. The eyes have an appetite (vv. 82, 123; 1 John 2:16) and we must be careful where we focus them (v. 37). Eyes that feast on the vanities of this world will never see the wonders in God's Word.

Like the patriarchs of old, we are also *strangers* in this world (vv. 19–20; 39:12; 105:12, 23; Gen. 23:4; Ex. 2:22; Lev. 25:23; Heb. 11:8–9, 13–16; 1 Peter 1:1; 2:11), and we need the Lord's guidance as we walk the pilgrim path. The laws for driving in Great Britain are different from the laws in the United States and it is dangerous to confuse the two. God's people are being led on the narrow road that leads to life, while the people of the world are on the broad road that leads to judgment (Matt. 7:13–14). Just as the cloud and fiery pillar led Israel in their wilderness journey (Num. 9:15–23), so the Scriptures lead us (v. 105). The psalmist felt a crushing burden to read and ponder God's ordinances, and unlike many travelers today, he was not afraid to ask the Lord for directions. If we take time to meditate on the Word and seek the Lord, He will show us the path of life (16:11).

Because we serve a different Master, obey a different set of laws, and have our citizenship in a different country (Phil. 3:20), we are different from the lost people whom Jesus called "the children of this world" (Luke 16:8). We will not conform to the world (Rom. 12:2), and the world opposes and persecutes us because of this. Therefore, we are *sufferers* who bear reproach for Jesus Christ (vv. 21–14; Matt. 13:20–21; Heb. 13:13). The psalmist called these persecutors "the arrogant [proud]" (v. 21) and described them as disobeying God's law (vv. 126, 158), ignoring it (v. 139), wandering from it (vv. 21, 118), and forsaking it (v. 53). Because they reject God's Word, they reject God's people and mock them (v. 51), lie about them (v. 69), try to trap them (v. 85), and oppress them without cause (vv. 78; 122). These are the "willful sins" that David wrote about in 19:14. This opposition was in high places among the rulers (vv. 23, 161), which would mean the nobles and officers of the land. The psalmist wanted God to remove the reproach they had put on him like a garment (v. 22; see 35:26; 109:29; 132:18), but the psalmist's suffering gave him opportunity to bear witness to nobles and kings (v. 46; and see Matt. 10:18; Acts 9:15; Phil. 1:12–18; 4:22). The writer needed wisdom to know how to handle these difficult situations and he found counsel in God's Word (v. 24). Instead of listening to the enemy's slander, he meditated on God's truth. That is a good way to keep your mind clean and confident (Phil. 4:4–7).

### Daleth (vv. 25–32)—Down but Not Out

The previous section ended with the psalmist delighting in God's Word, and this one opens with him down in the dust! The enemy attacks us the hardest when we are enjoying the blessings of God, and we must expect it. When things are going well and we "feel good," it is dangerous to relax and lay aside the armor (Eph. 6:10–18). "We must be as watchful after the victory as before the battle," said Andrew Bonar, and he was right. When he found himself down, the psalmist knew what to do—he prayed!

"Revive me" (v. 25; see 143:11). His enemies were slandering his name (v. 23), restricting him (v. 61), lying about him (v. 69), causing him to suffer (v. 83) and be despised (v. 141), and even threatening his life (v. 109), so it is no wonder that he felt like an insect in the dust. But when we seem to be at our worst, the Lord comes along with the very best and gives us the grace that we need (2 Cor. 1:3–11; 12:1–10). The *New International Version* translates the Hebrew word "preserve my life," but much more is involved in this request. It involves saving his life, of course, but also invigorating him and breathing new life within him. He prayed this prayer often (vv. 25, 37, 40, 50, 88, 93, 107, 149, 154, 156, 159), and the Lord answered him each time.

"Teach me" (vv. 26–27). Too often we ask, "How can I get out of this trouble?" when we should be asking, "*What* can I get out of this experience?" In times of trouble, we need God's wisdom lest we waste our suffering (James 1:2–8). The psalmist knew there were still lessons to learn in the school of life and he did not want to miss them. He talked to the Lord about what was happening to him, and the Lord answered by giving him wisdom and strength. By faith, he expected to see God's wonders displayed in the midst of his battles.

"Strengthen me" (vv. 28–30). Throughout the psalm, the writer makes it clear that he is suffering because of his commitment to God and His Word (vv. 28, 50, 67, 71, 75, 83, 92, 107, 143, 153). He was actually risking his life to obey the Lord (v. 109). Yet he did not rage against his enemies and seek to destroy them; rather, he wept over them and turned them over to God (vv. 115, 136). All he wanted was strength to keep on living for the Lord and magnifying His Word. He discovered that God's grace was indeed all that he needed (2 Cor. 12:9). He would walk in the way of God's truth and avoid the enemy's way of deception (vv. 29–30, 104, 128). When we find ourselves pressured by the enemy, our first response is usually to pray that God will change them, when perhaps our best response would be that God would change us and enable us to overcome.

"Defend me" (vv. 31–32). The writer did not want to bring shame to the name of the Lord (vv. 31, 46, 78, 80), so he turned the situation over to Him by faith. If we think up clever schemes to defend ourselves and slander others, then the Lord will not be able to defend us (Rom. 12:17–21). As we hold to His Word and trust His promises, the Lord is able to work in His way and in His time. Faith delivers us from the confinement of the enemy's plots and sets us free to enjoy a larger place. He has gone from biting the dust (v. 25) to running freely in the way of the Lord! (See vv. 45, 96; 4:1 and 18:36.)

### He (vv. 33–40)—Ending Well

Paul (2 Tim. 4:6–8) and Jesus (John 17:4) both ended well, to the glory of God, but not every believer achieves that coveted goal. A good beginning ought to lead to a good ending, but that is not always the case. Lot, Samson, King Saul, Ahithophel, and Demas all made good beginnings, but their lives ended in tragedy. The psalmist wanted to end well (v. 33), but ending well is the consequence of living well. What are the essentials for a consistent life that ends well?

*Learning (vv. 33–34).* We must pray for spiritual enlightenment so we may learn God's Word and the way of His Word. It is not enough to read the Bible, outline the books, get answers to questions, and be able to discuss theology. We must come to understand the character of God and the workings of His providence (27:11; 86:11; 103:7). Just as children come to understand the character of their parents and what pleases them, so we must get to know God better and discern His desires. We have a complete revelation of the Lord and His will in the Scriptures, but we need inner illumination to discover what it means to our own lives. Our prayer "Teach me" must be balanced with "Give me understanding," and both must lead to obedience.

*Obeying (v. 35).* What we learn with our mind and apprehend with our heart must motivate the will to do what God commands.

But our obedience cannot be that of a slave obeying a master in order to avoid discipline. It must be the obedience of a grateful child who delights to please his or her parents. "Doing the will of God from the heart" (Eph. 6:6). This was the way Jesus obeyed His Father: "I delight to do Your will, O my God, and Your law is within my heart" (Ps. 40:8). "I always do those things that please Him" (John 8:29). If we want to know God's truth, we must be willing to obey God's will (John 7:17).

*Delighting (vv. 36–37)*. These verses warn us that our hearts and minds ("eyes") must be focused on the truth of God and not material wealth and the vanities of the world (vv. 51, 157). Outlook determines outcome. Abraham looked for the heavenly city and ended well; Lot looked at Sodom and ended badly (Gen. 13; Heb. 11:8–16). What the heart loves and desires, the eyes will see (101:2–6; Num. 15:37–41; Jer. 22:17). To have one eye on the world and the other on the Word is to be double-minded, and God does not bless double-minded people (James 1:5–8).

*Fearing (vv. 38–39)*. The fear of the Lord is the fear that conquers every fear. The fear of man is the fear that leads to bondage and defeat (Prov. 29:25). The psalmist was not afraid of his enemies; he was afraid of disgracing the Lord and bringing dishonor to His great name. The psalmist claimed the promises of God and trusted God to deal with his enemies; for we live on promises, not explanations. Our faith is tested by the promises of God and our faithfulness is tested by the precepts of God, and both are important. (For more on God's promises, see vv. 41, 50, 58, 76, 82, 116, 123, 140, 148, 154, 162, and 170.) It is not our promises to Him (v. 57) but His promises to us that really count.

*Longing (v. 40)*. To have a deep longing for God's truth is the mark of a maturing believer. His soul was "consumed with longing" and he even "fainted with longing" (vv. 20–21 NIV), so much so that he even "panted" for God's commands (v. 131). He longed for the day when God's salvation would be revealed (v. 174; Rom. 8:18–23). Meanwhile, his longing was satisfied by the living Word of God, which is the believer's honey (v. 103), bread

(Matt. 4:4), milk, and solid food (1 Cor. 3:1–3; Heb. 5:12–14; 1 Peter 2:1–3).

### Vau (vv. 41–48)—Walking and Talking

We hear several voices in this section, and it begins with God speaking to us (v. 41). He does this, of course, as we read His Word and meditate on it. He speaks in love and in mercy, and even the warnings come from His compassionate heart. The Word of God is the expression of the love of God to us (33:11) and it should result in love from our hearts to the Lord, to His people, and to the lost. God's Word shares God's promises, and promises always imply future hope. Scripture is "the word of his promise" (1 Kings 8:56), and all His promises have their realization in Jesus Christ (2 Cor. 1:20). The Scriptures are also "the word of this salvation" (Acts 13:26), for the Word declares that Jesus is the only Savior and we can trust in Him. What a wonder that God has spoken to us! (Heb. 1:1–2). Are we listening?

But while God is speaking, the enemy is also speaking (v. 42). We have learned that the writer of this psalm was oppressed by enemies who lied about him, slandered his name, and even threatened his life. Our main weapon against these attacks is "the sword of the Spirit, which is the word of God" (Eph. 6:17), for only God's truth can silence the devil's lies (Matt. 4:1–11). We need God's truth in our hearts, not only to keep us from sin, but also to equip us to answer those who oppose us or ask us why we believe as we do (1 Peter 3:15).

God's people speak to the Lord (v. 43). Like Nehemiah, we can send up "telegraph prayers" to the Lord right in the midst of our work and our battles (Neh. 2:5; 4:4; 5:19; 6:9, 14; 13:14, 22, 31). When we are confronted by the enemy, the Lord will not give us words we have never pondered from the Scriptures, but His Spirit can remind us of what we have read and learned (John 14:25–26). The writer connected God's Word with his mouth, because the word "meditate" in the Hebrew means "to mutter." The ancient Jews spoke the Word audibly as they meditated and prayed (Josh. 1:8).

Our lives speak for the Lord (vv. 44–45) if our "walk" agrees with our "talk." The best defense of the faith is a transformed life that is compassionate toward others. Our obedience to the Lord and our loving ministry to others (Matt. 5:13–16) demonstrates the reality of our faith far better than anything else. Because we know and obey "the word of truth" (v. 43), we are able to enjoy freedom from the bondage of sin (v. 45), for it is the truth that makes us free (John 8:32; James 1:25; 2:12).

Finally, God's people speak to others (vv. 46–48). If we truly love God and His Word, we will not be ashamed to share the Word even with important people like kings (vv. 6, 80; Rom. 1:16; Phil. 1:20; 2 Tim. 1:12; 2:15; 1 Peter 4:16). When we delight in the Word, love it, and obey it, sharing the message with others comes naturally. To witness means to tell others what we have seen and heard concerning Jesus Christ (Acts 4:20) and what He has done for us. A satisfied Christian is an awesome witness whose testimony God can use to convict and convert others. We do not worship the Bible but we do honor God's Word and lift our hands to the Lord in praise and thanksgiving for His gift. In many churches, the entire congregation stands when the Scriptures are brought in and publicly read. (See 28:2, 63:4, 134:2 and 141:2.)

The basic Christian virtues (1 Cor. 13:13) are seen in those who live by God's Word: faith (v. 42), hope (v. 43), and love (vv. 41, 47, and 48). Love is mentioned three times because "the greatest of these is love." (On loving God and His Word, see vv. 97, 113, 119, 127, 140, 159, 163, 165, 167; 1 Tim. 1:5.)

### Zayin (vv. 49–56)—The Ministry of Memory

If the psalmist was a priest or a Levite, and he probably was, then he was required to be an expert on the book of Deuteronomy. Deuteronomy means "second law." The book records Moses's "farewell speech" that he gave to prepare the new generation of Israelites for the conquest of Canaan. After forty years of wandering, the nation would stop being nomads and would become settlers, but new generations would come along and be prone to forget the lessons of the past. In Deuteronomy, you find the word "remember" fifteen times and the word "forget" fourteen times. Some things in the past we must forget (Phil. 3:12–14), but some things we must never forget. "He who does not remember the past is condemned to repeat it" (George Santayana).

God remembers His people (vv. 49–51). When applied to the Lord, the word "remember" means "to pay attention to, to work on behalf of." Being omniscient, God cannot forget anything, but He can decide not to "remember it against us" (Isa. 43:25; Jer. 31:34; Heb. 8:12; 10:17). That is the negative side; the positive side is that He "remembers" to do us good and give us His blessing. He remembered Noah and delivered him (Gen. 8:1); He remembered Abraham and delivered Lot (Gen. 19:29); He remembered Rachel and Hannah and enabled them to conceive (Gen. 30:22; 1 Sam. 1:19). Remembering is not recalling, for God never forgets; it is relating to His people in a special way. The psalmist prayed that God would use the Word to work on his behalf. The writer had hope because of the promises God had given to him, and he prayed that those promises would be fulfilled. When Daniel found in the prophecy of Jeremiah the promise of Israel's deliverance from captivity, he immediately began to pray for the promise to be fulfilled (Dan. 9). True faith not only believes the promises but also prays for God to work. In his believing and praying, the writer found encouragement ("comfort" comes from the Latin meaning "with strength"), and he did not abandon his faith or run away from his problems. He was revived with new life!

His people remember God's Word (vv. 52–54). How could this spiritual leader know the "ancient laws" that God gave Moses centuries before? The nation had preserved the Word (Deut. 31:24–29) and taught it to each new generation (Deut. 4:1–14), and this is the obligation of the church today (2 Tim. 2:2). Unless the Word of God is honored, taught, and obeyed in a church, that congregation is one generation short of extinction. The psalmist was indignant at what the worldly people ("the

arrogant") were doing as they abandoned Israel's spiritual heritage (vv. 53, 104, 128, 163), and he wept over their evil deeds
(v. 136). Anger alone can be very destructive, but anger plus love
produces anguish, and anguish can lead to constructive action.
His response was to turn God's statutes into songs and to use the
Word to praise the Lord (v. 54; Eph. 5:19; Col. 3:16). He did not
consider God's law a burden to bear; he saw the Word as a blessing to share—and he sang it! Praise that is not based on the truth
of Scripture is unacceptable to the Lord. We are on a difficult pilgrimage from earth to heaven, and we need God's songs to
encourage us and to help us witness to others along the way
(Acts 16:22–34). We are strangers on the earth, and the Bible is
our guidebook to this world (vv. 19, 64) and to ourselves (v. 64).

His people remember His name (vv. 55–56). The name of
God—Jehovah, Yahweh—is full of meaning and power. To translate it only as "I AM" is to miss much of the dynamic that it
contains (Ex. 6:1–3). We might paraphrase it, "I am present, I am
actively present, and I can do what I choose when I choose to do
it." God's name Yahweh speaks not only of His existence and His
eternality, but also of His sovereignty, His power, and the
dynamic working out of His will in this world. The ancient
Jewish people so revered His name that they feared to use it and
substituted Adonai, lest they sin against their God. In the book
of Psalms alone, there are more than one hundred references to
the name of the Lord. We are to love His name (5:11), sing
praises to His name (7:17; 9:2; 18:49), and glorify His name
(29:2). It is through His great name that we triumph over our
enemies (44:5; 54:1; 118:10–12), so we should always call on His
name for help (116:4, 13, 17). To remember His name is to
encourage our hearts to trust Him, obey Him, and not be afraid.
"And those who know Your name will put their trust in You, for
You, LORD [Yahweh], have not forsaken those who seek you"
(9:10 NKJV).

To remember God's name is to ask Him to remember us and
work on our behalf. We must do this when we are in the darkness and afraid (v. 55), or when we are lonely and discouraged

(42:6). "The name of the LORD is a strong tower; the righteous run to it and are safe" (Prov. 18:10). If you want to know how strong His name is, study the names of God in the Old Testament and the "I AM" statements of Jesus in the Gospel of John. But be sure to imitate the psalmist and make it your practice to trust and honor His name in every aspect of life (v. 56 NIV), not just during emergencies.

### Heth (vv. 57–64)—God Is All We Need

Whenever the people of Israel failed God and turned to idols for help, it was evidence that they did not really believe Jehovah was adequate to meet their needs. In the time of Elijah, Israel tried to remedy the drought by turning to Baal, the Canaanite storm god, but it was the Lord who sent the rain in answer to the prophet's prayer. When the enemy threatened to invade their land, the leaders of Israel often ran to Egypt for help, as though Jehovah was unconcerned and unable to deliver them. The psalmist in this section makes it clear that the Lord God Almighty is all we need.

God is our portion (vv. 57–58). This is real estate language and refers to the apportioning of the land of Canaan to the tribes of Israel (78:55; Josh. 13–21). The priests and Levites were not given an inheritance in the land because the Lord was their inheritance and their portion (Num. 18:20–24; Deut. 10:8–9; 12:12). Jeremiah, the priest called to be a prophet, called the Lord "the Portion of Jacob" (Jer. 10:16; 51:19; Lam. 3:24), and David used the same image in Psalm 16:5–6. The "lines" in 16:6 refer to the property lines of one's land, the inheritance given by God. Believers today have a rich spiritual inheritance in the Lord Jesus Christ, for God's fullness is in Him and we are "complete in him" (Col. 2:9–10). He is our life (Col. 3:4) and our "all in all" (Col. 3:11). Because we are in Him, we have "all things that pertain to life and godliness" (2 Peter 1:3). Our riches in Christ are revealed in the Word, which is our "spiritual bankbook," and His wealth can never diminish. The psalmist had made promises to obey the Lord (vv. 8, 15–16, 32–34, 47, 106, 115), but that is not how we get our wealth from the Lord. What He provides for us is a gracious gift, not a loan, and we are not required to promise to repay Him (Rom. 11:33–36). Accept the inheritance He has given you, rejoice in it, and trust Him to supply every need.

God is our Master (vv. 59–61). The land inherited by the Israelites actually belonged to the Lord (Lev. 25:23) and He cared for it (Deut. 11:8–17). If the people obeyed the terms of the covenant, God would bless the people and their labors in the land, but if they turned to idols, He would chasten them, first in the land and then in other lands. Loving obedience was the condition for God's blessing, even as it is today. Our mind belongs to Him ("I considered my ways") and our feet belong to Him ("turned my steps"). Our time belongs to Him and we must not delay obeying His will (v. 60). In ancient days, no servant could say "No," no servant could linger or postpone doing the master's will, and no servant could give excuses or say "I forgot." The servant's responsibility is to hear the master's orders, remember them, and obey them immediately.

God is our greatest joy (vv. 61–64). It should be the Christian's greatest joy to know God, love Him, hear His voice, and obey His will. Praying to Him and praising Him should be more refreshing to us than sleep. Being with His people should satisfy our hearts, and we should see the love and glory of God in all of creation. Whether we are lying on our bed at midnight, meditating on His Word (vv. 55, 62, 147–148), fellowshipping with God's people, or taking a walk in God's glorious creation, we love God, listen to Him, and thank Him. "All who fear you" is a fine description (vv. 63, 74, 79, 120), for the fear of God ought to mark the people of God. In spite of the disobedience of mankind and the ravages of sin that destroy God's creation, the earth is still full of God's lovingkindness, and though we are pilgrims and strangers on this earth, God is our home (90:1) and we have nothing to fear.

### Teth (vv. 65–72)—God Is Good, All the Time
The emphasis in this psalm is on what is good in the life of the believer. The Hebrew word *tob* is used six times in these eight

verses and can be translated good, pleasant, beneficial, precious, delightful, and right. God does what is good because God *is* good and because what He does is "according to his word" and His Word is good (v. 39). Neither His character nor His Word will ever change, so, "God is good all the time."

God does what is good (v. 65–66). The phrase "according to" is used frequently in Psalm 119 to relate a request or a fact to the Word of God. God acts according to the precepts, promises, and principles revealed in His Word, and we should pray and act accordingly. To ask God for something that is not according to His will and His Word is to ask ignorantly and selfishly (James 4:3), and if He gives the request to us, *we will be sorry and wish we had not prayed.* This happened to Israel when they asked God for flesh to eat (106:15; Num. 11:31–35). Therefore, we should pray the prayer of verse 66, for the better we know God's Word, the better we can pray in God's will and obey God's will.

God overrules evil and from it brings good (vv. 67–71). The psalmist had disobeyed the Word and gone astray. His sin was probably not a flagrant act of rebellion but of ignorance (Lev. 5:17–19; Num. 15:28), and God in His love sent affliction to discipline him (Heb. 12:1–11). At the time, this discipline was not pleasant, but it brought God's servant back to the place of obedience, so it was worth it (vv. 71, 75). However, there are times when we are *obedient* and we still experience suffering, but God uses that suffering to mature us and teach us His Word. Spurgeon said that the promises of God shine the brightest in the furnace of affliction. There are times when suffering comes from the enemies of God, whose hearts are insensible ("covered with fat"; 17:10; 73:7), but the Lord can even use godless opposition for our good and His glory (Rom. 8:28; 1 Peter 1:6–9 and 4:12–19). The most evil act ever performed on this earth was the crucifixion of the Lord of Glory on a cross, yet God used that to bring His salvation to the world.

God uses the Word to show us good (v. 72). The word "better" ("precious" NIV) is *tob* in the Hebrew. This is the second time in the psalm that the writer has compared God's truth to treasure (v. 14), and he will use this image again in verses 127 and 162. David used it in 19:10. The person of faith does not live by the priorities and values of the world (Heb. 11:24–27) but puts the will of God ahead of everything else. When we find the good treasures of truth in the precious Word of God, we rejoice in the goodness of the Lord and have no desire to wallow in the things of this world. No matter what our situation may be, we can affirm from our hearts, "God is good—all the time!"

### Yodh (vv. 73–80)—Read the Instructions

Led by God's Spirit, the author wrote this long psalm to convince us to make knowing and obeying the Word of God the most important activities in our lives. In the previous section, he reminded us how necessary God's Word is when we are experiencing difficulties, but it does not stop there. We need God's Word for all of life. He mentioned several ministries of the Word that are necessary in the life of the faithful child of God.

We learn about ourselves (v. 73). When you purchase a new appliance, you take time to read the owner's manual. The Bible is the owner's manual for God's people. It is the only book that tells the truth about where we came from, why we are here, what we must do to succeed in life, and where we are going. God made us (139:13–18) and knows us better than we know ourselves, and He shares this knowledge in His Word. As we read, we "see ourselves" in the people and circumstances described in the pages of the Bible. We do not see "past history" but present reality! Unbelievers have no idea what the world and its people are really like, for the "real world" and the "real people" are presented in the pages of the Bible. The Bible is a mirror in which we see ourselves—and do something about what we see (James 1:22–27).

We become a blessing to others (vv. 74, 79). When we hope in God's Word, we have joy in life, and this helps us to encourage others. "Be kind, for everyone you meet is fighting a battle" (Ian Maclaren). Are people happy to see us arrive or are they happier when we leave? When our friends and acquaintances have burdens, do they turn to us for help, or do we add to their burdens? We are commanded to bear our own burdens coura-geously and to help others bear their burdens (Gal. 6:2, 5).

We receive God's best in our afflictions (vv. 75–78, 80). Life is difficult and we must accept from the hand of God both the pleasant experiences and the unpleasant (Job 2:1–10; Phil. 4:10–13). In the dark hours of life, the Word is a light that shows us the way (v. 105), and we do not go stumbling down the wrong paths. We have the love of God to comfort us and the promises of God to encourage us. We may not delight in our circum-stances, but we pray that God will use them to spread the Gospel and glorify His name (Phil. 1:12–16). The enemy attacks us, but we turn to the Word and find the help that we need. Our deter-mination in Christ is that we shall not be ashamed. God's decrees are perfect and they come from His loving heart (33:11), so we have nothing to fear.

When all else fails, read the instructions.

### Kaph (vv. 81–88)—Faith and Patience

The focus is on the responses of the believer while he waited for the Lord to judge his enemies and deliver him from persecu-tion and danger. His oppressors were also the enemies of the Lord and of Israel, so his concern was more than personal. Satan has been seeking to exterminate the Jews (v. 87) since the time the nation was in Egypt, and he will continue until the end-times (Rev. 12). The Christian life is a battleground, not a playground and we must expect tribulation (John 16:33).

*Fainting but hoping (vv. 81–83)*. His inner person was exhausted from longing for God to work. His eyes were strained from watching for some evidence of His presence (Lam. 2:11). He felt like a dried-up wineskin that had been thrown aside as useless. However, he never gave up hope, for no matter how dark the hour, the future is our friend because Jesus is our Lord. "It is always too soon to quit" (V. Raymond Edman).

*Questioning but waiting (vv. 84–85)*. "How long?" he asked in verse 84, and "When" in verses 82 and 84. These questions have often been asked by suffering saints (see on 6:3), even by the martyrs in heaven (Rev. 6:9–11), because they are the natural response of people who are suffering. (See Jer. 12:3–4; 15:15; and 20:11–12.) It is difficult for most people to wait for the things they can see—a traffic jam to end, a checkout line to speed up, an important letter or e-mail to arrive—and it is even more difficult to wait for our unseen Lord to work out His will. It is through "faith and patience" that we inherit what God has appointed for us (Heb. 6:12; see Rom. 15:4). Our trials will produce patience if we trust in the Lord (James 1:3–4). The enemy may be digging pits, but the Lord will see to it that they fall into them first (9:15; Prov. 26:27).

*Trusting and reviving (vv. 86–88).* Is the enemy spreading lies about you? God's Word is dependable and can be trusted (vv. 128, 142, 151, 160). Do you feel like your defeat is very near? Rest on His promises and rely on His love. When the Father allows His children to go into the furnace of affliction, He keeps His eye on the clock and His hand on the thermostat. He knows how long and how much. To walk by faith will bring unrest and weakness, but to meditate on the Word will bring peace and power. Once again, the psalmist prayed for new life (see v. 25) and the Lord revived him. "Your Father in heaven loves you too much to harm you, and He is too wise to make a mistake" (Robert T. Ketcham).

### Lamedh (vv. 89–96)—Change and the Changeless

The familiar hymn "Abide with Me" says, "Change and decay in all around I see." If that was true in 1847 when Henry Lyte wrote those words, how much truer it is today! To younger people, change is a treat, but to older folks, change is a threat. We like to relax in our comfort zone and resist the dramatic changes going on around us and within us. But if we do, we fail to grow spiritually and we miss the opportunities God gives us to reach others with the Gospel. The psalmist made some wonderful affirmations, which if heeded, will anchor us to the eternal and enable us to be used of God during these turbulent times.

*God's Word is settled (v. 89).* Ever since Satan asked Eve,

"Indeed, has God said ...?" (Gen. 3:1), the enemy has been attacking the Word of God. Atheists, agnostics, philosophers, scientists, and garden-variety sinners of all kinds have ignored the Bible, laughed at it, and tried to do away with it, but it still stands. Though born in eternity, God's Word is rooted in history and speaks to every generation that will listen. The Word is "founded forever" (v. 152) and will endure forever (v. 162). (See Matt. 24:34–35.) Build your life on the Word of God and you will weather all the changes of life!

*God is faithful (v. 90a).* Pause and read Psalm 90 and see what Moses had to say about the eternal God and the changes of life. From generation to generation, He is God, and we can commit ourselves, our children, our grandchildren, and our great-grandchildren to His care. Abraham, Isaac, and Jacob were three decidedly different kinds of men, but God was the "God of Abraham and of Isaac and of Jacob."

*God's creation is established (vv. 90b–91).* Until that last day when God's fire purifies all things and He ushers in a new heaven and earth (2 Peter 3; Rev. 21–22), this present creation will stand. The laws that He built into creation will also stand, whether scientists understand them or not. People may abuse and waste the earth and its resources, but God's creation will continue to serve the Creator. Everything in creation serves the Lord except human beings made in the image of God. What a tragedy! This is still our Father's world and we can trust Him to manage it wisely.

*God's peace is available (vv. 92–95).* We do not go to the Bible to escape the realities of life but to be strengthened to face life and effectively serve God. We may not be able to delight in what is going on in the world, but we can delight in what God says in His Word. The Word equips us to deal with the changes of life and the crises that come. The verb "sought out" in verse 94 means "to consult, to inquire, to beat a path, to read repeatedly. Here is a believer who beat a path to the Bible, read it over and over, studied it, and when he had to make a decision, carefully consulted it. Philosophies change, political expedients fail, promises and contracts are broken, but the Word of God still stands.

*God wants us to get out of our rut (v. 96).* So much truth is buried in this verse, you could meditate on it for hours. Whatever mankind does will never reach perfection, because our human work comes from our limited mind, strength, and ability. Perhaps the psalmist was reading the book of Ecclesiastes, for the limitations of human achievement is one of the themes of that book. "Vanity of vanities, all is vanity!" In contrast to the limits of mankind, God's Word and works have no limits. His commandment (singular—it is one united Book)—is limitless, boundless, immeasurable. Though Jesus lived, taught, and died in the little land of Palestine, His life and ministry have reached a whole world. Mary gave her sacrificial offering to Jesus in a home in Bethany, but what she did has blessed generations of people around the world (Mark 14:1–9).

Why should God's people stay in a rut when the Word of God is so boundless and there are no limits to what He can do! We may not like all the changes going on in the world, but we need not be frustrated and afraid. Although the news coverage was not as good, the situation was not much different in the days of the apostles, and they turned the world upside down! God is on the throne; He holds the world in His hands; His promises can never fail; so, let's get moving!

### Mem (vv. 97–104)—Beyond Bible Study

Never have there been so many tools available for serious Bible study, and we are grateful for them. However, the Word of God is unlike any other book: we must be on good terms with the Author if we are to learn from what He has written. Our relationship to the Lord is determined by our relationship to His will, and that is determined by how we relate to His Word. Too many believers have only academic head knowledge of the Word, but they do not know how to put this knowledge into practice in the decisions of daily life. What we all need is a heart knowledge of the Word, and this means being taught by God (v. 102). Here are the conditions we must meet.

*We must love His Word and meditate on it (vv. 97–100).* We

enjoy thinking about people and activities that we love, and meditation means loving the Lord by pondering His Word and allowing its truths to penetrate our hearts. (See vv. 48, 113, 127, 159, 165, 167; and 1:2.) This does not mean that we abandon our daily responsibilities or that we constantly quote Bible verses to ourselves and ignore our work. Rather, it means that our minds and hearts are so yielded to the Spirit that He can remind us of the Word when we need it and give us fresh understanding in the new challenges we face. There are many ways to learn truth. We can learn from our enemies in the encounters of life (v. 98), from our teachers in the explanations of life from books and lessons (v. 99), and from the older saints who have had the experiences of life and know the principles that work (v. 100). Joshua learned from serving with Moses, from the battles that he fought, and from the experiences, good and bad, that came to his life. But the most important thing he did was to meditate on the Word (Josh. 1:1–9), because his meditation helped him to test what he had learned in the other three "classrooms" and to put it all together into one balanced whole. God shares His truth with babes (Luke 10:21) and those who are humble enough to receive it (1 Cor. 1:18–2:8).

*We must obey His Word (vv. 101–102).* A true student of the Word is not a person with a big head, full of all sorts of knowledge, but one who has an obedient heart and loves to do God's will. While God's truth is food for our souls, it is not a "buffet" from which we select only the things we like. If the Bible tells us something is wrong, we stay off that path. If God tells us something is right, we do not abandon it. "Obedience is the organ of spiritual knowledge" (F. W. Robertson; John 7:17).

*We must enjoy His Word (vv. 103–104).* Honey would be the sweetest thing the psalmist could taste. However, the Word contains both sweetness and bitterness, and we must learn to receive both (19:10; 104:34; Prov. 16:24; Ezek. 2:9–3:15; Rev. 10). Samson got into trouble because of eating defiled honey from the carcass of a lion (Judg. 14:1–18). He was a Nazarite and was never to touch a dead body (Num. 6), so he defiled both himself and his parents, for Jewish people had to avoid dead animals (Num. 5:2; 9:10). God's Word is pure, not defiled, and gives us the sweetness and energy we need to obey His commands. The unsaved person finds the Bible boring, but the devoted child of God feeds on the Scriptures and enjoys the sweet taste of truth. This is what it means to go beyond Bible study.

### Nun (vv. 105–112)—We Will Be Faithful

It has well been said that the greatest ability is dependability, and this especially applies to the Christian life. We want God to be faithful to us, so is it wrong for God to expect us to be faithful to Him? Faithfulness is an evidence of faith, and faith comes from hearing and receiving the Word of God (Rom. 10:17; 2 Thess. 2:13). The psalmist described several areas of faithfulness in the life of the believer.

*Faithful feet (v. 105)*. Two familiar biblical images combine in this verse: life is a path (vv. 32, 35, 101, 128; 16:11; 23:3; 25:4) and God's Word is the light that helps us follow the right path (v. 130; 18:28; 19:8; 36:9; 43:3; Prov. 6:23; 2 Peter 1:19). The ancient world did not have lights such as we have today; the people carried little clay dishes containing oil, and the light illuminated the path only one step ahead. We do not see the whole route at one time, for we walk by faith when we follow the Word. Each act of obedience shows us the next step, and eventually we arrive at the appointed destination. We are told that this is "an enlightened age," but we live in a dark world (John 1:5; 3:19; 8:12; 12:46; Col. 1:13; 1 Peter 2:9) and only God's light can guide us aright. Obedience to the Word keeps us walking in the light (1 John 1:5–10).

*Faithful words (vv. 106–108)*. Making vows constantly to the Lord will not lift us to the highest levels of Christian living (Rom. 7:14–8:4), but when we do make promises to the Lord or to our friends, we should keep them (Matt. 5:33–37; Num. 30:2; Deut. 23:21; Eccl. 5:1–7). The Holy Spirit can help us fulfill new resolutions if we depend on His power. What we say when we are praying (v. 107) should also be truthful. To talk to God piously without being willing to obey Him in the matters we are praying about is to bring hypocrisy into our fellowship with God. After we have prayed, are we available to be a part of the answer (Eph. 3:20–21)? Perhaps the highest use of speech is in the worship of the Lord (v. 108), and we must see our words as sacrifices offered to the Lord (Hos. 14:1–2; Heb. 13:15). Do we sing to Him from the heart (Eph. 5:19)? Do we mean the words that we pray, sing, and read aloud from the litany? If worship is the highest use of words, then to be careless in worship is to commit a great sin.

A *faithful memory (vv. 109–110)*. The Old Testament believer did not have a pocket Bible that he could consult at will, for the Scriptures were written on large scrolls and deposited with the priests. This meant that the people had to listen carefully to the public reading of the Word and remember what they heard, an art that has almost vanished today. One of the ministries of the Holy Spirit is to bring God's Word to our remembrance when we need it (John 14:25–26; 16:12–15), but we cannot remember what we have never heard and learned (v. 11; Heb. 5:12–14). The psalmist was taking risks, just as we all do as we walk through the mine fields of this world, but he knew the Word would direct him.

A *faithful heart (vv. 111–112)*. What a precious treasure is the Word of God! (vv. 14, 72, 127, 162; 61:5). It is like a deep mine, filled with gold, silver, and precious gems, and we must take time to "dig" for these treasures (Prov. 2:1–9; 3:13–15; 8:10–11; 1 Cor. 3:9–23). A mere surface reading of Scripture will not put spiritual treasure into our hearts. Mining treasure is hard work, but it is joyful work when we "mine" the Bible, as the Spirit guides us into truth. Then, the Spirit helps us to "mint" the treasure so we can invest it in our lives (obedience) and in the lives of others (witness). Sometimes God takes us through the furnace of suffering so we can better receive the treasure into our own lives (1 Peter 1:6–12). The Word needs no purifying (v. 140; 12:6; 19:8), but we need to be cleansed so we can appreciate God's truth and appropriate it. Once your heart is set on obeying the Word, the life is on the right course (Matt. 6:33; Prov. 4:20–27).

## Samekh (vv. 113–120)—Dealing with the Enemy

If the life of faith consisted only of meditating on the Word and loving God, life would be easy, but people of faith have enemies, and life in this world is not easy. "Through many tribulations we enter the kingdom of God" (Acts 14:22 NKJV). Like the ten faithless men who spied out Canaan, if we look only at the enemy and ourselves, we will be discouraged and want to quit. But if like Caleb and Joshua, we look to the Lord, we can conquer the enemy (Num. 13:27–33). Four assurances in these verses help us face the enemy with courage and win the battle.

*God protects His people (vv. 113–115).* The "double-minded" were the people who were undecided and therefore uncommitted to the Lord (1 Kings 18:21; James 1:8; 4:8). Today, we would call them "half-hearted." There is nothing strange about believers experiencing both love toward God and His Word and hatred toward those who reject the Lord (vv. 104, 128, 163; 101:3; Amos 5:55; Mic. 3:2). "Hate evil, you who love the Lord" (97:10 NASB). If we love the Word, we will hate lies and oppose liars. The psalmist knew that his shelter and shield was the Lord alone, and he trusted in Him. He is not hiding in the Lord from fear of facing the enemy, because he addresses the enemy in verse 115. Only in the Lord could he find the help he needed. The Lord protects us that He might equip us to face the enemy and fight the battle (3:3; 27:5; 28:7; 31:20; 32:7; 33:20; 46:1–2; 61:4; 84:11; 91:1). The psalmist had his heart set on the Lord (v. 112), so there was no need to reconsider the matter. It was settled!

*God upholds the obedient (vv. 116–117).* The NASB and NIV each use "sustain" in verse 116 and "uphold" in 117, but the words are almost synonyms. "Sustain" pictures the believer leaning on the Lord for support and rest, while "uphold" mean that plus the idea of giving aid and refreshment. (For the first, see 3:6 and 37:17 and 24, and for the second, see Gen. 18:15.) When we feel like falling down and just giving up, the Lord comes to our aid in ways we could never fully understand.

*God rejects the wicked (vv. 118–119).* God's people in the Old Testament fought their enemies with swords and slings, but God's people today use the sword of the Spirit (Eph. 6:17; Heb. 4:12). It is a conflict between truth and lies, and God's truth must prevail. The writer described the enemy as sheep that had gone astray (vv. 10, 21, 176) and as cheap dross that must be discarded (Prov. 25:4; 26:23; Isa. 1:22, 25). God, in His judgments, purifies the saints but reveals the wickedness of the sinners, the way the refiner's furnace reveals the dross (Jer. 6:28–30; Ezek. 22:18–19; Mal. 3:2–3). "Their deceitfulness is useless" (v. 118 NASB) means that the thoughts and plans of the wicked are based on lies, but they are only deceiving themselves because their plans will fail.

*God alone should be feared (v. 120).* On the fear of God, see the comments on verse 63. The fear of the Lord is the fear that conquers every fear. "The Lord is my helper; I will not fear. What can man do to me?" (Heb. 13:6 NKJV; Ps. 118:6). The psalmist did not approach God as a criminal about to be slain but as a son showing loving respect to the father. God honors those who fear Him (15:4) and blesses them (115:13). If we fear the Lord, we depart from evil (v. 115; Prov. 3:7). This takes us back to verse 113: if we are single-minded, we will fear only the Lord and trust Him. "[T]he battle is not yours, but God's" (2 Chron. 20:15).

### Ayin (vv. 121–128)—Blessed Assurance

For the first time, the word "oppressors" and "oppress" appear in this psalm (vv. 121–122, and see 134). The word describes the abuse of power and authority, taking advantage of the underprivileged by either violence or deceit. The word includes the ideas of accusation and slander. The Jews were commanded not to oppress one another (Lev. 25:14, 17; Deut. 24:5–22), and this included the strangers in the land (Ex. 22:2; 23:9). Often, God's people suffer oppression while the guilty go free. When that happens, we need to remember the Lord and what He does for us.

*The Lord is the Rewarder (v. 121).* The psalmist was not boasting but affirming to the Lord that he was not guilty of anything that deserved punishment. He was a man of integrity who had a clear conscience; he had treated others justly and had practiced God's holy laws diligently. That in itself was a blessing, but God's people long to see justice reigning on the earth. When God rewards His people, it is a witness to sinners that their day of judgment is certain (58:10–11). "Therefore do not cast away your confidence, which has great reward" (Heb. 10:35 NKJV; Isa. 40:10; Rev. 22:12).

*The Lord is our Surety (v. 122).* The *King James Version* and *New American Standard Bible* are superior here to "ensure" in the *New International Version.* A person became surety when he or she pledged to pay another person's debt or fulfill a promise. When Jacob refused to allow Benjamin to go to Egypt for food with his brothers, it was Judah who willingly became surety for his youngest brother (Gen. 43:1–10; 44:18–34). Judah's passionate speech before his brother in Egypt assured Joseph that Judah had truly experienced a change of heart and that it was safe to reveal his identity to the men. To become surety for a friend's debts is forbidden in Scripture, lest you end up with a burden greater than you can handle (Prov. 11:15; 17:18; 22:26–27). But the Son of God became surety for those who have trusted Him! (Heb. 7:22). No matter how many promises we might make to the Lord, we can never fulfill them. But in His death on the cross, Jesus has paid the debt for us, and in His ministry of intercession at the throne in heaven, He is our living Surety. As long as He lives, our salvation is secure, and He lives "by the power of an endless life" (Heb. 7:16). So, no matter what people do to us and no matter how we feel, our Surety is secure and we remain in the family of God. Jesus has taken the responsibility for our salvation, and He will never fail.

*The Lord is our Master (vv. 123–125).* Whenever people attack us, they also attack the Lord, for we belong to Him. When Saul of Tarsus persecuted Christians on earth, He also persecuted their Lord in heaven (Acts 9:1–5). God cares for His servants. He does not always prevent us from being oppressed, but He always has a good reason for permitting it to happen. He is a loving Master who teaches us His will and gives us the discernment we need to handle the problems of life. Even more, He gives us promises that we can claim and thereby find the strength and wisdom we need. God's servants do not live by explanations; they live by promises.

*The Lord is the Final Judge (vv. 126–128).* In our impatience, we sometimes want God to work immediately and set everything right, but His ways and times are not always the same as ours. Faith and patience go together (Heb. 6:12), and God's delays are not God's denials. The day will come when the truth will be revealed and sin will be judged; meanwhile, instead of complaining about what we have paid or lost, let us rejoice in the wealth that we have in God's Word, wealth that can never be taken from us. All of God's precepts concerning all things are always right, so we can depend on the Scriptures and have the guidance that we need. If we love the Word, we will hate the wrong paths of sinners and stay away from them. We do not even put *one foot* on the path of the wicked! (Prov. 1:13).

### Pe (vv. 129–136)—A Chain Reaction

This section begins with the wonder of God's Word and ends with the weeping of the writer because the arrogant disobey the Word. Just as love and hate (vv. 127–128) and joy and affliction can exist in the same heart (vv. 111, 107), so can awe and anguish. In fact, when we begin to see the beauty and wonder of the Scriptures, we also begin to understand the ugliness of sin and the cheapness of what the world has to offer. This section describes a "spiritual chain reaction" in the life of the psalmist, one that can occur in our lives if we ponder the wonder of God's Word.

*Wonder leads to obedience (v. 129).* People obey God's Word for different reasons, some because of fear of punishment, others to secure blessings, and still others because they love God and want to please Him. The psalmist stood in awe at the wonder of God's Word—its harmony, beauty, perfection, practicality, power, and revelations. The longer I read and study the Bible, the more wonderful it becomes, and a God who wrote a book that wonderful deserves my obedience. To obey the Word is to become part of that wonder, to experience power and spiritual transformation in our lives.

*Obedience leads to understanding (v. 130).* The light of the Word comes into our hearts and minds and brings spiritual insight and understanding (2 Cor. 4:1–6). The word "entrance" (KJV) is translated "unfolding" in the *New American Standard Bible* and the *New International Version*; it means "disclosure" and "opening up" as in Luke 24:32 and 35. When Spirit-led teachers and preachers "open up" the Word, then the light of God's truth shines forth and brings about spiritual transformation (v. 135; 2 Cor. 3:18).

*Understanding leads to deeper desire (v. 131).* As a suffocating person pants for air or a thirsty person for water, so the child of God pants for the Word of God, and nothing else will satisfy. "I have treasured the words of His mouth more than my necessary food" (Job 23:12 NASB). When we lose our desire for God's Word, then we are vulnerable to the substitutes the world has to offer (Isa. 55:1–2).

*Desire leads to love for God (v. 132).* Just as children long to share the love of their parents, so the child of God experiences God's love through the Word (John 14:21–24). To love God's name is to love God, for His name reveals all that He is. The psalmist is here claiming the covenant promises that the Lord gave to the nation of Israel (69:36). Had Israel loved the Lord and kept the terms of the covenant, God would have blessed them and exhibited to them His power and mercy.

*God's love leads to guidance and freedom (vv. 133–134).* When we experience the love of God in our hearts, we keep His commandments (John 14:15), and obedience to His commandments sets us free from the slavery of sin (Rom. 6). The word "dominion" means "autocratic rule," but sin is not supposed to have dominion over us (Rom. 6:12–16). But there is more: we are also set free from the oppression of people and the enslavement it can bring (v. 134). When you are the servant of Jesus Christ, you are free from slavery to people. "You were bought with a price; do not become slaves of men" (1 Cor. 7:23 NASB).

*Freedom in Christ brings us God's blessing (vv. 135–136).* When God hides His face from His people, He is disciplining them

(13:1; 80:3–7), but the shining of His face upon them is a sign of His blessing (4:6; 67:1; Num. 6:25). To seek His face is to seek His blessing (v. 58). As we walk with the Lord in freedom, we walk in the light and have nothing to hide. But enjoying His freedom and blessing does not eliminate the burden we carry because of the wickedness in the world (v. 136). A broken heart and a blessed heart can exist in the same person at the same time. Jeremiah wept over the sins of a nation about to be destroyed (Jer. 9:1, 18; 13:17; Lam. 1:16), and Jesus wept over Jerusalem because they had rejected Him (Luke 19:41–44). The apostle Paul wept over lost souls (Rom. 9:1–3) as well as over professed believers in the church who were living for the world and the flesh (Phil. 3:17–21). If our enjoyment of God's Word and God's gracious blessings has truly reached our hearts, then we ought to have a burden for the lost and want to try to reach them for Christ.

### Tsadhe (vv. 137–144)—In God We Trust

The Spirit of God uses the Word of God to implant faith in our hearts (Rom. 10:17), and the more we live in God's Word, the stronger our faith will become. Some people have no faith (Mark 4:40), others have little faith (Matt. 8:26; 14:31), and a few have great faith (Matt. 8:10; 15:28). Like a mustard seed, faith has life in it, and if the seed is planted and cultivated, it will grow and bear fruit (Matt. 17:20). The message in this section of the psalm is that you can depend on the Word of God, so—have faith!

*God's Word is trustworthy no matter what people do (vv. 137–139).* The psalmist had worn himself out trying to convince people to trust God's Word (see 69:9; John 2:12), but they ignored both him and the Scriptures. He must have felt that his ministry had failed, but he had been faithful even as the Word is faithful. God and His Word are righteous and what He says is right. His Word is fully trustworthy. Though intellectual giants may attack it and even ridicule it, the Word stands and will be here long after they are dead and their books have been forgotten. People may sin and die, but God's righteousness and righteous Word remains (vv. 137, 138, 142, 144).

*God's Word is trustworthy no matter what people say (vv. 140–141).*

Over many centuries, the Scriptures have been thoroughly tested in the fires of persecution and criticism, the way a goldsmith tests precious metals (12:6–7; 18:30), and the Word has been found pure. One of the joys of the Christian life is to find new promises in the Word, test them in daily life, and find them trustworthy. The enemy wants to forget the Word (v. 139), but we remember the Word and depend on it. The world may look upon God's people as "small and despised," but when you stand on God's promises, you are a giant.

*God's Word is trustworthy regardless of how you feel (vv. 142–143).* You may experience trouble and distress, as did the psalmist, and still find delight in God's truth. Our feelings change but God's Word never changes. God's Word is not only true, but it is truth (v. 142 NASB; John 17:17). The Word of God is truth, the Son of God is truth (John 14:6), and the Spirit of God is truth (1 John 5:6). The Spirit of truth wrote the Word of truth, and that Word reveals the Son of God. When your feelings deceive you into concluding that it is not worth it to serve the Lord, immediately turn to the Scriptures and delight in your Lord.

*God's Word is trustworthy no matter how long you live (v. 144).* When we read the Word to ourselves, we see words in ink on paper. When we read the Word aloud, we hear puffs of sound that quickly disappear. Paper and ink and puffs of sound may not seem very lasting, but the Word of God is eternal and fixed forever (vv. 89, 160). To build your life on God's Word means to participate in eternity (Matt. 7:24–29; 1 John 2:17). It is not the length of life but the depth of life that counts, and depth comes from laying hold of God's Word and obeying it. Jesus spent only thirty-three years on this earth, and His public ministry lasted only three years, yet He accomplished a work that is eternal.

### Qoph (vv. 145–152)—A Primer on Prayer

The writer prayed throughout this entire psalm, but in these verses he concentrated on prayer and cried out to God day and night. From his experience, we receive some basic instructions about successful prayer.

*Pray wholeheartedly (vv. 145–146)*. We must seek God with our whole heart (vv. 2, 10, 58) and obey Him with our whole heart (vv. 34, 69). "In prayer, it is better to have a heart without words than words without a heart" (John Bunyan). In the Old Testament sanctuary, the golden altar of incense represented intercessory prayer (Ex. 30:1–10). The special incense was burned on the altar, and the fragrant smoke rising heavenward pictured prayer going up to the Lord (141:1–2; Rev. 8:3–4). The devotion of the heart is what "ignites" our prayers and enables us to present our requests to the Lord. The phrase "and I will keep" may be translated "that I may keep." The psalmist was not bargaining with God ("Answer my prayers and I will obey you") but dedicating himself to God to obey Him no matter how He answers his prayers. Before we can pray as we ought, we must pray for ourselves that God will give us a heart ignited by the fire of the Spirit.

*Pray without ceasing according to the Word (vv. 147–148)*. Two important elements of successful prayer are involved here. The first is that we constantly cultivate an attitude of prayer and remain in communion with the Lord. At morning and during the watches of the night (sunset to 10 P.M., 10–2, 2 until dawn), the psalmist prayed to the Lord. Jesus called this "abiding" (John 15:1–11). To "pray without ceasing" (1 Thess. 5:17) does not mean to walk around muttering prayers. It means to "keep the receiver off the hook" so that nothing comes between the Father and us.

The second element in successful prayer is the Word of God, for apart from God's Word, we cannot know God's will. Each verse in this section mentions the Scriptures and the writer's devotion to God's Word. We must balance the Word and prayer in our devotional life and ministry, for all Bible and no prayer means light without heat, but all prayer and no Bible could result in zeal without knowledge. Samuel emphasized both the Word and prayer in 1 Samuel 12:23 and so did Jesus in John 15:7. The spiritual leaders in the early church gave themselves to prayer and the Word (Acts 6:4). When we meditate on the Word, the

Father speaks to us, and when we pray, we speak to the Father. We need both instruction and intercession if we are to be balanced children of God.

*Pray as an act of love (v. 149)*. This verse combines both love and law, for if we love the Lord, we will keep His commandments. Too often, we think of prayer as an emergency measure, rushing into God's presence and crying for help. But what would you think of children who spoke to their parents only when they needed something? Prayer is more than asking; prayer is loving. If we love the Word of God, we must also love the God of the Word and express that love to Him. To tell Him we love Him only because we want to receive something is to practice prayer on a juvenile level. When we share our love with the Lord, we receive new life from Him.

*Pray with your eyes open (vv. 150–152)*. As he prayed, the psalmist saw his enemies drawing near, so he asked for God to draw near to help him. The familiar phrase "watch and pray" goes back to when Nehemiah was leading the people in rebuilding the walls of Jerusalem and restoring the gates. The enemy did not want the holy city to be rebuilt, so they used fear, deceit, and every kind of ruse to hinder the work. What was Nehemiah's defense? "Nevertheless we made our prayer to our God, and because of them [the enemy] we set a watch against them day and night" (Neh. 4:9 NKJV). Jesus (Matt. 26:41; Mark 13:33), Paul (Col. 4:2), and Peter (1 Peter 4:7) commanded God's people to "watch and pray," to be on guard and pray with intelligence and alertness. We are soldiers in a battle and we dare not go to sleep while on duty.

### Resh (vv. 153–160)—Strength for the Journey

Have you noticed that the writer became more urgent as he drew near the end of the psalm? The Hebrew alphabet was about to end, but his trials would continue, and he needed the help of the Lord. The last three stanzas all speak of persecution and trials, yet the writer still trusted the Lord. The Christian life is like the land of Canaan, "a land of hills and valleys" (Deut. 11:11), and we cannot have mountaintops without also having valleys. The key phrase in this stanza is "revive me" (vv. 154, 156, 159), which means "give me life, lift me up and keep me going." He had prayed this prayer before (vv. 25, 37, 40, 88, 107, and 149), and the Lord had answered. The psalmist not only prayed but also gave reasons why the Lord should answer.

*Revive me, for you are my Redeemer (vv. 153–155).* "Look upon [consider] my affliction" is a request for the Lord to "see to" his needs. Abraham used this word when he answered his son's question in Genesis 22:8—"The Lord will see to it," in other words, provide the sacrifice. Our wonderful Lord not only "sees" the need but can "see to" providing what is needed. "The eyes of the Lord are on the righteous, and His ears are open to their cry" (34:15; 1 Peter 3:12). The word "redeem" speaks of the kinsman redeemer who could rescue a family member in need, as Boaz rescued Ruth. (See Lev. 25:23–34.) In His incarnation, Jesus entered the human family and became our kinsman, and in the crucifixion, He paid the price to redeem us from sin, death, and hell. "Plead [defend] my cause" ties in with Jesus as our Kinsman Redeemer and also as our Surety (v. 122), Mediator, and Advocate, who represents us before the throne of God (1 John 2:1–2). In our affliction, it is comforting to know that the Son of God intercedes for us, hears our prayers, and meets our needs.

*Revive me, for you are merciful (vv. 156–158).* If we prayed on the basis of our own merit, God could never answer, but we come to the Father in the name of the Son (John 14:14; 15:16) and with the help of the Spirit (Eph. 2:18; Rom. 8:26–27). God in His grace gives us what we do not deserve, and in His mercy He does not give us what we do deserve. His throne is a throne of grace where grace and mercy are abundantly available to us (Heb. 4:16). The psalmist was still disgusted with the way the unbelievers lived (v. 158; see 53, 136), but their bad example did not change his own convictions.

*Revive me, for your Word can be trusted (vv. 159–160).* "The sum of your word is truth" (v. 160 NASB) and this means all of it can be trusted. The totality of God's written revelation is not just true—it is truth. To love the Word is to obey it, and to obey it is to receive life from it. The Bible is not a magic book that conveys divine life to anyone who picks it up and reads it. God's living Word communicates His life and power to those who read it, meditate on it, and obey it because they love God and His Word. When Jesus raised the dead, it was through speaking the Word (Luke 7:11–17; 8:40–56; John 11:38–44; see John 5:24), and His Word gives us life today when we find ourselves in the dust (v. 25).

### Shin (vv. 161–168)—Blessed Are the Balanced

During our time of study in Psalm 119, we have noticed that the writer practiced a balanced life of faith, and this quality is seen especially in this stanza.

*Respect and rejoicing (vv. 161–162).* The princes began their campaign against him by speaking against him (v. 23), but now they were persecuting him in a direct way. But the psalmist was not afraid of his persecutors; he stood in awe of God's Word. Once again we learn that when we fear God, we need not fear anyone else. He respected the Word and rejoiced in the Word at the same time, for the joy of the Lord and the greatness of the Lord are friends, not enemies. The princes wanted to rob him, but he found great wealth in the Word of God (see vv. 14, 72). The promises of God in the Bible are better than money in the bank, because they will never lose their value, and nobody can take them from us.

*Love and hate (v. 163).* "You who love the Lord, hate evil" (97:10). He loved God's law but hated every false way (vv. 97, 104, 127–128). He loved God's law but hated double-minded people (v. 113). Here he declared that he loved God's law but hated falsehood. Whoever loves and practices a lie will not enter the heavenly city and will be banished from God's presence forever (Rev. 21:17; 22:15).

*Praise and poise (vv. 164–165).* The devoted Jewish worshiper would praise God and pray three times a day (55:17; Dan. 6:10–11), but the psalmist went beyond that and worshiped seven times a day. The phrase means "often, many times, beyond what is expected." The legalist would set a goal and be proud that he reached it; the Spirit-filled believer sets no goal but goes beyond any goal he might have set. Just as prayer can bring peace to our hearts (Phil. 4:4–7), so praise can bring peace as well. Focusing on the Lord, asking for nothing, and totally lost in our praise of Him, has a way of making the problems look much smaller and the future much brighter. But praise also helps us to have poise in our Christian walk and to not stumble (Jude 24) or cause others to stumble (1 Cor. 8:13; Rom. 14:13). The singing saint is a stable saint, walking on a level path even when the enemy digs pits and sets up obstacles.

*Walking and waiting (vv. 166–168)*. Like the psalmist, we are waiting for "the salvation of the Lord," when the Lord shall come and set His creation and His people free (Rom. 8:18–25; 13:11; Heb. 9:28; 1 Peter 1:9). This is the "blessed hope" that every believer anticipates and longs for (Titus 2:13). But as we wait and hope, we must walk and work, for we want to be found faithful when Jesus comes (Matt. 24:45–51). When we love His Word, we will also love His appearing (2 Tim. 4:6–8) and live like those who are ready to meet their Lord (1 John 2:28).

### Tav (vv. 169–176)—Hear My Prayer!

Except for 174, each of the verses is a prayer to the Lord, and the focus is on His wonderful ability to meet our needs as we trust Him. The word "your" ["Thy"] is often repeated and helps us understand the requests the psalmist was making.

*I need your Word (vv. 169–72)*. We never outgrow our need for God's Word, no matter how long we have been walking with Him. There is always something new to learn and we often see new applications of old truths. Believers who boast that they "know the Bible from cover to cover" are only revealing how little they know about God's Word, for we shall spend eternity learning from His Word. The psalmist asked for understanding and deliverance, for he knew that the truth would set him free (John 8:32). After learning the statutes of God, he began to praise the Lord, for study and worship belong together. After Paul discussed the wonderful decrees of the Lord (Rom. 9–11), he broke out in worship and praise (Rom. 11:33–36).

*I need your hand (v. 173).* We all know that "God is spirit" (John 4:24) and therefore does not have a body with hands, feet, and so forth. In order to reveal Himself to us, He uses the familiar to explain the unfamiliar, and therefore the Bible describes Him in human terms. The hand of the Lord is mentioned only here in the psalm, but it is found many times in the book of Psalms. The idols of the heathen have hands that do not move or feel (115:7), but God's hand is active on the behalf of His people. We are the sheep of His hand (95:7), an image that Jesus used in John 10:28–29.

*I need your salvation (v. 174).* In his case, "salvation" meant deliverance from his enemies who were threatening him, but "salvation" can mean freedom from worry, the healing of a sickness, the provision of funds to pay a bill, or deliverance from Satanic oppression. As we saw in verse 166, our ultimate salvation is the return of Jesus Christ to deliver all creation from the bondage of sin.

*I need your help (v. 175).* The writer prayed "Help me!" in verse 86, but God's people are always crying for help. "My heart trusted in Him, and I am helped" (28:7 NKJV). God's hand can help us (v. 173), but so can God's judgments. "Judgments" is a synonym for the Word of God, but it can also refer to the working of God's providence in this world (105:7; Rom. 11:33). Of course, the two go together, because God always obeys His own Word when He works in this world. God helps us as He arranges the affairs of this world and of our lives, for there are no accidents in the life of the believer—only appointments. Our Father watches over us and accomplishes His will (23:3; John 10:4; Rom. 8:28).

*I am your servant (v. 176).* He did not say that he had greatly sinned against the Lord or that he was rebelling against God's will. At this point, he felt his own weakness and ignorance and expressed it in terms that were meaningful to him. In verse 110 he affirmed that he had not strayed away, but now he realized the danger of feeling overconfident (1 Cor. 10:12). During the spiritual journey recorded in this psalm, the psalmist had experienced his ups and downs, but he had always stayed himself on the Word of God, and he did this to the very end. He opened the psalm with a benediction (v. 1), but he closed it with a warning, and both are important to the balanced Christian life. God gives us promises and assurances so we will not despair, but He gives us warnings that we might not presume. He was still the servant of God and not the servant of sin, and he still remembered God's Word, so he would not stray for long. The Good Shepherd would find him and lead him back to the fold. He would anoint his wounds with healing oil and give him a long refreshing drink of water (23:5).

### The Pilgrim Psalms (Pss. 120–134)

Each of these fifteen psalms is called "A Song of Degrees." The Hebrew word translated "degrees"[2] or "ascents" comes from a root that means "to go up," as ascending a stairway. Ten of the psalms are anonymous, four are attributed to David (122, 124, 131, 133) and one to Solomon (127). These psalms were selected to form a "hymnal" to be used by the people who went to Jerusalem for the three annual feasts (Ex. 23:14–19)—Passover in spring, Pentecost in early summer, and Tabernacles in the autumn. The pilgrims sang these songs together as they journeyed in family groups to Jerusalem (Luke 2:41–52), and this helped to focus their minds on what the Lord had done for their nation. The sanctuary is mentioned in 122:1 and 9; 132:7–8; and 134:1–2, and Mount Zion and Jerusalem are mentioned in 122:2–3, 6; 125:1–2; 126:1; 128:5; 129:5; 132:13; 133:3; and 134:3. Three special themes are repeated: (1) the afflictions that Israel experienced at the hands of the other nations, (2) the gracious way God cared for and protected His chosen people, and (3) the blessing of being in Jerusalem. Israel had suffered contempt and scorn (123:3–4), near extinction (124:1–5; 130:1), traps (124:6–7), bondage (126:1, 4), and affliction (129:1–3), yet she is still here!

Under the leadership of Moses, the Israelites were a nomadic people for forty years. But after they settled in Canaan, the Lord required them to go to Jerusalem three times a year. This reminded them that, spiritually speaking, they were still a pilgrim people and needed to depend on the Lord. "For we are aliens and pilgrims before you," said David (1 Chron. 29:15; and see Pss. 84:5–7 and 119:19 and 54.) Too many believers today want to be "settlers," not pilgrims and strangers (Heb. 11:8–10, 13–16; 1 Peter 1:1; 2:11). We are happy to settle down in our comfort zones and live as though Jesus never died, Jesus is not coming again, and our lives will never end. We are guilty of what Eugene Peterson calls "the tourist mindset," content to make occasional brief visits with the Lord that are leisurely and entertaining, all the while conforming to this world and enjoying it. (See A Long Obedience in the Same Direction, IVP, p. 12.) Our citizenship is in heaven (Luke 10:20; Phil. 3:20; Heb. 12:22–24), and that should make a difference in our lives on earth. We need to "feel temporary" as we make this pilgrim journey called life.

## Psalm 120

The psalm begins with distress (v. 1), concludes with war (v. 7), and in between deals with deception and slander. It hardly seems a fit hymn for a group of pilgrims to sing as they made their way to the sanctuary of God. However, it appears that the author of this psalm was in the same situation as the writer of Psalm 42: circumstances prevented him from attending the feast, so he had to stay home among people who made life difficult for him (see 42:3, 9–10). The singing of this psalm would remind the pilgrims that they were indeed privileged to be able to go to Jerusalem and that others would have liked to go with them. It also reminded the travelers that when they returned home, they needed to carry some of the blessing to those who stayed behind and to help make life easier for them. The psalm reminds believers today that worship is a privilege and the blessings we receive must be shared. When we find ourselves experiencing distress and disappointment, we have three responsibilities to fulfill if our burdens are to become blessings.

### We Must Pray (vv. 1–2)

The opening phrase can be translated "I cried" or "I cry," because the past and the present are combined in the tense of the verb. (Compare NASB and NIV.) The writer had prayed in a previous time of trouble, and the Lord had answered him, so now he had confidence to pray again. Instead of complaining about his situation, he shared it with the Lord and, in this psalm, shared it with us. His problem was that people were lying about him and slandering his name. (See 5:9, 12:1–8; 26:24; 31:18; 52:3ff; Prov. 10:18 and 26:24.) It's possible that he was involved in some kind of litigation and the opposition had bribed false witnesses to testify against him. He did not dare go to Jerusalem for fear his enemies would take advantage of his absence and do even more damage.

### We Must Trust God (vv. 3–4)

It is not likely that the psalmist was actually addressing his enemies, but this is the message God gave him in answer to his prayers. The writer did not need to attack the enemy, because the Lord would do it for him. *Arrows* and *fire* are images of their evil lying words, images that occur frequently in Scripture (55:21; 57:4; 59:7; 64:3–4; Prov. 16:27; 25:18; 26:18–19; Jer. 9:3, 8; James 3:6). The writer was confident that God would punish the enemy with their own weapons, but the consequences would be far worse. The arrows would be sharpened and shot at them by a mighty warrior, probably a reference to the Lord God Himself (24:8; Isa. 9:6, "Mighty God"). The broom tree is a desert shrub that affords shade (1 Kings 19:4), and its roots can be made into excellent charcoal. There is so much godless speech in our world today that believers must be careful what they hear and how it affects them. We must not only turn away our eyes from beholding vanity (119:37) but also turn away our ears from hearing foolishness. "Take heed what you hear" (Mark 4:24). When we are slandered and lied about, we must leave the matter with the Lord and trust Him to work.

### We Must Patiently Endure (vv. 5–7)

In the ancient Near East, Meshech was located in Asia Minor, to the northwest of Israel, and Kedar was a nomadic nation in northern Arabia, southeast of Israel. Meshach was a Gentile nation (Gen. 10:2) and the people of Kedar were descended from Ishmael, Abraham's son by Hagar (Gen. 16; 25:13, 18). Both peoples were at great distance from Israel and were considered enemies of the Jews. The writer was not actually dwelling with these people, because he could not live in two places at once, especially places thousands of miles apart. Rather, he was dwelling with Jewish people *who were behaving like people who lived outside the covenant blessings of God.* Any Jew who feared God and respected the Ten Commandments would not bear false witness against another Jew or seek to slander his or her name. It would be difficult to dwell with these foreign peoples, but it would be even more difficult to dwell with Jewish people who acted like foreigners.

Believers today must not only live with unbelievers but also with professed believers who live like unbelievers. Paul sometimes shamed the believers to whom he wrote by comparing them to the Gentiles, meaning "the outsiders, the unsaved" (1 Cor. 5:1, 12–13; Eph. 4:17; Col. 4:5; 1 Thess. 4:12; 1 Tim. 3:7). The psalmist was a peacemaker and tried to encourage his godless Jewish neighbors to be peaceable, but they were more intent on making war. His loving words only made them more and more angry. After over fifty years of ministry, I am convinced that most of the problems in families and churches are caused by professed Christians who do not have a real and vital relationship to Jesus Christ. They are not humble peacemakers but arrogant troublemakers. Until God changes them or they decide to go elsewhere, the dedicated believers must be patient and prayerful. This is the way Joseph dealt with his brothers in Canaan and his false accusers in Egypt. It is also the way David dealt with King Saul and Jesus dealt with His enemies (1 Peter 2:18–25).

# Psalm 121

This may have been used as an antiphonal psalm that the pilgrims sang as they journeyed to Jerusalem to celebrate a feast. The leader of the company opened with verses 1–2, which are in the first person, and different people or groups answered him with verses 3–4 and so on, which are in the second person. The theme is God's protection over His people; the word "keeps" (watches over) is used six times. Safety is something about which the pilgrims would be especially concerned as they journeyed on the roads through the hill country. A pilgrim could stumble and hurt himself, or someone might suffer sunstroke, or a chilly night of camping out might give somebody a bad cold. There was always the possibility of robbers swooping down. But the message of the psalm applies to God's pilgrims today and gives us the assurances we need as we journey in this life.

### "My Father's Creation Is Before Me" (vv. 1–2)

The opening line can be translated "I lift up my eyes" (NIV) instead of "I will lift" (KJV, NASB). If Jehovah created the heavens and the earth, then He is a God of power, wisdom, and glory, and we have nothing to fear. Satan and his demonic army may be at work opposing the saints, but this is still our Father's world. The apostate Jews worshiped other gods at the shrines ("high places") in the hills (2 Kings 16:4; Jer. 3:23; 13:27; 17:2; Hos. 4:11–13), but the faithful people of God looked above the hills to the great God who created all things. When the travelers caught sight of Jerusalem, situated on the mountains (87:1; 125:1–2; 133:3), they knew that God dwelt there in His sanctuary and provided the help they needed (3:4; 20:2; 46:1; 124:8; 134:3; 1 Kings 8:29–53). Everything in the heavens and on the earth bears witness to the great Creator who is also our heavenly Father, so why should we fear? (See 33:3; 89:11–13; 96:4–5; 104:2–9; 115:15; 124:8; 134:3; 136:4–9.)

### "My Father's Eyes Are upon Me" (vv. 3–4)

The word translated "moved" means "to slip and slide, to stagger, to be shaken." How easy it would be to sprain an ankle or even fall and break a bone while walking on uneven rocky paths. The Lord is concerned about our feet and our walk. (See 31:8; 56:13; 66:9; 125:1; 1 Sam. 2:9; Prov. 2:8; 3:21, 23, 25–26.) "Keep" means "to guard and protect" and is used six times in the psalm (vv. 3, 4, 5, 7 [two times] and 8). It is first used in the Bible in Genesis 2:15 where the Lord put Adam in the garden "to keep it." This means to guard and protect it and take good care of it. Even while we sleep, God watches over us because He does not go to sleep. (See 1 Kings 18:41.) The Lord promised to keep Jacob, who became the father of the twelve tribes of Israel (Gen. 28:15; 48:15–16), and He protects Jacob's descendants as well (Deut. 32:10). "The eyes of the Lord are on the righteous, and His ears are open to their cry" (34:15 NKJV; 1 Peter 3:12). "I will instruct you and teach you in the way which you should go; I will counsel you with my eye upon you" (Ps. 32:8 NASB).

### *"My Father's Presence Is Beside Me" (vv. 5–6)*

Our Keeper is not only on the throne looking down on us, but He is at our side to shield us from all harm. This does not mean that obedient believers never find themselves in difficulty or danger, or that they will never feel physical and emotional pain. The things that God permits to happen to us in His will may hurt us *but they will not harm us.* David had many experiences that brought heartache and even threatened his life, but the Lord enabled him to turn those seeming tragedies into beautiful psalms that encourage us today. The Lord at our right hand provides the "shade" that we need (17:8; 36:7; 57:1; 63:7; 91:1; Isa. 25:4; 49:2; 51:16).

In writing about the sun and the moon, the psalmist was saying several things. To begin with, in that part of the world, the burning sun is menacing (2 Kings 4:18–19; Jonah 4:8), but at night, the sudden drop in temperature is both uncomfortable and unhealthy, if you lack warm covering. Day and night, our Father is with us to shelter us from that which could harm us. The Jewish people followed a lunar calendar (81:3), so the writer was also referring to days (the sun) and months (the moon). From day to day, from month to month, from season to season (Gen. 1:16–18), from year to year, our Father is with us in the many challenges and changes of life. The psalmist did not believe the superstition that the phases of the moon affected the minds and bodies of people. The English word "lunatic" comes from the Latin word *luna*, which means "moon"; and the word "epileptic" comes from a Greek word that means "moon-struck" (see Matt. 4:24 and 17:15). Whether by day or by night, in heat or cold, whatever the changes might be, the Father's presence provides all that we need. We need not be afraid of sudden attacks that can come in the day or the night, for "the shadow of the Almighty" covers us (see Ps. 91).

### "My Father's Care Is Around Me" (vv. 7–8)

We need not fear life or death, today or tomorrow, time or eternity, for we are in the loving care of the Father. "All evil" means anything that could harm us, but in His grace, He turns into good the things we think are evil. Joseph had to endure the slander and hatred of his brothers, thirteen years of separation from his father, the false accusations of his employer's wife, and years in prison, all because of his brothers' sins. But in the end, Joseph was able to say, "[Y]ou meant evil against me; but God meant it for good" (Gen. 50:20 NKJV)—and Paul said the same thing in Romans 8:28!

The phrase "going out and coming in" refers to the daily activities of life (Deut. 28:6; 1 Sam. 29:6; 2 Sam. 3:25). Yes, the Father is concerned about our tasks and our schedules and even the so-called "minor details" that we too often take for granted. Orthodox Jews take Deuteronomy 6:9 and 11:20 literally and affix small metal boxes containing Scripture portions to the right-hand doorpost of the house, and they touch the box reverently each time they go in and out of the house. These boxes are called *mezuzas*; the word means "doorpost." Some Jewish people also attach *mezuzas* to the right-hand doorposts of individual rooms in the house. What a delight it is to know that, as we go in and out of the house, to and fro in the city, and even fly from city to city and country to country, the Father is with us and cares for our every need. "Casting all your care upon Him, for He cares for you" (1 Peter 5:7 NKJV). And His loving care will go on forever! (v. 8). "You will guide me with Your counsel, and afterward receive me to glory ... . My flesh and my heart fail; but God is the strength of my heart and my portion forever" (73:23, 26 NKJV).

"Who can mind the journey when the road leads Home?"

## Psalm 122

Three of the "Pilgrim Psalms" are assigned to David. This one focuses on Jerusalem (vv. 2, 3, 6) and the house of God (vv. 1 and 9). Psalm 124 describes God's protection of Israel from her enemies, and 131 speaks of David's submission to the Lord. Some deny David's authorship of 122 and move the psalm to the times of Ezra and Nehemiah, but such a move seems contrary to what the psalm says. David's dynasty did not exist in the post-exilic days (v. 5), nor was Jerusalem the well-built city in post-exilic times that it was even during the reign of David (v. 3; 2 Sam. 5:9, 11). The phrase "house of God" was used for the tabernacle (1 Sam 1:7, 24; 2 Sam. 12:20), so it could certainly be used for the tent David pitched for the ark in Jerusalem (2 Sam. 6). The psalm speaks of a united people, which was true in David's time, but the kingdom was divided after Solomon's death (1 Kings 12:25–33) and the tribes were hardly a strong united nation during the post-exilic days. The fact that King Jeroboam set up his own religion after the kingdom divided is evidence that the tribes must have been going up to Jerusalem annually during the reigns of David and Solomon. In the days of the monarchy, the throne and the temple were separated, but today, the Lord Jesus Christ is both King and Priest (110; Heb. 7–9), and God's people are citizens of "Jerusalem which is above" (Gal. 4:25–26; Phil. 3:20; Heb. 12:22–29). One day there will be a new Jerusalem, a holy city prepared by God for His people (Rev. 3:12; 21:1–10).

Believers today need not make long pilgrimages to "holy places" in order to worship God, for the Lord does not dwell in man-made buildings (Acts 7:48–50). Nor do we need the kind of "religious entertainment" that draws people to some meetings. The key thing is the heart. From David's words in this psalm, we can easily discern the kind of heart believers need if we are to please God in our worship.

### A Heart for God (vv. 1–2)

"Let us go" sounds tame, like an invitation to a tea. "We will go" is the better translation. Whether this was an invitation to someone living far from Jerusalem, or to David living in Jerusalem, the statement expressed determination and dedication. After the tent had been set up and the ark placed in it, no doubt David frequently went there to worship God, for David's love for God's house was well-known (27:4; 65:4; 2 Sam. 7:1–3). He rejoiced at an opportunity to go with other worshipers to praise the Lord. Nothing is said here about a pilgrimage, although this psalm is placed among the "Songs of Ascent." David lived in Jerusalem and had to go but a short distance to reach the tent and the ark. Though he lived in the holy city, David did not take this privilege for granted, for he had a heart for God and for God's house. David was a man after God's own heart (1 Sam. 13:14). The pilgrim coming from a distance would not complain about the journey, for his heart was set on the Lord. Love makes burdens lighter and distances shorter. Note that Jerusalem is mentioned not only in verses 2, 3, and 6, but also in 125:1; 126:1; 128:5; 129:5;, 132:13; and 133:3.

### A Heart for Praise (vv. 3–5)

The Lord had told His people that one day there would be a central place where they would worship (Ex. 23:14–19; Deut. 12:5–7, 11–14, 17–19; 14:23; 16:2, 16), and that place was Jerusalem. The Lord instructed David that the place on Mount Moriah where he had built the altar was to be the site for the temple (1 Chron. 21–22), and He also gave David the plans for the structure (1 Chron. 28). Jerusalem had been a Jebusite stronghold before David captured it and made it his capital city, "the city of David" (2 Sam. 5:6–10). His choice was a wise one, for not only was Mount Zion an almost impregnable citadel, but it was located on the border of Judah and Benjamin and helped to bind the northern and southern tribes together. King Saul was from Benjamin, and David was from Judah.

When the psalmist looked at the city, he thought of unity and security. Just as the stones of the walls and houses were "bound firmly together," so the people were bound together in their worship of the Lord and their respect for the throne. The twelve separate tribes, plus the tribe of Levi, shared the same ancestors and history, participated in the same worship in the same holy city, and were governed by the same divine laws. The church today already has spiritual unity (Eph. 4:1–6), but we must endeavor to maintain it and demonstrate it before a watching world (John 17:20–23). As for security, Jesus promised that the very forces of hell could not stand before the onward march of His church (Matt. 16:18).

But it was the praise of Jehovah that was central (v. 4). God had commanded that His people go to Jerusalem for the feasts of Passover, Pentecost, and Tabernacles (Ex. 23:14–19; John 4:20–21), and the people went as worshipers and not sightseers. Yes, there was much to see in Jerusalem, but giving thanks to the Lord was their most important task and their greatest privilege. At the same time, the people were giving allegiance to the dynasty of David, for the same Lord who assigned the feasts also established the throne. In Romans 13, Paul makes it clear that the Lord established the system of governmental authority that we have, and we must respect the offices even if we cannot always respect the officers. Though there is a separation of church and state in modern democracies, there must never be a separation of God and country. Regardless of our political affiliation, our most important civic duty is to pray for those in authority (1 Tim. 2:1–6).

### A Heart for Prayer (vv. 6–9)

The name "Jerusalem" means "foundation of peace," and yet the city has been a center of conflict for centuries. If we understand biblical prophecy correctly, there can be no peace in Jerusalem or on earth until the Prince of Peace reigns on David's throne (Isa. 9:6–7; Luke 1:26–33). So, when we pray for the peace of Jerusalem, we are actually praying, "Thy kingdom come" (Matt. 6:10) and "Even so, come, Lord Jesus" (Rev. 22:20). Jesus wept over the city because they were ignorant of the peace God had for them (Luke 19:41–48) and had rejected their own Messiah (John 11:47–48). But our intercession must not be perfunctory prayers; they must come from our heart because we love God and love His people. Note the fruit of the Spirit in this psalm: love (v. 6), joy (v. 1), and peace (vv. 6–8; Gal. 6:22).

The "prosperity" mentioned in verse 6 does not refer to material wealth, but primarily to the spiritual enrichment that comes to those who love God, His Son (born a Jew), His Word (a Jewish book), and His chosen people. "Salvation is of the Jews" (John 4:22). To promise that all who pray for the peace of Jerusalem will become wealthy is to misunderstand the promise. Paul prayed for his people (Rom. 10:1) and yet materially was a poor man (2 Cor. 6:10). Christian believers have a debt to Israel for the untold spiritual wealth they have given us (Rom. 15:25–27). It is selfish to want personal prosperity when the emphasis here is on the city of God, the chosen people of God (vv. 6–8), and the house of God (v. 9). But there is an application to believers today, for we are God's people, citizens of the heavenly country, and we must pray for one another and for the ministry of the churches. We belong to each other, we need each other, and we must help each other. We must pray for peace within and among the churches. We must pray for the needs of "our brothers and friends," and surely we must pray for the lost.

A heart for God will surely be a heart filled with praise and prayer.

## Psalm 123

It is not until we read verse 4 that we discover the burden of the writer: the constant persecution of the people of Israel, being treated with scorn and contempt. In Psalm 124, Israel was almost swallowed up, drowned, and imprisoned in a trap. Captivity is the theme of 126, and 129 compares their suffering to a farmer plowing their backs. Has any nation ever suffered the way Israel has suffered? Of course, God's people today are also suffering because of their commitment to Christ (John 16:30). According to missiologists, more Christians were martyred in the twentieth century than in all the previous centuries combined! Some students assign this psalm to the time of King Hezekiah, when the Assyrians were attacking Jerusalem and making humiliating speeches about the Jews (Isa. 36–37). But during the post-exilic years, Israel also suffered the ridicule and scorn of their Gentile neighbors (Neh. 2:19; 4:1–4, 7ff). This psalm speaks about the God who is enthroned in heaven whose hand would work for His people, and you find both of these themes in Ezra and Nehemiah. The "hand of God" is found in Ezra 7:6, 9, 28; 8:18, 22, 31 and Nehemiah 2:8, 18. "The God of heaven" is mentioned in Ezra 1:2; 5:11–12; 6:9–10; 7:12, 21, 23 and Nehemiah 1:4; 2:4. The psalm begins in the first person singular (I, my), but then changes to the plural (we, our, us). Perhaps this was a communal prayer, begun by a priest or Levite (v. 1), continued by a choir (v. 2), and closed by the congregation (vv. 3–4).

When we find ourselves among the slandered, ridiculed, and persecuted, where do we turn for help? The psalm gives three answers to that question.

### We Look by Faith to God's Throne (v. 1)

Of course, with our human eyes, we cannot see God on His throne, but with the eyes of faith we see Him as we believe the Word. "My eyes are toward the Lord" (25:15 NKJV). To look toward the Lord means to trust Him and turn our problems over to Him by faith. "Looking unto Jesus, the author and finisher of our faith" (Heb. 12:2 NKJV). God's throne is mentioned often in the book of Psalms (9:4, 7; 11:4; 45:6; 47:8; 93:2; 97:2; 103:9), and to believers today, His throne is a throne of grace (Heb. 4:14–16). The life of faith begins by looking to the Lord by faith and trusting Him for salvation (Isa. 45:22). The life of faith continues as we keep our eyes of faith on Jesus (Heb. 12:2), and it will climax with faith becoming sight and we'll see Jesus in His glory (1 John 3:1–2).

### We Look by Faith to God's Hand (v. 2)

In eastern countries, masters often commanded their servants by means of hand signals, so the servants kept their eyes on the master's hand. This is what gave them direction for their work. But the master's hand was also the source of their provision, what they needed for their daily sustenance. Finally, the master's hand protected them in times of danger. The *New Jewish Publication Society* translation reads "they follow their master's hand." So it is with God's people today: our direction, provision, and protection all come from our Master's hand and His hand never fails. Even the heart of a king is in the hands of the Lord (Prov. 21:1), so God's feeble remnant in Jerusalem did not have to fear the nations around them.

### We Look for God's Mercy and Grace (vv. 3–4)

The exiles from Israel had spent seventy years in Babylon. Most of the older ones died and at least two new generations were born. Now, about 50,000 of these people were trying to rebuild their temple, restore their city, and revitalize their nation. This was not an easy task, and the nations around them did not want Israel back on the scene again. The Persian rulers who had promised to help them did not always keep their promises, or the local Persian officers interfered with the announced plans. It was another evidence of the hatred the Gentiles had for the Jews. "We have endured much contempt" (v. 3). (See 31:11, 18; 44:13; 119:22, 141; Neh. 2:19; 4:1–4, 7ff; Lam. 3:15, 30.) But God chooses and uses the despised things of this world (1 Cor. 1:28). After all, our salvation was purchased by One who was "despised and rejected of men" (Isa. 53:3).

We are not only subjects of the King (v. 1) and servants of the Master (vv. 2–3), we are also the children of a gracious Father who hears the cries of His children and comes to their aid. He has grace and mercy for each situation. In those post-exilic times, God's chosen people were being maligned, ridiculed, and opposed, but God gave them the grace they needed to finish the temple and restore the worship. The enemy was smug and complacent, but God was not at work in their midst. The nation of Israel continued, and one very special day, the promised Messiah was born into the human race in the little town of Bethlehem. If you find yourself laughed at and criticized because you belong to Jesus Christ, you are part of a very elite group, *and you do not have to be embarrassed or start looking for a place to hide!* There is grace available at the throne of grace from the God of all grace, so lift your eyes of faith to Him.

## Psalm 124

The contempt and ridicule of Psalm 123 has now been mixed with anger (v. 3) and become open hostility. When David began his reign in Jerusalem, the Philistines attacked him twice, and the Lord gave David great deliverance (2 Sam. 5:17–25). This psalm may have been his song of thanksgiving to the Lord. Note the "flood" image in 2 Samuel 5:10 and 124:4–5. However, when Nehemiah and the people were repairing the walls and gates of Jerusalem, the surrounding nations ridiculed them (Neh. 2:19–20; 4:1–5) and then threatened to attack them (Neh. 4:7–23). Nehemiah's words "Our God will fight for us" (Neh. 4:20) remind us of 124:1–2 and 8. We may not have entire nations and armies opposing us, but we do face emergencies that are more than we can handle. That is when we turn to the Lord for help, because He is on our side and helps us with these emergencies.

### The Sudden Attack (vv. 1–2)

The phrase "rose up" gives the image of a sudden ambush, a sneak attack that might have defeated Israel, except the Lord was on their side. "If God is for us, who can be against us?" (Rom. 8:31 NKJV; Ps. 56:9; 118:6; Gen. 31:42). Our enemy Satan does not give advance warning of his attacks; therefore, we must be sober and vigilant (1 Peter 5:8), put on the whole armor of God (Eph. 6:10–18), and be alert in our praying. God promised His chosen people that He would curse those who cursed them (Gen. 12:3), and He has kept that promise. The invading armies, such as Assyria and Babylon, did not conquer the Jews because their armies were too great for God, but because God's people were great sinners and the Lord had to chasten them. If we are walking with the Lord, we need not feel unprepared for the enemy's sudden attacks.

### The Deepening Flood (vv. 3–5)

Here is a situation where we stand helpless as the problem gets worse and worse. During the rainy season, and when the mountain snow melts, the dry riverbeds in Israel quickly become filled with water and flash floods threaten houses and people. Jeremiah compared the enemy invasions to sudden floods (Jer. 47:1–4), and Job 27:19–20 uses the same image on a personal level. (See also 18:4, 16; 32:6; 69:1–2, 15; 88:17.) This image of the persecution of the Jews is also seen in Revelation 12:13–17. The psalmist feared that the raging waters of persecution would sweep over him and his people and that they would be swallowed up forever. Jeremiah pictured the Babylonian captivity of Israel as Nebuchadnezzar swallowing the nation (Jer. 51:34, 44). But if the Lord is on our side, He will provide a way of escape.

### The Menacing Beast (v. 6)

A sudden attack by a wild beast is a biblical picture of persecution (7:1–2; 10:8–11; 27:1–2; 57:4). There are twelve words in the Hebrew language for lions, which indicates that the Jewish people in that day took wild beasts seriously. Jeremiah compared Babylon to a lion (Jer. 4:7; 51:38), and Peter compared Satan to a prowling lion (1 Peter 5:8). Like a cunning animal, Satan stalks us and waits until we have relaxed our guard, and then he pounces. But the Lord is stronger than Satan, and if we are abiding in Him, we can win the victory.

### The Hidden Trap (vv. 7–8)

We must use the Word of God to throw light on our path so we can detect and avoid the devil's traps (119:105; 91:1–3; 1 Tim.

3:7; 6:9; 2 Tim. 2:24–26). The picture is that of a helpless bird who walked into the trap in order to eat the food. Satan always has fascinating bait to offer. The Lord may allow us to fall into a trap, but nobody can keep us when He wants us to be free. The Lord not only opened the trap but broke it so it cannot be used again! The death and resurrection of Jesus Christ has broken the dominion of sin and death and we can walk in freedom through Jesus Christ.

Praise God, we are not helpless! "Our help is in the name of the Lord" (v. 8).

## Psalm 125

Three kinds of people are mentioned in this psalm: those who trust in the Lord (v. 1), who are also called righteous and good (vv. 3–4); those who compromise with the enemy (v. 3); and those who deliberately go on the wrong path (v. 5). We could probably call them the faithful, the backslidden, and the apostate. This psalm was probably composed during the post-exilic period of Ezra and Nehemiah. Nehemiah mentions all sorts of people who made his work difficult for him, beginning with Shemiah, the "secret informer," and Noadiah, the hireling prophetess (Neh. 6:10–14). Eliashib was a compromising high priest (Neh. 13:4–9), and one of his grandsons married into the family of an enemy of the Jews (Neh. 13:28). There were also many unnamed Jewish men who entered into mixed marriages that were contrary to God's law (Neh. 13:1–9, 23–31; Ezra 9–10). Thank God for the faithful who believe God and obey His Word! The psalm names the benefits that faith and faithfulness bring to God's people.

### Faith Keeps Us Standing (vv 1–2)
Spiritual security and stability belong to those who walk by faith. The city of Jerusalem was firmly established and could not be shaken. For one thing, it was built on a solid foundation of rock that went deep into the ground. The city was surrounded by a number of hills and probably two sets of walls. Even more,

Jerusalem was home to the holy temple of Jehovah and the throne of David. God's glory and God's authority dwelt among His people.

The writer did not say that God's people *should be* like Mount Zion but that they *are* like Mount Zion. We are built upon the solid Rock, Jesus Christ (1 Cor. 3:11; 1 Peter 2:4–8). He dwells within us and He surrounds us with His protection and mercy. As people of faith, we shall not be moved (16:8; 21:7; 62:6). Like Paul, we say, "None of these things move me" (Acts 20:24). We have a marvelous standing, for we stand in God's grace (Rom. 5:2; Gal. 5:1), and we stand by faith (Rom. 11:20). We take our stand on the truths of the Word of God (2 Thess. 2:15) and stand in the will of God (Col. 4:12). It is God who enables us to stand (2 Cor. 1:21, 24), and because He does, we are able to accomplish the work He wants us to do (1 Cor. 15:58). When we begin to trust ourselves or other people, and we bypass the Lord, then we begin to waver, stumble, and fall.

### Faith Keeps Us Obeying (v. 3)

The land of Israel belongs to the Lord and He allowed His people to dwell there as long as they obeyed His covenant (Lev. 25:2, 23, 38). The land was assigned by lot to the various tribes (Josh. 14–19) and was never to be sold to anyone outside the tribe. But over the years, their sins defiled the land and the Lord finally had to send the people to Babylon to give the land the rest and cleansing it needed. While the people were away, some of the land was taken over by strangers, including Gentiles from neighboring nations, and this had to be straightened out when the exiles returned. Israel was under Persian rule during the postexilic years, and the Persian officers could do as they pleased. Some of the Jews became weary of this arrangement and capitulated to the Persians. "If you cannot whip them, join them." But the "scepter of wickedness" was wielded not only by Persians but also by greedy Israelites who disobeyed God's law and exploited their own people (Neh. 5). The prevalence of evil makes it easier for everybody to sin (Matt. 24:12), but the Lord will not permit this to go on forever. The people who trust God will obey His Word no matter what others may do, and they will not succumb to temptation (1 Cor. 10:13).

### Faith Keeps Us Praying (v. 4)

Jesus taught us to keep on praying and not become discouraged if the answer is long in coming (Luke 18:1–8). The times may be bad, but there are always good people in bad times, people who trust God and obey His will. No matter how depressing the times may be, people of faith pray and receive good things from the hand of their Father (Luke 11:9–13). To live by faith is to keep our eyes on the Lord (123:1; Heb. 12:1–2), rest on the promises of His Word, and do what is right no matter what others may say or do. Faith means living without scheming.

### Faith Keeps Us Hoping (v. 5)

People of faith know that God will one day judge the disobedient, no matter how much they seem to get away with resisting God and abusing others. The future is your friend when Jesus is your Lord. It is not easy to walk on the narrow way, but it leads to life, while the broad way leads to destruction (Matt. 7:13–27). They may be enjoying the pleasures of sin now, but what will the outcome be? "Mark the blameless man, and observe the upright; for the future of that man is peace. But the transgressors shall be destroyed together; the future of the wicked shall be cut off" (37:37–38 NKJV).

The life of faith is not easy, but the life of unbelief is much harder—in this life and in the life to come.

## Psalm 126

Some students connect this psalm with the sudden deliverance of Jerusalem from the Assyrian siege during the reign of Hezekiah (Isa. 36–37). But the Hebrew verb translated "turned again" in v. 1 (KJV; "brought back" NASB, NIV) and "turn again" or "restore" in verse 4, is also used to describe the return of the Jewish exiles from Babylon (Ezra 2:1; Neh. 7:6; Isa. 10:22; Jer. 22:10). Cyrus gave his decree in 537 B.C., an event prophesied by Isaiah (44:24–45:7). Isaiah also prophesied the joy of the people at their liberation (Isa. 48:20; 49:8–13; 51:11; 54:1; 55:10–12) and the witness of this remarkable event to the other nations (Isa. 43:10–21; 44:8, 23; 52:7–10). But once the exiles were back in their land, their joy began to subside, for life is not always easy when you are making a new beginning after a time of discipline. But life is so arranged that we must often make new beginnings, and the Lord helps us by giving us special encouragements.

### Within Us, the Joy of Freedom (vv. 1–3)

The generation of Jews that conquered the Promised Land was true to the Lord, and so were their children, but the third generation broke the covenant and turned to idols (Judg. 2:7–23). God punished His people *in the land* by allowing seven nations to invade, rob, and destroy. When Israel's rebellion became so great that the land itself was being defiled, God took them *out of the land* and sent them to Babylon for seventy years. Now they had been set free and they could not believe what was happening. Yes, they knew that both Isaiah and Jeremiah had promised this "second exodus," but it was too good to be true. During long years of waiting, they had dreamed of returning home, and now the dream had become reality. God in His grace had forgiven them (Isa. 40:1–2; 44:21–22) and they could make a new beginning. The Jews had lost their song in Babylon (137:1–5), but now they were shouting, laughing, and singing! What a witness of God's faithfulness to keep His promises!

The surrounding nations, some of whom hated Israel, were utterly astonished at this event and openly confessed that the God of Israel had done great things for them. The Jews replied that indeed He had done great things for them, and they gave God the glory. "If you can explain what is going on, God did not do it" (Dr. Bob Cook). This confession of the greatness of God was made by others in Scripture: Moses (Deut. 10:21), Job (Job 5:8–9), Samuel (1 Sam. 12:24), David (2 Sam. 7:21–23), the prophet Joel (Joel 2:21), Mary (Luke 1:49), and the unnamed demoniac whom Jesus healed (Luke 8:39). This ought to be the confession of every Christian and of every local church.

### Around Us, the Promise of Life (v. 4)

"Turn again our captivity" (KJV) can also be translated "restore our fortunes." The captivity had ended and the Jews were praying for the blessing of the Lord on their life in the land. However, not all the Jews had left Babylon, for while many came during the reign of Cyrus (Ezra 1–3), others followed during the reigns of Darius (Ezra 6) and Artaxerxes (Ezra 7–8). It was important that the people return to their land and get to work, but it was also important that God bless their work (127:1–2). If the Lord did not keep His covenant and send the early and latter rains (Lev. 26:4; Deut. 11:10–12; 28:12), there would be no crops and their labors would have been in vain. Each raindrop was but a tiny thing, but when dropped on the earth, it was the promise of life. How gracious of the Lord to send "showers of blessing" (Ezek. 34:26) to His people! How important it is that God's people pray for His blessing and prepare themselves to receive it (2 Chron. 7:14; Mal. 3:8–12). In Scripture, water for drinking is a picture of the Spirit of God and the refreshing life that He brings to those who seek Him (John 7:37–38).

### Before Us, the Challenge of Work (vv. 5–6)

"Faith without works is dead" (James 2:26), so after we have praised God and prayed, we must get to work, for work is a blessing, not a curse. God gave our first parents work to do in the garden before sin ever entered the human race (Gen. 2:15). In Scripture, the people God commissioned for special service were busy when He called them: Moses was caring for sheep (Ex. 3); Gideon was threshing wheat (Judg. 6); David was tending the family flock (1 Sam. 16); Nehemiah was serving the king (Neh. 1); Peter, Andrew, James, and John were busy in their fishing business (Luke 5:1–11); and Matthew was in his tax office (Matt. 9:9).

The returned remnant experienced some bad seasons (Hag. 1:9–11), but the promise came that God would send the rains and the harvests (Hag. 2:15–19). God would keep His covenant promises if His people would keep His covenant commands. The grain that the farmer sowed might have been used to make bread for his family, so it is no wonder he was weeping as he toiled. Tears and rejoicing often went together at that time (Ezra 3:8–13; 6:16, 22), but the farmer was trusting God to multiply the grain so that he would have both bread for his family to eat and seed to sow the next season (2 Cor. 9:10–11). In His covenant, God gave the promise of adequate food for the people (Deut. 28:1–14), and the sower was claiming that promise. It pleases the Lord when we water with our tears the seed of the Word that we sow. We cannot reap if we do not first sow the seed, and the seed must be watered with our tears and our prayers.

Some blessings God sends suddenly (vv. 1–3), some come in the course of time (v. 4), and some come as we patiently sow and weep (James 5:7). But His promise is secure: "in due season we shall reap if we do not lose heart" (Gal. 6:9 NKJV).

## Psalm 127

No amount of human sacrifice or toil can accomplish much unless God's blessing is upon His people. That is the major message of this psalm. It is assigned to Solomon, who was both a builder and a father, but the message also seems to fit the post-exilic times of Nehemiah. The population of Jerusalem was small and the people had to build and repair the buildings. Houses were desperately needed for families or else the struggling Jewish nation had no future (Neh. 7:4). Surrounded by numerous enemies, Jerusalem needed strong gates and walls and watchmen on the alert day and night (Neh. 4:9ff; 7:3). Note that the psalm deals with the same elements Jeremiah wrote about in his letter to the Jewish exiles (Jer. 29:4–7). But the psalm also speaks to us today and reminds us of some privileges we have as the people of God in a dangerous and demanding world.

### Building (v. 1a)

A wrecking crew or a demolition team can destroy in a few hours or days what it took engineers and builders months to plan

and construct. Even a weak little child can heedlessly destroy
something valuable, and some adults go through life just tearing
things down. God had called us to build—our lives, our homes,
our churches, and the kingdom of God around the world. Before
commencing His public ministry, Jesus was a carpenter (Mark
6:3), and He is currently building His church in this world
(Matt. 16:18). The apostle Paul saw himself as a builder (Rom.
15:20, 17), and he warned that it is a dangerous thing to destroy
the local church (1 Cor. 3:11–17). Whether we are building
structures with bricks and mortar and steel, or building lives,
families, and churches with truth and love, we cannot succeed
without the help of the Lord. Jesus said, "Without Me you can
do nothing" (John 15:5 NKJV).

### Guarding (1b)

Strong walls around the city and alert watchmen on those
walls are essential if we are to protect what we have built—and
how foolish it is to build and not protect! Many a child and many
a ministry has been lost to the enemy because the watchmen did
not stay awake and warn that the enemy was approaching.
Building and battling go together; this is why Nehemiah's men
had their tools in one hand and their swords at their side (Neh.
4:17–18). Jesus joined the two in Luke 14:25–33. The famous
British preacher Charles Haddon Spurgeon called his publication *The Sword and The Trowel* because its purpose was to build
believers and the church and to fight sin and false doctrine. As
he awaited execution in a Roman prison, Paul encouraged
Timothy to preach the Word and to be "watchful in all things"
(2 Tim. 4:1–5). If parents, teachers, and church leaders do not
courageously maintain the walls and guard against the enemy,
our building will be in vain.

### Enjoying (v. 2)

If verse 1 warns against overconfidence ("We can do it without God's help!"), verse 2 warns against overwork and anxious
toil ("I have to do it all right now!"). This verse does not say it is
wrong for people to get up early, work hard, and make sacrifices

(see 2 Thess. 3:6–15). It only warns us that our work must be a blessing we enjoy and not a burden we endure. Yes, both physical and mental toil are a part of this fallen world (Gen. 3:17), but doing God's will is nourishment, not punishment. Work suited to our gifts and personalities is food for our souls (John 4:34), but the anxious laborer eats "the bread of sorrows"—sorrow while working and sorrow while trying to rest at night as he worries about the next day. God gives us "richly all things to enjoy" (1 Tim. 6:17), and this includes earning our daily bread. Note in Ecclesiastes how much Solomon had to say about enjoying life and labor (2:24; 3:12–15, 22; 5:18–20; 8:15; 9:7–10; 11:9–10).

God's special name for Solomon was "Jedidiah—beloved" (2 Sam. 12:25). But *all* of God's people are "God's beloved" (Rom. 1:7; Col. 3:12; 1 Thess. 1:4; 2 Thess. 2:13) because they are accepted and blessed in the Beloved One, Jesus Christ (Eph. 1:6 NASB; Matt. 3:17; 17:5). The last line of verse 2 is translated and interpreted several different ways, but the thrust of it seems clear. We get tired *in* God's work but we do not get tired *of* God's work, because the Lord who gives us the strength to work also gives us the rest we need. "The sleep of a laboring man is sweet" (Eccl. 5:12). But even as we sleep, God works for us in different ways, for He never slumbers or sleeps (see Mark 4:26–29). As we go to bed at night, we may look back at the day and wish we had worked better and harder, accomplished more and had fewer interruptions, but we can commit the day's work to the Lord and not fret. After a hard day's ministry, Jesus was able to go to sleep in a boat on the sea in a terrible storm! (Matt. 8:23–27).

### Conserving (vv. 3–5)

It does no good to build and guard our houses and cities if there are no future generations to inherit them and keep the family, city, and nation going. There were few people living in Jerusalem in the post-exilic age (Neh. 7:4), and it was important that the young people marry and have families. Among the Jews, it was unheard of that a husband and wife not want children or that a child be aborted. "Children are *the* blessing for the Jew," writes Rabbi Leo Trepp. "Each child brings a blessing all his own, our ancestors would say. We rejoice in children because we are a people, a historical people" (*The Complete Book of Jewish Observance*, p. 217). Children are precious—a heritage—and make the home a treasury. But they are also useful—like fruit and arrows—and make the home a garden and an armory. If we do not raise our children to know and love the truth, who will plant the seeds of truth and fight the battles against lies and evil in the years to come? (For other comparisons, see 128:3 and 144:12.) The city gate was the place where important legal business was transacted (Deut. 21:19; Ruth 4:1ff; Amos 5:12), and it was helpful to have a godly family to back you up. Also, the enemy would try to enter at the city gate, and the more sons to fight at your side, the better was the opportunity for victory. It is in the family that we preserve the best of the past and invest it in the future. Every baby born is God's vote for the future of humankind and our opportunity to help make some new beginnings.

Not everyone is supposed to get married, nor are all married couples able to have children. But all adults can value the children, pray for them, be good examples to them, and see that they are protected and cared for and encouraged in their spiritual upbringing. Remember what Jesus said about this in Matthew 18:5–6.

## Psalm 128

Because families traveled together to the annual feasts in Jerusalem, it is only right that another psalm be devoted to parents and their offspring. The previous psalm pictured children as a rich heritage and as arrows for defeating the enemy (127:3–5). This psalm uses agricultural images for both the wife and the children. In one form or another, the word "bless" is used four times, but it is the translation of two different Hebrew words. In verses 1–2, it is the word *asher* which is often translated "happy" (Gen. 30:12–13), and in verses 4–5, it is *barak*, which means "blessed of the Lord." The latter word is used by the Lord when He blesses people; the former word is used to describe the good that comes when people do that which pleases the Lord. Like

127 and Jeremiah 29:4–7, this psalm deals with protection (v. 1), working (v. 2), the family (vv. 3–4, 6), and God's blessing on Jerusalem (v. 5). While the writer includes all who fear the Lord (v. 1), the psalm is addressed especially to the man of the house (v. 3). We see a happy man and woman as they go through several stages in life.

### Godly Believers (v. 1)

In the ancient Near East, marriages were arranged primarily by the parents, but the stories of Jacob (Gen. 28–30) and Ruth indicates that love was not entirely lacking in these marriages. Here we have a Jewish couple who truly feared the Lord and wanted to establish a home that Jehovah could bless. To fear the Lord means to reverence Him and seek to please Him by obeying His Word. In the background is the covenant God made with Israel (Lev. 26; Deut. 38–30). If they obeyed, God would meet their needs; if they disobeyed, He would chasten them. This is the Old Testament version of Matthew 6:33. It takes three to form a happy marriage: a man and woman who love the Lord and each other, and the Lord who performed the first wedding back in the Garden of Eden.

### Successful Workers (v. 2)

It is the Lord who gives His people "power to get wealth" (Deut. 8:18). How easy it is for us to think that our planning, skill, and hard work accomplished it all, but such is not the case. As we saw in the previous psalm, without the blessing of the Lord, all our labor is in vain. Each Jew was required to give tithes to the Lord, but the Lord wanted the workers to share the fruit of their labor. If the nation turned to other gods, one of the first places the Lord would send judgment was in the home and field (Lev. 26:14ff; Deut. 28:30–34).

### Happy Parents (vv. 3–4)

Both the vine and the olive tree were important to the economy of Israel, the vine providing wine and the olive tree supplying fruit and oil (104:14–15). A husband's love for his wife is illustrated by the vine and the olive tree (Song. 7:6–9). Jewish couples wanted large families and considered each child a blessing from the Lord. The phrase "within your house" refers to the wife's apartment at the back of the tent, as far from the tent door as possible. The faithful wife is not unhappy in her own house, caring for children she dearly loved. The unfaithful wife leaves the safety and sanctity of her apartment and goes seeking for victims (Prov. 7:10–13). The olive shoots around the base of the parent tree, fresh and vigorous, picture the children around the family table. It takes patience to care for them as they grow, but the efforts are rewarding. How shocked those ancient families would be if they visited a modern home and watched parents and children scattering in all directions and rarely eating a leisurely meal together.

### Useful Citizens (v. 5)

The Jewish people are proud of their heritage and want to see God's very best blessings come to Jerusalem. They realize how enriched they are from Zion. They long for each of their children to bring honor to Israel, and they pray for the peace and prosperity of Israel and Jerusalem. Many of the psalms end with a prayer for the land and the city (14:7; 25:22; 72:18–19; 106:48; 130:7–8; 125:5; 131:3; 134:3; 135:21; 148:14). True patriotism begins in the home, where love of God, family, and country are bound together.

### Contented Grandparents (v. 6)

From bride and groom to grandparents in just six verses! How time flies! Three generations are represented in the psalm, and all of them walking with the Lord. We are so prone to remember that God judges the succeeding generations if they imitate the sins of their ancestors, that we forget that He also passes along the blessings when the ancestors have been godly (Ex. 34:67; Num. 14:18–19; Deut. 5:9–10). It is often the third generation that abandons the faith (Judg. 2), so we must pray much for our children and grandchildren, that the Lord will keep His good hand of blessing on their lives for His glory.

"Blessed is the nation whose God is the Lord" (33:12).

# Psalm 129

The destruction of Jerusalem by the Babylonians was described by the prophets as "plowing" (vv. 3–4; Isa. 51:23; Mic. 3:12; Jer. 26:17–18), so this psalm was probably written after the exiles returned to the land. There they were surrounded by enemy peoples who hated them, so the theme was appropriate. The psalmist speaks for the nation and states that, no matter how severe the persecution, nothing can destroy the people of Israel. But God's church has also suffered severe persecution throughout the centuries, and faithful individual Christians face personal hostility. "Yes, and all who desire to live godly in Christ Jesus will suffer persecution" (2 Tim. 3:12 NKJV). The psalm gives three instructions that we should follow when we find ourselves suffering for Jesus Christ.

### Accept It (vv. 1–2)

Persecution is not something "strange" in the life of either Israel or the church (1 Peter 4:12). To ask, "Why, Lord?" is to confess our ignorance of the place of God's people in this present evil world. When the Lord called Abraham, He revealed that some would bless the Jews and others curse them (Gen. 12:1–3). Isaac was persecuted by Ishmael (Gen. 21:8–21; Gal. 4:21–31), and the Jews were terribly oppressed in Egypt (88:15; Hos. 11:1). However, the more they were persecuted, the more they increased (Ex. 1:9–14), and there the family of Jacob was molded into the nation of Israel. Israel has suffered more than any nation in history, *yet Israel has not been destroyed!*

Egypt tried to drown the Jews (Ex. 1:15–22), but the Lord drowned Egypt's crack troops (Ex. 14:19–31). The Assyrians tried to starve them into surrender, but God wiped out the Assyrian army (Isa. 37–38). Nebuchadnezzar, ruler of Babylon, tried to burn them up, but the Lord delivered them (Dan. 3). Belshazzar blasphemed the God of Israel and defiled the holy vessels of the temple, but that very night, the Medes and Persians killed him. The Persian soothsayers tried to throw Daniel to the lions, but God rescued him and the beasts killed the soothsayers instead

(Dan. 6). Hitler killed over six million Jews in his gas chambers, but he was soundly defeated, and the nation of Israel was born a few years later. The church of Jesus Christ has experienced persecution, but it still stands and will stand until Jesus returns (Matt. 16:18). Every true believer can identify with Paul's testimony in 2 Corinthians 4:7–12. When it comes to suffering for the sake of the Lord, we must, first of all, accept it.

### Benefit from It (vv. 3–4)

As you read these verses, you can almost feel the sharp cutting edges of the plow. *Their enemies treated Israel like dirt and walked on them!* (See Josh. 10:24 and Isa. 51:23.) Some students see in the plowing image a picture of prisoners being whipped, leaving long deep gashes on their backs. If that is a part of the picture, then our Lord endured the same suffering—and yet His stripes bring spiritual healing to those who trust Him! (Isa. 50:6; 53:5). The nation of Israel has been plowed long, deep, and often, but what a harvest of blessing it has brought to the world! The day came when God cut the cords that tied the oxen to the plow, and then Israel was free (see 124:7). The exiles returned to their homes wiser and better people because they had felt the pain of the plow. Instead of blaming God for their suffering, they confessed, "The Lord is righteous."

The plowing image is a good one for believers today, for it reminds us that there can be a glorious harvest, *but it depends on the seeds that we plant.* Of itself, suffering does not produce blessing. If we plant seeds of hatred and resentment, then suffering will produce bitterness. But if we plant faith, hope, love, and the precious promises of the Word, then the harvest will bless us and help others, and it will bring glory to God. (See 1 Peter 4:12–19.) God permits people to treat us like dirt, and we must accept it, but we have the privilege of transforming it by the grace of God into character that honors the Lord.

### Commit to the Lord (vv. 5–8)

The harvest image continues, but moves from the fields to the housetops. Roofs were flat and usually composed of a mixture of mud and mortar, wood and thatching. It would be easy for wind-blown seeds to settle on the roofs, take root in the shallow soil, grow quickly, but not last. Jesus used this image in his parable about the sower (Matt. 13:5–6, 20–21). Where there has been no plowing, you will not get much of a harvest. The psalmist prayed that those who hated Zion would perish quickly like the useless grass on the roof. But why would anybody want to hate the Jews? Is this hatred born of envy? The most logical answer is that Satan hates Israel and has always been at war with her (see Rev. 12). Satan is also at war with the church (John 15:18–15; 17:14; 1 John 3:13).

Instead of returning evil for evil, the Jews committed the con-flict to the Lord and trusted Him to vindicate His own people (Rom. 12:17–21). Jewish harvesters often blessed one another as they worked in the fields (Ruth 2:4), but no blessing would be given to Israel's enemies, for they were rebelling against the God of Israel. First, these enemies would be turned back in disgrace because they could not eradicate Israel, then they would wither away, and finally they would be mowed down and used for fuel. But the people of Israel can always say to the world, "We bless you in the name of the Lord," because Israel has brought to the world the knowledge of the true and living God, the Scriptures, and the Savior. "Salvation is of the Jews" (John 4:22).

When people treat you like dirt because you belong to Jesus, remember the ABCs of this psalm: accept it, benefit from it, commit it to the Lord.

## Psalm 130

The sixth of the seven Penitential Psalms (see 6), Psalm 130 emphasizes what God does for helpless people who cry out to Him for mercy. Perhaps the Jewish pilgrims used this psalm to confess their sins and seek God's forgiveness and blessing as they made their way to the sanctuary. (See Heb. 10:19–25 for the kind of preparation believers today need when they approach the Lord.) No matter what our need, when we call upon the Lord in faith, He hears us and makes the changes needed in our lives.

## From Death to Life (vv. 1–2)

The picture is that of a person drowning and unable to stand on the bottom or swim to safety. (See 40:2; 69:1–3, 13–15; Isa. 51:10; Ezek. 27:34.) The tense of the verb "cry" indicates that the writer had been crying in the past and continued to cry out as he wrote the psalm, because without God's merciful intervention, he would die. But he remembered the prayer of Solomon when the king dedicated the temple, and he knew that God's eyes were upon him and His ears open to his cries (2 Chron. 6:40; Ps. 34:15; 1 Peter 3:12). Five times he addressed Jehovah, the God of the covenant (LORD) and three times Adonai, the Master (Lord). We can cry out to God from the depths of disappointment and defeat and from the depths of fear and perplexity. Like a heavy weight, sin drags its victims to the depths, but God made us for the heights (Isa. 40:31; Col. 3:1).

## From Guilt to Forgiveness (vv. 3–4)

The psalmist moved from the sea to the courtroom, but there the sinner could not stand because of guilt. The only way we can get rid of the sin record is to come to God for His gracious forgiveness, and this forgiveness is made possible because of the work of Christ on the cross (32:1–2; Rom. 4:1–8). The word translated "mark" means "to observe and keep a record," and God is able to do that (90:8; 139:23–24; Jer. 2:22; 16:17; Ezek. 11:5; Hos. 7:2). Sinners cannot stand before the holy Judge and argue their own case (1:5; 143:2; Ezra 9:15; Nah. 1:6; Mal. 3:2). But God is ready to forgive (86:5; Neh. 9:17), and faith in the Savior brings forgiveness to the soul. God casts our sins behind His back and blots them out of His book (Isa. 38:17; 43:25; 44:22). He carries them away as far as the east is from the west (103:11–12), casts them into the sea (Mic. 7:19), and holds them against us no more (Jer. 31:34; Heb. 10:17). But forgiveness is not a blessing to be taken lightly, for it cost God His Son; therefore, we ought to love and fear God (76:7). If you take seriously the guilt of sin, you will take seriously the grace of forgiveness. Salvation is a serious and costly transaction.

### From Darkness to Light (vv. 5–6)

From the courtroom we move to the city walls where the watchmen are alert as they peer through the darkness to detect the approach of any danger. Nothing they do can make the sun come up any sooner, but when the day dawns, the guards rejoice that the city has been safe another night. When the Lord forgives sinners, it is for them the dawning of a new day as they move out of darkness into God's marvelous light (1 Peter 2:9; Luke 1:76–79; see comments on Ps. 27). The forgiven sinner is content to wait on the Lord for whatever He has planned for that day. This is not the waiting of *hopeless resignation* but of *hopeful anticipation*, for each new day brings new blessings from His hand (119:74, 81, 82; Lam. 3:22–26). If you find yourself forgiven but still in the darkness, wait on the Lord and trust His Word, but do not try to manufacture your own light (Isa. 50:10–11).

### From to Bondage to Freedom (vv. 7–8)

Our final visit is to the slave market and the theme is *redemption*, which means "setting someone free by paying a price." Israel knew a great deal about God's redemption, for at the Exodus, God's power had set them free from Egyptian tyranny (Ex. 12–15). They had no hope and could not free themselves, but the Lord did it for them. He gave His people "abundant redemption" that included freedom from slavery, victory over their enemies, and a Promised Land for their home. The slave has no hope, but the child in the family looks forward to receiving an inheritance. All who trust Jesus Christ are children in God's family and not slaves, and their future is secure (Gal. 3:26–4:7). The psalmist saw a future redemption for the people of Israel, as did Paul (Rom. 11) and the prophets (Isa. 11, 60, 65–66; Zech. 12:10–14:21). Christian believers look forward to the coming of Christ and the redemption He will bring (Rom. 8:18–30).

# Psalm 131

If anyone in Israel had reasons to be proud, it was David. The eighth son of a common citizen, he began as a humble shepherd and yet became Israel's greatest king. A courageous soldier, a gifted general and tactician, and a sincere man of God, it was David who defeated Israel's enemies, expanded her boundaries, and amassed the wealth that Solomon used to build the temple. He wrote nearly half of the psalms, and though (like all of us) he was guilty of disobeying the Lord, he was always repentant and sought God's merciful forgiveness. It was for David's sake that the Lord kept the light burning in Jerusalem during the years of Judah's decay, and it was from David's line that Jesus Christ came into this world. Except for a few lapses into selfishness and sin, David walked with the Lord in a humble spirit. In this brief psalm, he tells us the essentials of a life that glorifies God and accomplishes His work on earth.

### Honesty—Accept Yourself (v. 1)

We move toward maturity when we honestly accept who we are, understand what we can do, accept both and live for God's glory. Rejecting or hating ourselves, fantasizing about ourselves, and envying others are marks of immaturity. David had seen some of this kind of behavior in his own son Absalom as well as in King Saul. A proud heart refuses to face reality, a high look covers up hidden inadequacy, and arrogant ambition ("going to and fro constantly") impresses some people but leads ultimately to embarrassing failure (Jer. 45:5). When you accept yourself and your lot and thank God for the way He made you, you do not need to impress people. They will see your worth and love you for who you are. (See 16:5–6; Prov. 18:12; Phil. 4:11–12; Heb. 13:5.) Spoiled children want to be seen and heard and they get involved in things they cannot handle. David did not promote himself; it was all God's doing.

### Humility—Accept God's Will (v. 2)

The simile of the weaned child is a beautiful picture of the meaning of humility and maturity. Hebrew children were weaned at ages three or four, and this experience marked the end of their infancy. But most children do not want to be deprived of mother's loving arms and satisfying breasts, and they feel rejected and unwanted. But after the crisis of birth, each child must eventually be weaned and learn the first lesson in the school of life: growing up involves painful losses that can lead to wonderful gains. The Hebrew word for "wean" means "to complete, to ripen, to treat kindly." The English word may be a contraction of the Scottish phrase "wee one," or it may come from a Teutonic word that means "to be accustomed." Maturing people know that life is a series of gains and losses, and they learn how to use their losses constructively. If children are to grow up and not just grow old, they must be able to function apart from mother. This means weaning, going to school, choosing a vocation, and probably marrying and starting a new home. They must learn that there is a difference between cutting the apron strings and cutting the heartstrings and that these separations do not rob them of Mother's love.

God's goal for us is emotional and spiritual maturity (1 Cor. 13:11; 14:20; Eph. 4:13–15), and God sometimes has to wean us away from good things in order to give us better things. Abraham had to leave his family and city, send Ishmael away, separate from Lot, and put Isaac on the altar. Painful weanings! Joseph had to be separated from his father and his brothers in order to see his dreams come true. Both Jacob and Peter had to be weaned from their own self-sufficiency and learn that faith means living without scheming. The child that David described wept and fretted but eventually calmed down and accepted the inevitable. The word describes the calming of the sea or the farmer's leveling of the ground after plowing (Isa. 28:25). Instead of emotional highs and lows, the child developed a steady uniform response, indicating a giant step forward in the quest for maturity. Successful living means moving from dependence to independence, and then to interdependence, always in the will of God. To accept God's will in the losses and gains of life is to experience that inner calm that is so necessary if we are to be mature people.

### Hope—Anticipate the Future (v. 3)

Infants do not realize that their mother's decision is for their own good, for weaning sets them free to meet the future and make the most of it. The child may want to keep things as they are, but that way lies immaturity and tragedy. When we fret over a comfortable past, we only forfeit a challenging future. In the Christian vocabulary, hope is not "hope so." It is joyful antici-pation of what the Lord will do in the future, based on His changeless promises. Like the child being weaned, we may fret at our present circumstances, but we know that our fretting is wrong. Our present circumstances are the womb out of which new blessings and opportunities will be born (Rom. 8:28).

## Psalm 132

It is not likely that this is a post-exilic psalm. The ark is men-tioned (v. 8), and after the destruction of the temple, the ark disappeared from the scene. Also, the writer referred in verse 10 to a king from David's dynasty, and there was no Davidic king after Zedekiah, until Jesus came to earth. Nobody in post-exilic Jerusalem was anointed as king. Since verses 8–10 are quoted by Solomon in his prayer at the dedication of the tem-ple (2 Chron. 6:41–42), perhaps this psalm was written for that occasion. It could well have been a litany, with the worship leader opening (vv. 1–5) and the people responding (vv. 6–10). The leader then quoted God's words to David (vv. 10–12), and the people or a choir closed with a recital of God's promises to Israel (vv. 13–18). Note especially the references to David in Solomon's prayer (2 Chron. 6:3–11, 15–17). Psalm 132 also parallels Psalm 89 but is more optimistic in outlook. Note in 89 the use of anointed (v. 20; 132:10), enemy (vv. 22–23; 132:18), horn (v. 24; 132:17), and throne (v. 29). (For other "Zion psalms," see 24, 48, 68, and 89.) The completion of the temple was no assurance of God's blessing on Israel, for the important thing was that the people fulfill their responsibilities toward the Lord.

### Give God His Rightful Place (vv. 1–5)

The ark represented God's throne on earth (80:1 and 99:1 NASB, NIV) and its rightful place was in the Holy of Holies of

God's sanctuary. Unless God is on the throne of our lives, no enterprise we attempt can be really successful. The ark had been in several places before Solomon put it into the temple (2 Chron. 5). The ark went before the children of Israel as they followed the cloud and pillar of fire through the wilderness, and it also went before them into the water as the people crossed the Jordan River and entered Canaan. It is possible that the ark was temporarily at Bethel (Judg. 20:27) and then Mizpah (Judg. 21:5), but it finally rested at Shiloh (1 Sam. 1–3). The wicked sons of Eli used the ark as a "good luck charm" and took it into battle against the Philistines, but the Philistines captured it (1 Sam. 4–5). Frightened by the judgments God sent, the Philistines returned the ark to the Jews, and for twenty years it rested in the house of Abinadab in Kirjath Jearim (1 Sam. 6:1–7:2). When David became king, he wanted the ark in Jerusalem and prepared a tent for it, but his first attempt failed (2 Sam. 6:1–11). The ark remained in the house of Obed-Edom for three months, and then David successfully brought God's throne to Jerusalem (2 Sam. 6:12–19; 1 Chron. 15–16). It appears that the tabernacle of Moses and its holy furniture were in Gibeon (1 Chron. 21:29).

David had two great ambitions: to bring the ark to Jerusalem and then to build a glorious temple to house it. He even made a vow to the Lord, and the Lord permitted him to fulfill the first desire but not the second (2 Sam. 7). David had gone through much hardship with reference to the building of the temple (v. 1; 1 Chron. 22:14), for the wealth he turned over to Solomon came from the spoils of his many battles. The worship leader called on God to "remember—pay attention to" what David had done, for humanly speaking, without David there would have been no temple. Even purchasing the property on which the temple was built cost David a great deal of pain (2 Sam. 24). The words spoken in verse 4 do not mean that David forsook sleep all those years but simply expressed the passion of his heart and the desire to accomplish his goal quickly (Prov. 6:4). "The Mighty One of Jacob" (vv. 2, 5) is an ancient name for Jehovah, for Jacob used it in his last words to his family (Gen. 49:24; and see Isa. 1:24; 49:26; 60:16).

### Express to God Your Joyful Worship (vv. 6–9)

We get the impression that the ark was almost forgotten during the years it was in the house of Abinadab in Kirjath Jearim ("city of woods"). The city was only eight miles northwest of Jerusalem, so distance was no problem. Did some of the people in David's hometown of Bethlehem (Ephrathah—"fruitful land") "start the ball rolling" and encourage the king to act? At any rate, once the ark was back in Jerusalem, the people felt drawn to go on pilgrimage to the city. When Solomon put the ark into the Holy of Holies, the glory of God moved in, just as when Moses dedicated the tabernacle (1 Kings 8:1–11; Ex. 40). (On "footstool" see notes on 99:4–5.) The statement in verse 8 is taken from Numbers 10:33–36 and reminded the worshipers of God's guidance and power exhibited in the days of Moses. The prayer for the priests in verse 9 is answered in verse 16. A holy priesthood was important to the prosperity of Israel, but so was a nation dedicated to the Lord. The Lord could now "rest" in His house after many years of wandering from place to place (2 Sam. 7:6; 1 Chron. 28:2).

### Remind God of His Faithful Covenant (vv. 10–12)

God's covenant with David (2 Sam. 7) assured Israel that one of David's descendants would sit on the throne, and now Solomon was king, "God's anointed." So it was for David's sake, not Solomon's, that God blessed the king and the people. The prophet Isaiah called this "the sure mercies of David" (Isa. 55:3). The psalmist reminded the Lord of His covenant, because he wanted someone from the Davidic dynasty to sit on the throne of Israel. Ultimately, this promise was fulfilled in Jesus Christ, the Son of David, whose throne and kingdom are forever (2 Sam. 7:11–17; Acts 13:26–39; Luke 1:30–33). If David's successors wanted the blessing of God, they needed to obey the law of God, and many of them did not. Believers today are united with the Lord in a new covenant that Jesus made in His own blood (Matt.

26:26–30; Heb. 12:24), and He will never break that covenant. The psalmist used David's name when he prayed to the Lord, but we pray in the name of Jesus (John 14:13–14; 15:16; 16:23–26). The Father is faithful to His Son, and the Son is faithful to the covenant He made in His own blood.

### Trust God for His Bountiful Blessings (vv. 13–18)

God not only chose Israel to be His people and David and his descendants to be His kings, but He chose Zion to be the site of His temple and His throne (the ark). David had desperately wanted to build God a house, but was forbidden to do so, but he gathered the wealth needed, received the plans from the Lord, and bought the property on which the temple would stand. This purchase grew out of the sin David committed when he took a census of the people (2 Sam. 24). When the fire from heaven consumed his sacrifice, David knew that this was the place God had chosen. Other nations had temples, but none of those temples had the glory of the true and living God dwelling in them.

God spoke to the people in verses 14–18 and reaffirmed His covenant with Israel (Lev. 26; Deut. 27–30), for the people as well as the kings were obligated to obey the Lord if they expected to experience His blessing (v. 12). God promised to dwell with Israel, provide their food, bless their worship, and defeat their enemies. Two special images are seen here—the lamp and the sprouting horn (v. 17)—and both refer to David and to the promised Messiah, Jesus Christ. The burning lamp symbolized the king (2 Sam. 21:17), the preservation of life (18:28–30), and the perpetuation of the royal dynasty (1 Kings 11:36; 15:4; 2 Kings 8:19; 2 Chron. 21:7). The sins of some of David's successors deserved radical punishment, but for David's sake, the Lord allowed them to reign from David's throne. A horn is a symbol of power and strength, and the sprouting of the horn of David is a picture of the coming of the promised Messiah. The Hebrew word for "sprout" is translated "branch" in Isaiah 4:2, Jeremiah 23:5 and 33:15, and Zechariah 3:18 and 6:12, and refers to the Messiah, "the Branch." The word translated "flourish" or "shine" in verse 18 can also mean "to blossom," and is used that way in Numbers 17:8, the blossoming of Aaron's rod. This, too, is a Messianic image. So, the psalm ends by pointing to Jesus Christ.

The psalm concerns itself with David and God's covenant with him, but it points to David's greater Son, Jesus Christ, and His covenant with His church. The psalmist was concerned about the ark of the covenant, but the ark points to Jesus Christ who today is enthroned in the Holy of Holies in heaven. We see, not the earthly Zion, but the heavenly Zion (Heb. 12:22–24), and we rejoice that we are "a kingdom of priests" because of the grace of God (Rev. 1:5–6). Let us give God His rightful place, worship Him joyfully, rest on His faithful covenant, and trust Him for the promised blessings for those who willingly obey His will.

# Psalm 133

David was king of Judah and Benjamin and ruled in Hebron for seven-and-a-half years. He inherited a divided nation and almost a civil war, but then the Lord gave him a united kingdom (2 Sam. 5; 1 Chron. 12:38–40). He could well have written this psalm when he began his reign in Jerusalem. The people usually journeyed to Jerusalem in family groups (see Luke 2:41–52), so this psalm perfectly suited the situation. It applies to individual believers and churches today, for we also have our "family quarrels" and need to learn to walk together in love. Maintaining the spiritual unity of God's people is the work of every believer, with the help of the Holy Spirit (Eph. 4:1–6), and three ministries of the Spirit are illustrated in this psalm.

### We Are Born of the Spirit (v. 1)

When you read the Scriptures, you cannot help but discover that the "brothers" did not always live in unity. Cain killed Abel (Gen. 4), Lot quarreled with Abraham (Gen. 13), Joseph's brothers hated him and sold him into slavery (Gen. 37), and the brothers did not even get along among themselves! (Gen. 45:24). Miriam and Aaron criticized their brother Moses (Num. 12), and some of David's children turned against him (2 Sam.

13–18; and note 2 Sam. 12:10). Our Lord's own disciples frequently quarreled over which one of them was the greatest (Matt. 18:1ff; Mark 9:33ff; Luke 22:23ff), and Paul and Barnabas argued over John Mark and finally broke company and chose new ministry companions (Acts 15:36–41). The church began in visible unity (Acts 2:1, 44, 46), but when you read Paul's epistles, you find a sad story of rivalry and division, and it is not much better today.

It was one thing for the Jewish clans to spend a few days together while traveling to Jerusalem and quite something else to dwell together at home for the rest of the year! Yet they all had a common ancestor in Abraham; they spoke a common language; they worshiped the same God; they were children of the same covenant; they shared a common land; and they were governed by the same holy law. Christians today have experienced the same spiritual birth, worship the same God, declare the same gospel message, preach from the same Scriptures, and are headed for the same heavenly city, but, alas, there is often more division among us than unity! Yet all of us know that spiritual oneness in Christ (Gal. 3:26–29; Eph. 4:1–6) is both "good and pleasant." There is an artificial "unity" that is based on "least common denominator" theology and is more organizational uniformity than the kind of spiritual unity for which Jesus prayed (John 17:11, 21–23). This we must avoid. Those who have truly been "born of God" (1 John 2:29; 3:9; 4:7; 5:1, 4, 18) belong to the same family and need to love one another.

### We Are Anointed by the Spirit (v. 2)

At his ordination, the high priest was anointed with the special oil that was compounded according to the directions God gave Moses (Ex. 30:22–33). He and the other priests were also sprinkled with the oil and the blood from the sacrifices (Ex. 29:1–9, 21). In Scripture, oil is a symbol of the Holy Spirit (Isa. 61:1–3; Zech. 4; Luke 4:17–19; Acts 10:38), for this anointing was given to priests, prophets, and kings, all of whom needed the Spirit's help to be able to minister effectively (1 Sam. 16:13). We often hear Christians pray for "an anointing of the Spirit" on God's servants, yet each true believer has already been anointed of God. This anointing establishes us so that we do not fall (2 Cor. 1:21–22) and enlightens us so that we do not go astray (1 John 2:20, 27). Every believer needs this strengthening and teaching ministry of God's Spirit.

When the high priest was anointed, the oil ran down his beard to the front of his body and over his collar. This suggests that the oil "bathed" the twelve precious stones that he wore on the breastplate over his heart, and this "bathing" is a picture of spiritual unity. When God's people walk in the Spirit, they forget about the externals and major on the eternal things of the Spirit. Externals divide us—gender, wealth, appearance, ethnic prejudices, social or political standing—while the Spirit brings us together and we glorify Christ.

### We Are Refreshed by the Spirit (v. 3)

The Jews were basically an agricultural people and they depended on the early and latter rains and the dew to water their crops (Deut. 11:10–17). In Scripture, dew symbolizes the life-giving Word of God (Deut. 32:2), the blessing of God that brings fruitfulness (Gen. 27:28, 39; Deut. 33:13, 28), and God's special refreshing on His people (Hos. 14:5; Zech. 8:12). How often we need the refreshment of the Holy Spirit that comes silently but bountifully, like the dew upon the grass! When things are "dry," they begin to wither and fall apart, but when the dew comes, it brings new life and things hold together. Life means unity, death means decay, and the difference is the dew from heaven. Hebron in the far north was the highest of their mountains, nearly ten thousand feet, and Zion was one of the lesser mounts in the land. They were 200 miles apart, yet God sent His dew to both of them! Travelers report that in some parts of the Holy Land, the morning dew is like a hard rain that fell in the night, saturating everything. The dew speaks of fruitfulness and the anointing oil speaks of fragrance, for the unity of God's people is both "good and pleasant."

What does the word "there" refer to in verse 3? Probably two things: (1) Zion and Jerusalem, for it is there God commanded His blessing (132:13–18; Lev. 25:21; Deut. 28:8), for "salvation is of the Jews" (John 4:22); and (2) where there is unity among His people (v. 1). The Holy Spirit is grieved by the sins that bring division (Eph. 5:25–32). Both images—the oil and the dew—remind us that unity is not something that we "work up" but that God sends down. When we get to the heavenly Zion (Heb. 12:18–29), there we will enjoy perfect unity "life forevermore." But why not seek to have that kind of unity today? "Will You not revive us again, that Your people may rejoice in You?" (85:6 NKJV)

## Psalm 134

This last psalm of the "Songs of Ascents" series is quite brief, but it deals with a vast subject: worshiping the Lord and sharing His blessings with others. It is a short psalm—117 is the shortest—but it deals with a subject that could fill volumes. The psalm closes the collection with a benediction and leads into a series of psalms that emphasize praising the Lord. The inferences we draw from this psalm ought to encourage us in our own pilgrim journey and make us a blessing to others.

### A God Who Never Sleeps (v. 1)

As you review these fifteen psalms, you see that the pilgrims had a variety of experiences on their journey, but they arrived safely in the Holy City, fulfilled their obligations, and were now preparing to return home. It was night and they wanted to make one last visit to the temple. Directed by the high priest, the temple priests and Levites were responsible to make sure everything was in order for the next day's ministry. They also checked the building to see that nothing dangerous or defiling had gotten past the doorkeepers and was hidden in the sacred precincts. The pilgrims heard a temple choir singing the praises of Jehovah, and their ministry would continue all night. Pagan temples were silent at night, because their gods had to rest (1 Kings 18:27), but "He who keeps you will not slumber. Behold, He who keeps Israel shall neither slumber nor sleep" (121:3–4 NKJV). The Lord gives sleep to His beloved people, but He stays awake and guards the city and watches over the family (127:1–2). He also hears the praises of His people.

"The Lord that made heaven and earth" (v. 3) also made the day and the night (Gen. 1:14–19), and the darkness and the light are both alike to Him (139:11–12). When we go to sleep, we know that the Father is caring for us, and when we awaken, He is there to greet us (91:1–6). If we awaken in the night, we can fellowship with Him and meditate on His Word (119:55, 62, 157–148). If God never slumbers nor sleeps, why should we stay awake all night, tossing and turning and fretting? "Be still, and know that I am God" (46:10).

### A Worship That Never Ends (v. 2)

Visitors at churches sometimes ask, "When does the worship service end?" If you had asked that question of a priest or Levite in the temple in Jerusalem, he would have replied, "Never!" David arranged that the temple choirs praise the Lord day and night (92:1–2; 1 Chron. 9:33; 23:30). While you and I are asleep in our part of the world, somewhere else on the globe, believers are worshiping God. Even more, our High Priest in heaven intercedes for us and enables us to pray and to worship. Some people find it difficult to stay awake and alert during an hour's church service. What would they do if the Lord commanded them to praise Him all night long? "Any man can sing in the day," said Charles Spurgeon, "but he is the skillful singer who can sing when there is not a ray of light by which to read—who sings from his heart ... ."

God gives us "songs in the night" (42:8; 77:6; Job 35:10; Isa. 30:29), when circumstances are difficult and we cannot see our way. He gave David songs in the darkness of the cave when his life was in danger (142:7–11), and He gave Paul and Silas songs while they suffered in the Philippian jail (Acts 16:25). Our Lord sang a song in the night before He went out to Gethsemane and then Calvary (Matt. 26:30). The greatest responsibility and highest privilege of individual believers and of churches is to worship God, for everything that we are and do flows out of worship. Yet today, worship is often trivialized into cheap, clever entertainment, and the sanctuary has become a theater. As the choir in the temple lifted their hands to heaven (see on 28:2), they were pointing to the Source of all good things and praising Him for His mercy and grace. True worshipers lift "clean hands and a pure heart" to the Lord (24:4; James 4:8), for the Lord looks on the heart. We will worship God for all eternity (Rev. 4–5), so we had better start learning now.

### A Blessing That Never Stops (v. 3)

As the pilgrims left the temple, a priest on duty called, "May the Lord bless you from Zion" (NASB; see 20:2; 128:5). The pronoun "you" is singular, for the blessing of God is for each of us personally. It is also singular in the priestly benediction found in Numbers 6:22–27. To leave God's house with God's blessing upon us is a great privilege, but it is also a great responsibility, for we must share that blessing with others. If it is a joy to *receive* a blessing, it is an even greater joy to *be* a blessing. Spiritually speaking, God blesses us from Zion, for "salvation is of the Jews" (John 4:22). From the day He called Abraham and gave him His covenant (Gen. 12:1–3), God has blessed the nations because of the Jewish people, for they have given us the knowledge of the true and living God as well as the gifts of the Word of God and the Savior. If God never sleeps and our worship never ends, then the blessing will not stop. Like the precious gift that Mary of Bethany gave to Jesus, the fragrance of the blessing will reach around the world (Mark 14:1–9).

## Psalm 135

The emphasis of the psalm is on praising the Lord because of who He is and what He has done for His people. It opens with the command to "praise the Lord" repeated four times and concludes with the command to "bless the Lord," also repeated four times. "Jehovah" is found thirteen times in the psalm, and the familiar phrase "praise the Lord" ("hallelujah") is repeated eight times. The psalm has been called "a mosaic" because it contains numerous quotations from other parts of Scripture, no doubt collected by a temple liturgist who, led by the Spirit, put the material together for a special occasion of worship. Some students think that the occasion was the one described in Nehemiah 9, and the use of the phrase "our God" (vv. 2, 5) is characteristic of the book of Nehemiah (4:4, 20; 6:16; 9:32; 13:2). (See also Ex. 5:8; Deut. 31:7; 32:3; Josh. 24:18.) The Jewish people spoke of Jehovah as "our God" to affirm their separation from the false gods of the nations around them (vv. 15–18; 48:14; 67:6; 77:13; 115:3; 116:5). This psalm is an inspired statement of faith and believers today can shout a hearty "Amen!" to its affirmations.

### The Lord Is Our God—He Chose Us (vv. 1–4)

It was God's election of Israel that set them apart from the rest of the nations, for they are "his people" (vv. 12, 14; 100:3; Deut. 32:9, 36, 43, 50). Israel is His treasured possession (v. 4; Ex. 19:5; Deut. 7:6; 14:2) and He gave them their land (v. 12). His temple stood in Jerusalem and His priests offered Him praise and sacrifices. The Jewish people were set apart to honor the name of the Lord and to bear witness to other nations that Jehovah is the one true God. Why did God choose Israel? Because "the Lord is good" (v. 3). The church today is an elect people, saved by the grace of God (Rom. 1:6; 8:30; Eph. 1:4) and called to glorify God (1 Peter 2:9–12). All believers are priests of the Lord and we must worship Him as He has instructed in His Word.

### The Lord Is Sovereign—He Does What He Pleases (vv. 5–12)

The Lord is great (115:3; Ex. 15:11; 18:11), greater than the false gods of the nations. Their gods can do nothing (vv. 15–18), but Jehovah can do anything He wants to do! God showed His power over the gods of Egypt and Canaan by defeating their armies and giving Israel their possessions (vv. 8–12; Ex. 7–14; Num. 21:21–35). The Lord is ruler over all creation, from the heights of the heavens to the depths of the sea (Ex. 20:4). Even the weather is under His control (v. 7; 33:7; Job 38:22; Jer. 10:13;

51:16). Israel's exodus from Egypt is a fact of history, and Israel's faith is built on the revelation of the God of history, not the fantasies of the gods of mythology. The Christian faith is also built on solid historical facts (1 Cor. 15:1–8; 1 John 1:1–4).

### The Lord Is Compassionate—He Vindicates His People (vv. 13–14)

The name of Jehovah is glorious and renowned; it is everlasting. Few people today think or speak about the gods of the past, but the name of the Lord God is still revered. One poet wrote, "The great god Ra whose shrines once covered acres / Is filler now for crossword puzzle makers." People who take comparative religions courses in school recognize the names of the ancient gods and goddesses, but one does not have to go to university to know the name of Jehovah God or of Jesus. Yet this glorious God, whose name will live forever, has compassion for lost sinners and for His people. Many times during their history, the Israelites were rescued and vindicated by the Lord as He put their enemies to shame. (See 102:12; Ex. 3:15; Deut. 32:26; and Heb. 10:30.)

### The Lord Is the True and Living God—He Cares for Us (vv. 15–18)

With minor changes, these verses are quoted from 115:4–8. Dead idols cannot speak, see, hear, or breathe, and they cannot give life to their worshipers. Because Jehovah is the living God, He speaks to us in His Word, sees us in our every circumstance, hears our prayers, and comes to us when we need the help that only He can give. (See the comments on Ps. 115.)

### The Lord Be Praised—He Is with Us (vv. 19–21)

Israel could praise the Lord because He was present with His people. No other nation could claim that distinction. His glory led Israel through the wilderness, and that glory resided in the sanctuary until God had to depart because of the nation's sins (Ezek. 7–11). What other nation had the glory of God dwelling in their midst (63:2; Rom. 9:4)? The Lord is not a distant God; He is "a very present help in trouble" (46:1). Jesus is

"Immanuel—God with us" (Matt. 1:20–25; 28:20). "I will never leave you nor forsake you" (Heb. 13:5; Gen. 28:15; Josh. 1:5; Isa. 41:10, 17). Praise the Lord!

## Psalm 136

This is an antiphonal psalm, prepared to be used by a worship leader and a choir, or a worship leader and the congregation, or perhaps two choirs. The rabbis called it "The Great Hallel" (praise). The psalm reviews God's dealings with His people and turns history into theology and theology into worship. If our worship is not based on history—what God had done in this world—then it lacks a theological message and is not true worship at all. The refrain is a familiar one. It was sung at the dedication of Solomon's temple (2 Chron. 7:3, 6) and also by King Jehoshaphat's singers when Judah was attacked by Moab and Ammon (2 Chron. 20:21). (See also 106:1; 107:1; and 118:1 and 29.) The divine title "the God of heaven" (v. 26) suggests a post-exilic date, for "God of heaven" was a title used frequently in that period (Ezra 1:2; 5:11–12; 6:9–10; 7:12, 21, 23; Neh. 1:4; 2:4; Dan. 2:18, 19, 44). The focus is on giving thanks to God for who He is and what He has done for His people.

### The Creator—He Brings Forth (vv. 1–9)

The God of Israel is Jehovah, the God of the covenant, and He is good and merciful. The nations had their gods and lords (1 Cor. 8:5–6), but Jehovah alone is the God of gods and the Lord of lords. The dead gods of the nations (135:15–18) could never do the wonders that the Lord did, nor were they good and full of mercy (lovingkindness, covenant love, steadfast love). The apostle Paul joined mercy and grace in 1 Timothy 1:2, 2 Timothy 1:2, and Titus 1:4, and so did John (2 John 3) and Jude (Jude 2). God in His mercy does not give us what we do deserve, and in His grace, He gives us what we do not deserve, all for the sake of Jesus Christ. No wonder the psalmist gave thanks to the Lord!

The psalmist started at the beginning of time with the creation of the universe, recorded in Genesis 1. The Lord had the wisdom to plan creation and the power to execute that plan, and all He had to do was to speak the Word (33:6–9). Because humanity refused to be thankful for creation, mankind began that terrible descent into ignorance, idolatry, immorality, and ultimate judgment (Rom. 1:18ff). In the day or the night, whether we look up at the heavens or down at the earth and waters, we should see evidence of the hand of God and realize that a Creator brought it forth from nothing. In this creation is all that we need for life and work, so let us thank Him!

### The Redeemer—He Brings Us Out (vv. 10–12)

The psalmist wrote nothing about Israel's years of suffering in Egypt, or the Lord's judgments against the gods of Egypt (Ex. 12:12), but focused on the Exodus. "Brought out" is a phrase the Jewish people used to describe their deliverance (Deut. 1:27; 4:20, 37; 5:6; 16:1). By the time Israel crossed the Red Sea, the land of Egypt, its firstborn sons, its religion, and its army had been destroyed by the power of God. The Exodus marked the birthday of the nation of Israel, and from that time, the Jews looked back each year at Passover and remembered what the Lord had done for them. The Exodus is also a picture of the redemption we have in Jesus Christ, the spotless lamb of God who shed His blood to set sinners free (1 Peter 1:18–19; John 1:29; Eph. 1:7; Col. 1:14; Heb. 9:12). God's mighty arm was revealed at the Exodus (Ex. 15:16), but it was revealed even more at the cross (Isa. 53:1ff; Luke 1:51).

### The Shepherd—He Brings Us Through (vv. 13–16)

The Lord brought Israel through the sea (vv. 13–15) and through the wilderness (v. 16). A pillar of cloud guided them by day and a pillar of fire by night (Ex. 13:21–22). He led them to Sinai where they remained for over a year while Moses received and taught the divine law and supervised the construction of the tabernacle. The nation needed the discipline of the law and the delight of worship before they were ready to enter Canaan and take the land. Israel's unbelief and disobedience at Kadesh Barnea sent them back into the wilderness (Num. 13–14) where that rebellious generation died during the next thirty-eight years of wandering. Moses commanded the new generation to remember those wilderness years and obey the Word of God (Deut. 8). Indeed, the Lord Jesus Christ is our Shepherd in this life (23:1; 78:52–55; 80:1; John 10:11–14; Heb. 13:20; 1 Peter 5:4) and throughout eternity (Rev. 7:17).

### The Conqueror—He brings Us In (vv. 17–22)

As the forty years drew to a close, Moses led the people back to the gateway into the Promised Land, and on the way, Israel defeated great and mighty kings and took their lands (Num. 21). Reuben, Gad, and the half tribe of Manasseh claimed their inheritance east of the Jordan River (Num. 32; Josh. 18:7), but their men marched with Israel into Canaan and helped to conquer the enemy and claim the land (135:10–12; Josh. 22). The land belonged to the Lord but He gave it to Israel as their inheritance, and they would enjoy its blessings as long as they obeyed the covenant. Believers today have been delivered from sin through faith in Christ and are now in the "kingdom of the Son of His love" (Col. 1:13 NKJV). Canaan is not a picture of heaven, for there will be no wars in heaven. It pictures our present inheritance in Jesus Christ, an inheritance that we claim as we walk by faith and defeat Satan and his forces that want to keep us in bondage and spiritual poverty. This is the theme of Hebrews 1–4.

### The Deliverer—He Brings Us Back (vv. 23–25)

These verses summarize Israel's failure to serve God and how the Lord brought seven nations into the land to punish them. The record is in the book of Judges. The people would turn to idols and the Lord would chasten them, as He promised He would. Then the situation would become so unbearable that the people would repent and cry out for mercy, and the Lord would "remember them" (see 132:1) and rescue them (Judg. 2:11–23). This was no way to live in the wonderful land God had given them, but it describes many professed believers today. When things are going well, they forget the Lord, but when things grow worse, they turn to Him for help. The mention of food in verse

24 reminds us that the nations that invaded Israel either destroyed the crops or took them, leaving the land impoverished (Judg. 6:1–6). If we are truly thankful for our food, and acknowledge that God provides it, then we are not likely to turn away from Him and worship other gods. The creatures of the earth look to God for what they need and thank the Lord by obeying His will and bringing Him glory (104:10–18).

There is only one way to end a psalm like this: "O give thanks to the God of heaven! For His mercy endures forever" (v. 26 NKJV).

## Psalm 137

"Remember" and "forget" are used a total of five times in these nine verses. The American humorist Elbert Hubbard said, "A retentive memory may be a good thing, but the ability to forget is the true token of greatness." Sometimes we must remember to forget. A Jew, probably a Levite, wrote this psalm after he had returned home from Babylon with the remnant in 536 B.C. Twenty years later, Babylon was destroyed. The psalmist was with a group of former exiles (note the "we" and "us" in vv. 1–4), recalling some of their experiences, and from this encounter with the past, he learned some lessons about the human memory, himself, and the Lord.

### Memory Can Open Wounds (vv. 1–4)

Sitting was the official position for mourning, and the Jewish exiles felt and acted like mourners at a funeral. The two major rivers were the Tigris and the Euphrates, but Babylon had a network of canals that helped to turn the desert into a garden. Perhaps the Jews gathered by the canals because they needed water for their religious rituals (Acts 16:13). Whatever else they may have left back in Judah, they brought their harps with them, for music was important to their worship of the Lord (81:1–3). Music was also one way of expressing their grief and seeking the help of the Lord "who gives songs in the night" (Job 35:10). These former exiles remembered the times their guards demanded that they entertain them by singing one of the "songs of Zion." What biting sarcasm! The Babylonians knew how the Jews honored Mount Zion and the city of Jerusalem, and how they boasted of Zion's strength and security (46:5, 7, 10, 11; 48; 76:1–3; 87), but now, the city and temple were in ruins. In their sarcasm, the guards were asking, "Where is your God? Why did He not deliver you?" (See 42:3, 10; 79:10; 115:2.)

The exiles had refused to obey; they did not sing for their captors. Why? For one thing, the Babylonians wanted "the Lord's song" (v. 4), and the Jewish people were not about to use sacred temple hymns to entertain the pagans. How tragic it is today when music stars use "Amazing Grace" or "The Lord's Prayer" to entertain pagan crowds that know neither the Lord nor His grace. What did Jesus say about throwing valuables to dogs and pigs (Matt. 7:6)? But even more—their hearts were not in giving a concert. Their captors wanted "songs of mirth," and the exiles had no joy. They had lost everything but God and their lives, and being normal people, they were deeply pained in their hearts. Their city, temple, and homes had been destroyed, their people had been deported, and the throne of David had been cast to the ground. But even worse, they had seen the Babylonian soldiers get great glee out of throwing Jewish babies against the walls and smashing their heads (v. 9). It was one way the Babylonians could limit the future generation of their enemies.

Yes, memories can bring pain, and the pain does not go away when we try to "bury" the memories. Denial usually makes things worse. But the fact that the exiles could talk about these painful things indicates that they were facing them honestly and learning how to process this pain in a mature way. It takes time for broken hearts to heal, and Jesus can heal them if we give Him all the pieces (147:3; Luke 4:18).

### Memory Can Build Character (vv. 5–6)
Sometimes we have to lose things to really appreciate them. Here were the exiles in Babylon, mourning the loss of everything that was important to them, and asking themselves, "Did we really appreciate what the Lord gave us—our land, our city, the

temple, our home, our children?" At least one man made a vow when he was in exile, that he would always remember Jerusalem and make it the highest priority and greatest joy in his life. By "Jerusalem," of course, he meant the Lord Jehovah, the temple and its ministry, the city and its people, and the ministry of Israel to the world. Before he wrote about God's judgments on Edom and Babylon (vv. 7–9), he judged himself for his own carelessness and even asked God to punish him if he failed to keep his vow. As we look back on life and evaluate our experiences, it is important that we learn our lessons and grow in godly character. "So teach us to number our days, that we may gain a heart of wisdom" (90:12 NKJV). "I will pay You my vows, which my lips have uttered … when I was in trouble" (66:13–14 NKJV).

### Memory Can Encourage Faith (vv. 7–9)

These three verses have been a serious problem for the unlearned and a target for the unbelieving who are at war with God and the Bible. However, once this passage is understood, it should encourage the faith of God's people in times of upheaval when the Lord seems to be shaking everything (Heb. 12:25–29). The Babylonian guards were taunting the Jewish exiles, wanting them to sing about their God *who had not rescued them* and their city, *which was now a heap of ruins*. This was not a matter of politics but theology, nor was it a personal vendetta but an issue between two nations. As individuals, we have the right to forgive an offender, but if the judge forgives every criminal who appears in his court, the foundations of society would be undermined and chaos would result.

The law God gave to Israel is based on the *lex talionis*—the law of retaliation—and retaliation is not revenge. It simply means "to pay back in kind." In short, the punishment must fit the crime, and our courts still follow that principle. In eighthteenth century England, there were over 200 capital crimes for which the culprit could be hanged, but no nation follows that pattern today. "Eye for eye, tooth for tooth" (Deut. 19:16–21) is not brutality; it is justice. A point that is often ignored is that, though

Babylon was God's chosen instrument to discipline the Jews, *the Babylonians went too far and treated the Jews with brutality.* (See Isa. 47:1–7 and 51:22–23.) They abused the elderly, they murdered the babies and children, they violated the women, and they killed promiscuously. Though these practices may have been a normal part of ancient warfare (2 Kings 8:12; 15:16; Isa. 13:16; Nah. 3:10), Babylon went to the extreme in their inhumanity. But, let us be honest and admit that when nations today have done atrocious things—the Holocaust, for example—other nations have risen up in horror and demanded justice. If that response is correct for us, why is it wrong for the psalmist?

The psalmist knew from the prophets that God would judge Edom and Babylon, *so he prayed for the Lord to keep His promises.* Esau, father of the Edomites, was Jacob's brother (Gen. 25:30), and Esau's descendants should have shown mercy to their blood relatives. (On the future of Edom, see Isa. 63:1–6; Jer. 49:7–22; Ezek. 25:12–14 and 35:1ff; the book of Obadiah. As for Babylon's future, see Isa. 13, noting especially v. 16; and Jer. 50–51.) The psalmist knew these Scriptures and asked the Lord to fulfill them in His own time. "For the Lord is a God of recompense, He will surely repay" (Jer. 51:56 NKJV). Finally, the word "blessed" as used in verses 8–9 does not mean "happy" in the sense of Psalm 32:1, or even "favored by God" as in Psalm 1:1. It carries the meaning of "morally justified," as in Psalm 106:3—"Blessed are those who keep justice" (NKJV). It was not the Jewish people individually who punished Babylon but the God of Israel who answered their prayers and vindicated His people (Rom. 12:17–21). One day, He will vindicate His church and punish those who have persecuted and slain His servants (Rev. 6:9–17).

## Psalm 138

This is the first of eight psalms attributed to David. They form a special collection just before the five "Hallelujah Psalms" that climax the book. The psalm probably grew out of the opposition of the neighboring nations when David became king of a united Israel (2 Sam. 5; 8:1–14). It was God's plan that David reign over

Israel (v. 8), but the Jebusites, Philistines, and Moabites wanted a divided Israel with a weak leader. David knew God's will, prayed for God's help (v. 3), trusted God for victory (vv. 7–8), and defeated the enemy. The psalm does not mention the Lord until verse 4, but it is obvious that Jehovah is the object of David's prayers and praise. The psalm helps us understand better what really happens when God answers prayer.

### Answered Prayer Glorifies God's Name (vv. 1–3)

"The gods" are the false gods of the nations that attacked David (82:7). His victories over their armies were God's victories, and David wanted Jehovah to have the praise and glory (Jer. 50:1–2). The word translated "temple" means "sanctuary" and was applied to the tabernacle at Shiloh (see 1 Sam. 1:9; 3:3). The third line in verse 2 has been variously translated (except in the KJV and the NKJV) so as not to give the impression that God's Word is greater than God's character and reputation ("name"). The meaning seems to be: "I trusted your promises and prayed, and the Lord answered above and beyond anything that He promised." It is another way of expressing Ephesians 3:19–20. God gave David boldness to face his enemies and the strength to defeat them. God answered prayer and this brought glory to His name.

### Answered Prayer Gives Witness to the Lost (vv. 4–5)

Jehovah is not only higher than the gods of the enemy, He is also greater than their rulers. David's victories proved that. However, there were Gentile kings who rejoiced that David had won the battles— rulers such as Hiram (2 Sam. 5:11) and Toi (2 Sam. 8:9). David prayed that the day would come when all the kings of the earth would hear God's Word and praise the Lord for His promises to Israel. Beginning with Egypt, every nation that has opposed and persecuted Israel has gone down in defeat, as God promised to Abraham (Gen. 12:1–3). (See 68:29–32; 72:8–11; 96:1, 3, 7–8; 102:15–17.) The Messianic hope of Israel is their only hope and the only hope of the world. Jesus has come; He is "the ruler of the kings of the earth" (Rev. 1:5) and the King of Kings and Lord of Lords (Rev. 19:16). What a great day that will be when the kings of the earth join together with God's people in praising the Lord!

### Answered Prayer Accomplishes God's Purposes in Our Lives (vv. 6–8)

Jehovah is the Highest of the high and the Greatest of the great, but He is also willing to become the Lowest of the low and stoop down to meet our needs. To "look upon the lowly" means to pay attention to them and regard them with favor (11:4; 113:5–9; Isa. 57:15 and 66:2; Luke 1:47–55). The ultimate proof of this is the incarnation of Jesus Christ, for He became poor that we might become rich (2 Cor. 8:9) and became a servant that we might be set free (Phil. 2:1–12). He was lowly in His life and also in His death, for He who is perfect was treated like a criminal and nailed to a cross, and on that cross, He became sin for us (2 Cor. 5:21). David gave thanks that the Lord knew his need and came to his aid. In His covenant with David (2 Sam. 7), God revealed that He had a great purpose to fulfill through David's life, and He would not allow the enemy to thwart that purpose. This is true of believers today (Phil. 1:6 and 2:13; Eph. 2:10 and 3:20; Col. 1:29), and He will not forsake us. It has well been said that the purpose of prayer is not to get man's will done in heaven but to get God's will done on earth, and this was demonstrated in David's life.

# Psalm 139

What we think about God and our relationship to Him determines what we think about everything else that makes up our busy world—other people, the universe, God's Word, God's will, sin, faith, and obedience. Wrong ideas about God will ultimately lead to wrong ideas about who we are and what we should do, and this leads to a wrong life on the wrong path toward the wrong destiny. In other words, theology—the right knowledge of God—is essential to a fulfilled life in this world. David contemplated God and wrote for us a psalm whose message can only encourage us to be in a right relationship with Him.

### God Knows Us Intimately—We Cannot Deceive Him (vv. 1–6)

The verb "search" means "to examine with pain and care." The Jewish people used this word to describe digging deep into a mine, exploring a land, and investigating a legal case. Our friends see the outside but God sees the heart, and we cannot deceive Him. Adam and Eve tried it (Gen. 3:7–24), Cain tried it (Gen. 4:1–15), and even David tried it (2 Sam. 11–12), and all of them discovered that God knew all about them. "Understand" in verse 2 means "to distinguish and discern with insight" and not just gather raw data. "Compass" in verse 3 is a picture of winnowing grain, and "try" in verse 23 means "to test metal." The fact that God knows us intimately and exhaustively is asserted in verses 1, 2, 4, 14, and 23. He knows our actions, our locations, our thoughts and words, our ways, and our motives. "All things are naked and open to the eyes of Him to whom we must give account" (Heb. 4:13 NKJV). But even more, He knows what is best for us and does all He can to guide us that way. He hems us in behind and before and puts His hand on us to steady us and direct us. The word translated "beset" (KJV) or "enclosed" (NASB) means "to guard a valuable object," so God's knowledge and guidance are for our protection. What should be our response to this? We should be overwhelmed by the height and depth of God's knowledge and be thankful that He knows us perfectly. "I am not equal to it!" David exclaimed.

### God Is with Us Constantly—We Cannot Escape Him (vv. 7–12)

If God knows so much about us, perhaps the wisest thing is to run away and hide, but all "escape routes" are futile. If we go up to heaven or down to sheol, the realm of the dead, God is there; if we travel the speed of light to the east or west (the Mediterranean Sea was west of Israel), His hand will catch us and tenderly lead us. We cannot hide even in the darkness, for to the Lord, the darkness is as the light. *God wants to walk with us and guide us, because His plan for us is the very best.* Why should we want to run away and hide?

Adam and Eve tried it and failed (Gen. 3:8), and so did the prophet Jonah, who only went from bad to worse. We need God's presence with us if we want to enjoy His love and fulfill His purposes. (See Isa. 43:1–7; Ps. 23:4; Matt. 28:19–20.)

### God Made Us Wonderfully—We Cannot Ignore Him (vv. 13–18)

This is one of the greatest passages in literature about the miracle of human conception and birth. "In the presence of birth," said Eugene Petersen, "we don't calculate—we marvel." David declared that God is present at conception and birth, because we are made in the image of God and God has a special purpose for each person who is born. We live in and with our bodies all our lives, and we know how amazing they are. God formed us as He wants us to be, and we must accept His will no matter how we feel about our genetic structure, our looks, or our abilities. The verb "covered" (v. 13 KJV) means "woven together" (see Isa. 32:12), and "intricately wrought" in verse 15 is translated "embroidered" in Exodus. In the mother's womb, the Lord weaves and embroiders a human being, and abortion interrupts this miracle. What a tragedy!

But the Lord did more than design and form our bodies; He also planned and determined our days (v. 16). This probably includes the length of life (Job 14:5) and the tasks He wants us to perform (Eph. 2:10; Phil. 2:12–13). This is not some form of fatalism or heartless predestination, for what we are and what He plans for us come from God's loving heart (33:11) and are the very best He has for us (Rom. 12:2). If we live foolishly, we might die before the time God has ordained, but God's faithful children are immortal until their work is done. How can we ignore God when He has given us such a marvelous body and planned for us a wonderful life? Life is not a prison, it is an exciting pilgrimage, and the Lord has prepared us for what He prepared for us. Our responsibility is to yield ourselves to Him daily, ponder His thoughts found in His Word (92:5; Isa. 55:8–9), and walk in the Spirit. God thinks of us! (Jer. 29:11). Should we not think about Him?

### God Judges Righteously—We Cannot Dispute Him (vv. 19–24)

If we cannot deceive God, escape God, or ignore God, is it not sensible to obey God? Yes, it is reasonable, but there are those who prefer to oppose God and dispute what He says about them in His Word. David called these people wicked, violent, liars, blasphemers, and rebels, and he grieved because of them. God also grieves over sinners—the Father does (Gen. 6:6), the Son does (Mark 3:5; Luke 19:41), and so does the Spirit (Eph. 4:30). Yes, it is difficult to love rebellious sinners and still hate their sins, but we need more "holy hatred" in this day when blatant sin is a popular form of entertainment. (See 11:5; 45:7; 97:10; Amos 5:14–15; Rom. 12:9, 19–21.) Whenever we pray "Thy kingdom come," we are asking the Lord to judge the wicked, and we leave the matter in His hands. But David closed with a prayer for God to search His heart, know his anxieties and concerns, forgive him, and lead him. We must be cautious as we examine ourselves because we do not even know our own hearts (Jer. 17:9). It is best to open the Word and let the Spirit search us and speak to us, for then we discover the truth. We must never dispute with God, for He loves us and wants only the very best for us.

## Psalm 140

It seems likely that the circumstances behind this psalm occurred during David's years as a member of King Saul's official staff, when Saul's envy and paranoia were developing. In their attempt to please the king, some of Saul's officers spread lies about young David and even tried to set traps to make him look bad. God's people face similar situations today, for Satan is a murderer (John 8:44), a slanderer and accuser (Rev. 12:10), and a deceiver (2 Cor. 11:3). We learn four lessons from this psalm that encourage us to trust God and be faithful when Satan's servants oppose us.

### What Sinners Do to God's People (vv. 1–5)

David's presence among Saul's leaders was like light in darkness (Eph. 5:8ff) and health in a hospital. When confronted by a godly man like David, Saul and his leaders either had to change their ways or get rid of him, and they chose the latter course. They were evil men (v. 1) who planned evil (v. 2), spoke evil (v. 3), and practiced evil (vv. 4–5). Note that verse 3b is quoted in Romans 3:13 as part of the evidence Paul assembled that proves the depravity of the human heart. The phrase "the evil man" (v. 1 KJV) is collective, for the pronouns in the psalm are plural (vv. 2–4, 6, 8). What David needed from the Lord was wisdom to avoid their traps and protection from their violent plans. You meet the "hunting metaphor" in 9:16, 31:4, 19:110, 141:9, and 142:3, and the "sharp tongue" image is found in 52:2, 55:21, 57:4, 59:7, and 64:3. As God's people in an evil world, we must expect the opposition of the enemy and trust the Lord to enable us to overcome (John 16: 33).

### What God's People Should Do to Sinners (vv. 6–8)

First, we must affirm our faith in the Lord and not be ashamed to openly confess it. We must humbly ask Him for the help we need to live and work among difficult people who hate us and want to see us fail. Whenever David found himself in that kind of a situation, he gave himself to prayer and asked God for the wisdom to know what to do and the strength to do it. Here he asked God to put a helmet on his head and protect him from deception and danger (60:7; Eph. 6:17). He also prayed for his enemies, that their evil desires would change and their evil plans not succeed. If they succeeded, they would only become proud and go on to do greater evil. Our prayers for godless people must focus on changing their character, and not just stopping their persecution of believers. David obeyed Matthew 5:44.

### What Sin Does to Sinners (vv. 9–11)

Our enemies think they are hurting us, but they are really hurting themselves. The trouble they cause us will only come right back on their own heads, for it is an inexorable law of God that people reap what they sow. They dropped burning coals on David's head, but God would return the same to them (see 11:6; 18:8; 120:4; Prov. 25:22; Gen. 19:24). The destructive fires they lit with their tongues would burn them, and they would fall into the pits they had dug for David (v. 10; see 7:15; 9:15; 35:7–8; Prov. 26:27). They hunted David and set traps for him, but evil would eventually hunt them down and destroy them (v. 11). "Be sure your sin will find you out" (Num. 32:23).

### What God Does for His People (vv. 12–13)

We have read the whole story, so we know that God did maintain David's cause, defeat his enemies, and keep His promise to put him on the throne of Israel. David would establish a dynasty that would eventually bring the Savior into the world. He would write nearly half of the psalms, he would expand and defend the borders of the kingdom, and he would make the preparations necessary for the building of the temple. What a great man he was because he trusted in the Lord! David was grateful to God for His intervention, and he determined to live to glorify the God of Israel. David wrote, "The Lord will accomplish what concerns me" (138:8 NASB), and God honored His faith. For God's devoted people, the best is yet to come. Yield to Him and He will accomplish what He has planned for you, and you will be satisfied.

## Psalm 141

Even a casual reading of 140 and 141 reveals that the two are related and use a similar vocabulary—heart, tongue, hands, snares, the righteous, and so forth. The enemy was after David again and he needed immediate help. It has been suggested that David wrote this psalm after his cave experience with Saul (1 Sam. 24), but then he was not really in danger; or perhaps he wrote it when he was away from the sanctuary during Absalom's rebellion. Life is built on character and character is built on decisions. This psalm reveals David making a number of wise decisions as he faced the attacks of the enemy.

### "I Will Seek the Lord's Help" (vv. 1–2)

Whenever the enemy caused trouble, David's first response was to pray. "The Lord is my light and my salvation; whom shall I fear? The Lord is the strength of my life; of whom shall I be afraid?" (27:1 NKJV). He was a man with spiritual insight who understood that he could pray and worship God even if he was away from the sanctuary and had no priest to assist him (40:6–8; 50:8–9; 51:16–17; Isa. 1:11–17; Jer. 7:22–23; Hos. 6:6; Mic. 6:6–8; Mark 12:32–33). Each evening, the Jewish priest would offer a burnt offering on the brazen altar and also burn incense on the golden altar, but God accepted David's prayer and uplifted hands. Frankincense was usually included with the burnt offering. (See Ex. 30:1–10, 34–38; Lev. 2:2.) Incense is a picture of prayer going up to the Lord (Rev. 5:8; 8:4). David's hands were empty but his heart was full of love for the Lord and faith in His promises. Both Ezra (Ezra 9) and Daniel (Dan. 9) prayed at the time of the evening offering. After the second temple was built, this psalm was read when the evening sacrifices were offered and the lamps were lit in the holy place.

### "I Will Keep Myself from Sin" (vv. 3–4)

David faced a great temptation to compromise with the enemy, and he knew this was wrong. But, they were slandering him so why should he not slander them? But the problem was with his heart, not his mouth, and he prayed for a heart that would not be inclined to approve of their sins and imitate them (Prov. 4:23). David pictured his temptation as "eating their delicacies" (see Prov. 4:14–17). Times of testing become times of temptation when we stop believing and start scheming, when we ask "How can I get out of this?" instead of "What can I get out of this?"

### "I Will Gladly Accept Counsel" (v. 5)

"The righteous" can also be translated "the Righteous One," referring to the Lord; but either way, the message is the same. When we yield to God's will, the difficulties of life are tools that God uses to bring maturity to our lives. Often, the Lord sends people to speak to us, and their words hurt us, but they do not harm us (Prov. 9:8; 17:10; 19:25; 27:10). King Saul did not listen to rebuke and went from bad to worse. In the ancient world, honored guests at a meal were anointed with fragrant oil (Luke 7:44–46), but David knew that the enemy's delicacies and oil were but bait in the traps they had set for him (vv. 9–10). David would rather be admonished than anointed. As we face the problems and perils of the Christian life, it is important that we listen to wise counsel and obey it.

### *"I Will Let God Judge My Enemies" (vv. 6–7)*

These two verses have puzzled translators and expositors, but the general message seems clear. David continued to pray for his enemies, and he saw a day coming when God would judge them and vindicate his own cause (138:8; 140:12). Perhaps it is best to translate the verbs "Let the judges be thrown down ... let them learn that my words were true ... let them say, 'As one plows ... .'" To throw people from a cliff was a terrible form of execution (2 Chron. 25:12; Luke 4:29), but David is no doubt speaking in metaphorical language as in verses 1–5. When God has judged the leaders, their followers will agree that David's words were correct, especially when they see the unburied bones of those leaders bleaching in the sun. The scavenger birds and beasts will have stripped their corpses of flesh. If "they" in verse 7 refers to David's men, the idea may be that they are willing to die for David's cause and "plowed under," for this will eventually bring a harvest of righteousness to the land. The image is similar to that in 129:1–4. However, the first explanation is better.

### *"I Will Keep Going by Faith" (vv. 8–10)*

Fixing one's eyes on the invisible Lord means living by faith in His Word (Isa. 45:22; Heb. 12:1–2). God had anointed David to be king of Israel and nothing but David's own disobedience could frustrate that plan. Unlike Peter when he walked on the water in the storm, David did not take his eyes of faith off the Lord (Matt. 14:22–33). God was David's refuge and he was immortal until his work was done. If David had worried about the traps and hidden snares the enemy had set, he would have been paralyzed with fear; but he committed himself to the Lord and walked safely through the battlefield. Four simple words declare his faith, "I pass by safely" (v. 10 NASB). This reminds us of our Lord's experience in the synagogue at Nazareth, when the people became angry at His message and tried to throw Him from a cliff, but "He went His way" (Luke 4:28–30). Life goes on and there is work to do, so we must not allow tough situations to paralyze us but to energize us in trusting the Lord. Life's trials are not excuses for doing nothing; they are opportunities for claiming God's promises and experiencing His miraculous power.

## Psalm 142

This is the last of the psalms attributed to David that relate to the years in which he was fleeing from Saul (see 7, 34, 52, 54, 56, 57, and 59). Whether his "prison" (v. 7) was the cave of Adullum (1 Sam. 22) or a cave in En Gedi (1 Sam. 24), we cannot be sure, but it is obvious that he was in danger and was depressed and feeling abandoned. But he did what God's people must always do in times of crisis: he looked to the Lord for help. He knew very little about Saul and his plans, but he did know about Jehovah and His great promises, and because of his faith in these assurances, he triumphed over his feelings and his foes.

### The Lord Hears Our Prayers (vv. 1–2)

David not only cried aloud with his voice, but he cried earnestly from his heart. He was a godly young man who had faithfully served the Lord and his king, and yet there he was in a cave, hiding like a guilty criminal. Later in life, David would understand more fully that during those fugitive years in the wilderness, God was equipping him for the work he would do the rest of his life, but at the time, his situation was miserable. His feelings were so pent up within him that he "poured out" his troubles (43:4; 62:8; 102 title) and his inner turmoil ("complaint"). God knew David's difficult situation better than he did, but the Lord has ordained that our prayers are a part of His providential answers. When we need bread, our heavenly Father wants us to come and ask (Luke 11:9–13). The word "trouble" means "in a tight place, in narrow straits" (120:1; 138:7; 143:11). David would learn that those dangerous narrow places usually led to wider places and greater opportunities (18:18–19; 4:1; 25:17).

### The Lord Knows Our Circumstances (vv. 3–4)

In verse 3, the pronoun changes from "him" to "you" (see 23:4). David was a great warrior, but he was "feeling faint" within and was overwhelmed by all that was happening to him (77:3; 143:4; Jonah 2:7; Lam. 2:12). But what life does to us depends on what life finds in us, and David was a man with faith in his heart. He trusted God to show him the way to go and to protect him on the path. One day he would look back and realize that God's "goodness and mercy" had attended his way throughout his life (23:6). Were there hidden traps before him? Then the Lord would guide and protect him (140:5; 141:9). He had no bodyguard at his right hand, and nobody seemed to care whether he lived or died, but the Lord cared and stood at his right hand (16:8; 109:31; 110:5; 121:5). No matter the circumstances around us or the feelings within us, God cares for us (1 Peter 5:7). We can be confident that He is working all things together for His glory and our good (Rom. 8:28).

### The Lord Meets Our Needs (5–7)

He is our "refuge and strength" (46:1), so we have all the protection we need. The cave may have been his temporary home, but David knew that the Lord was his Rock and his fortress (90:1; 91:1–2). But the Lord was also his portion (16:5; 73:26), so his desperate situation really deprived him of nothing. In the Lord, we always have all that we need. The Lord was his deliverer, and time after time, often in the nick of time, David would behold the hand of God rescuing him from the hands of the enemy. As David prayed, he realized that it was the name and purposes of the Lord that were really important and not his personal safety, comfort, or promised kingship. He prayed to be delivered so that he might praise God and glorify Him. He looked forward to the day when prayer would give way to praise, and the people would gather around him and welcome him as their king. It would be a long and difficult journey, but the Lord would perfect what He had planned for him (138:8). Eventually, David was delivered and the nation surrounded him and received him as God's chosen ruler. The Lord gives bountifully to His children (13:6; 116:7; 119:17; Eph. 1:3). When He gave us Jesus Christ, He gave us all that we will ever need.

## Psalm 143

This is the seventh and last of the "penitential psalms" (see on Ps. 6). It is included primarily because David felt he needed to confess sins that were keeping him from enjoying God's help and blessing (vv. 1–2). He had concluded that the suffering he was experiencing from the attacks of the enemy were actually God's chastening, so he asked God for mercy. It is true that the Lord can use painful circumstances and difficult people to bring us to repentance, but sometimes those very things are God's "tools" to polish and mature us, not to punish us. In this psalm, David presents many requests to the Lord, all of which may be summarized in two prayers: "Hear me" (vv. 1–6) and "Answer me" (vv. 7–12). This kind of praying is a good example for us to follow.

### *"Hear Me"—Tell God Your Situation (vv. 1–6)*

The basis for David's prayer was the character of God, His faithfulness and righteousness, attributes that are mentioned again in verse 11. God is righteous in all that He does because He is holy, and He is faithful to His covenant and His promises. We plead these same attributes when we confess our sins to the Lord and claim His forgiveness (1 John 1:9). By calling himself God's servant (vv. 2, 12), David affirmed that he was a son of the covenant and could plead on the basis of God's Word. He also affirmed his own sinfulness (130:3–4; Job 9:32; 22:4; and see Rom. 3:20 and Gal. 2:16).

After focusing on God's character and his own needs, David told the Lord what he was enduring because of his enemies. The reference is probably to King Saul's relentless persecution during David's exile years. His vivid description almost helps us to feel the pain that David and his men were experiencing. They were crushed to the ground, lying in a dark grave like a corpse (v. 7; 7:5; 74:20; 88:5–6; Lam. 3:6), discouraged by a fainting ("stunned") heart that wants to give up, and wrapped up in a depressed spirit that is appalled and devastated. Those who believe that God's people never have their dark days and difficult weeks need to ponder this passage carefully.

What made this even more difficult was David's memory of "the good old days" (v. 5; see 77:5, 11–12). Was he remembering the peaceful days he spent as a shepherd, caring for his father's flock? But a lion and a bear attacked the flock (1 Sam. 17:34–36), so perhaps the "good old days" were not that good! Did he recall the days he served in Saul's court, playing the harp for the paranoid king and leading his soldiers out to victory? But Saul tried to kill David and even commanded his men to kill him. No, David remembered the great works of God recorded in the Scriptures—the Creation ("the works of His hands"), the call of Abraham, the pilgrimage of Jacob, the life of Joseph (from suffering to glory), the exodus from Egypt and the conquest of Canaan. David had his own "Hebrews 11" to encourage his faith. He stood in the cave and made it into a Holy of Holies as he lifted his hands expectantly to the Lord in praise and prayer. (See 28:2; 44:20; 63:4; 77:2; 88:9; 141:2.) The Hebrew text of verse 6 reads "My soul—for Thee," for there is no verb. The image of the parched land suggests the verb "thirsts," used by the *King James Version* and the *New International Version*, and the *New American Standard Bible* reads "longs for Thee." The idea is the same: David's hands were raised to God because he longed for Him and thirsted for fellowship with Him (42:2; 63:1; 84:2; 107:9; John 7:37–39; Rev. 21:6; 22:17). When we reach out to the Lord, it is because He has first reached out for us.

### *"Answer Me"—Wait for the Answer in Expectation (vv. 7–12)*

What were the answers for which David was waiting anxiously? The same answers we want to receive today. For one thing, *we want to see God's face (v. 7)*. David had often heard the priestly benediction declare that God's face would shine upon His people in gracious blessing (Num. 6:22–27), but if He was displeased, He would hide His face from them (10:1; 13:1; 69:17; 102:2). To know the shining of His face means to walk in the light of His countenance and enjoy the smile of God upon our lives, but the absence of that blessing was like a living death (28:1).

We also want *to hear God's Word* (*v. 8*). To see His smile and hear His voice gives us the strength we need to overcome the enemy. David moved from the darkness (v. 3) to the morning and the dawning of a new day (5:3; 30:5; 59:16; 88:13; 130:6; 90:14). The Word reminded him of God's unfailing love, and the Word strengthened his faith (Rom. 10:17) and gave him guidance on the dangerous path he had to take from the cave to the crown.

We also want the blessing of *experiencing the protection of God* (*v. 9*). Jehovah was David's "Rock" (18:2, 31, 46; 19:14), and he hid himself in "the cleft of the Rock" (Ex. 33:22) and was safe from the enemy. "Rock of ages / Cleft for me / Let me hide myself in Thee." Another answer we receive from the Lord is *a knowledge of the will of God* (*v.10*). His good Spirit (Neh. 9:20) teaches us from the Word and shows us the path we should take (119:105). A knowledge of God's will gives us confidence in the difficulties of life; it keeps us going when the going gets tough. Finally, God answers prayer by helping us *bring glory to His great name* (*vv. 11–12*). "For thy name's sake" was the great motivation of David's life and ministry (see 1 Sam. 17:26, 36, 45–47). "Hallowed be Thy name" is the first request in the Lord's Prayer, and it ought to be the motivation of all our prayers. David knew that he had a great work to do for the Lord, and he depended on the Lord to help him accomplish it and bring honor to His name.

## Psalm 144

David wrote this psalm to "bless the Lord" (vv. 1, 15) and honor Him for making him a successful warrior and king, and to pray for His continued blessing of his people. He was concerned about dangers around them (vv. 6–7, 11) and needs within the land (vv. 12–14). In writing this psalm, he used material from Psalm 18, his great song of victory when he became king, so perhaps 144 was written about that same time (1 Sam. 5, 8). During his years of exile, David had learned much about himself and about the Lord. In this psalm, he gave witness to Jehovah, the God of Israel, and reminded his people that their God was not like the gods of their neighbors.

### The Loving God Who Cares for Us Personally (vv. 1–4)

David had been a fugitive for perhaps ten years and then he reigned over Judah for seven years and six months. By the time he became king of all the tribes and made Jerusalem his capital, he had seen many battles and would fight many more. But God prepares and equips His leaders, and David had no fear of the future (18:34, 45; 55:21; 78:9). (For the image of God as Rock and fortress, see 18:2, and as shield, see 3:3.) The phrase "my goodness" (KJV) is translated "my lovingkindness" in the *New American Standard Bible* and "my loving God" in the *New International Version.* (See 18:2, 47.) The associating of love and war is unusual, but "You who love the Lord, hate evil" (97:10 NKJV). David inherited twelve tribes that did not always get along with each other, and during the years immediately following the death of King Saul, tribal rivalry and conflict created numerous problems. But God brought about political unity within the nation and gave David victory against the enemies outside the nation (18:47–48).

David's position and reputation did not go to his head, for he asked, "Who am I that God should do this for me?" The statements in verses 3–4 remind us of 8:4, and this is a reminder that we need, especially when we think we can handle life without trusting God. The Hebrew word translated "breath" is *habel,* the name of one of Adam's sons (Abel), and the word translated "vanity" thirty-eight times in Ecclesiastes. (See also 39:4–6, 22; 62:9; 78:33; 94:11.) The "shadow" image is found in 102:11, 109:23, Job 8:9 and 14:2, and Ecclesiastes 6:12 and 8:13. How helpless we are without the Lord!

### The Mighty God Who Delivers Us Victoriously (vv. 5–11)

David used these same vivid images in 18:8–9, 14–17, 45, and 50. The Jewish people did not forget God's dramatic appearance at Mount Sinai (Ex. 19:18–25 and 20:18–21), but here the mountains and "great waters" seem to stand for the enemies of Israel (104:32; Isa. 8:7; 59:19; 64:1–5; Mic. 1:4; Nah. 1:5; and Hab. 3:10). The "strange children" of verse 7 (KJV) are the outsiders who attacked Israel, the "aliens and foreigners." Some of them also tried to get into the nation and cause trouble (v. 11). They told lies and took oaths they never meant to keep. When they lifted their right hand in an oath, it was only deception. As he contemplated God's power and mercy, David sang a new song to the Lord (see 33:3), for he had experienced God's help in a new way, learned afresh the wonderful character of the Lord, and was making a new beginning as king of the nation. The plural "kings" refers to David's successors.

### The Gracious God Who Blesses Us Abundantly (vv. 12–15)

David never engaged in war just for the sake of conquest. His goal was to defend the land so the people could live peaceful and profitable lives. The people of Israel were God's people, and they had a work to accomplish on the earth. Therefore, they had to have children (v. 12), the necessities of life (v. 13), and peace in the land (v. 14). All of these blessings were promised to them in God's covenant (Deut. 28:1–14) if the people and their rulers obeyed the laws of the Lord. David mentioned the home and family first, for as goes the home, so goes the nation. He compared the sons to strong growing plants (127:3–5; 128:3) and the daughters to beautiful graceful statues that could support buildings. Then he moved to the fields to behold bountiful crops and multiplying flocks and herds. Once again, these blessings are all mentioned in God's covenant. Translations of verse 14 differ. Are the oxen heavy with young or bearing heavy loads because the fields are so fruitful? Is the picture that of a family of animals giving birth without losing any of their young, or was David describing a battle scene with the enemy breaking through the walls and the people crying out in the streets? "Breaking in" could describe the enemy coming through the walls, and "going out" the captives being led out as the people weep and express their sorrow. In His covenant with Israel, God promised them victory over the enemy, peace, prosperity, and a happy life. It is unfortunate that the nation rebelled against Jehovah and lost all those blessings in Babylonian captivity. "How blessed are the people whose God is the Lord!" for He cares for us personally, delivers us victoriously, and blesses us bountifully.

## Psalm 145

This is the last psalm in the book attributed to David, and it is also an acrostic. The Hebrew letter *nun* (our letter *n*) is missing at verse 14, although some early versions based on the Septuagint have a verse starting with *nun*. (See NIV marginal note.) This is the only psalm called "A psalm of praise." David mentioned several attributes of God, among them His greatness (v. 3), His grace, goodness and compassion (vv. 8–9), His glory and might (v. 11), His righteousness and kindness (v. 17), and His providential care (v. 20). Who could not praise a God with these wonderful characteristics? But along with telling us why we should praise the Lord, David tells us when we should praise Him.

### Praise God from Day to Day (vv. 1–2)

In heaven, we shall praise the Lord forever and forever, but now is the time to get prepared as we praise Him from day to day. No matter how dark and difficult the day may be, there is always something for which we can praise the Lord—even if it is only that the situation is not always this bad! Our universe operates a day at a time as the heavenly bodies move in orbit around the sun, and we are foolish to try to live two days at a time. "As your days, so shall your strength be" (Deut. 33:25 NKJV), and some of that strength comes from praising and thanking the Lord.

### Praise God from Generation to Generation (vv. 3–7)

One of the important obligations of the older generation is to pass on to the younger generation the truth about the Lord. Whether we admit it or not, every local church is one generation short of extinction, and we must obey 2 Timothy 2:2. (See 48:13; 71:18; 78:6; 79:13; 102:18; Ex. 3:15; 12:14, 17, 42; Judg. 2:10.) God is so great that the human mind cannot fathom Him (Isa. 40:28; Job 5:9; 9:10; 11:7; Rom. 11:33; Eph. 3:8), but the human heart can love Him and tell others how great He is. God's character and God's awesome works furnish us with more material than we could ever exhaust, and we will have all of eternity to keep learning more! But David was not writing only about theology; he was also writing about personal witness, what the Lord has done in our own lives. "Come, you children, listen to me; I will teach you the fear of the Lord" (34:11 NKJV). The older generation must reach back into their lives and "utter the memory" of God's great goodness (v. 7). The word translated "utter" means "to pour forth like a bubbling spring" (19:2; 59:7; 94:4; 119:17).

### Praise God from Nation to Nation (vv. 8–13a)

David knew his basic theology (v. 8; Ex. 34:6; Num. 14:18; Neh. 9:17), but he also knew that this wonderful truth must be shared with others. Jonah knew it but would not share it (Jonah 4). "All" is one of the key words of this psalm. God is good to all (v. 9) and His throne lasts for all generations (v. 13). He upholds all who fall (v. 14) and the eyes of all creatures look to God for their food (v. 15). He satisfies every living thing (v. 16) and helps all who call on Him (v. 18). One day all flesh will praise Him (v. 21). "Salvation is of the Jews" (John 4:22), but the message of salvation was not supposed to remain with the Jews. It was not sufficient for the people of Israel to praise God and teach their children to praise Him. They were obligated to share the truth about the Lord with their Gentile neighbors and let their light shine (Isa. 42:6). The psalm begins "I will extol Thee" but ends "All flesh will bless His name" (v. 21). The church today has a similar obligation and privilege. All of God's works in creation praise Him around the world, but for some reason, His own people do not follow this example. God has compassion on all—God loves a lost world (John 3:16)—and we keep it to ourselves! The glory and wonder of God's spiritual kingdom must be proclaimed from nation to nation as well as from house to house. (Note that v. 13 is quoted in Dan. 4:3.)

*Praise God from Need to Need  (vv. 13b–16)*
Our great God is not an "absentee landlord" who collects rent but never repairs the roof. He knows our every need and He is there to help those who call on Him—those who fall, those carrying back-breaking burdens, those who hunger, and certainly those who want to be saved from their sins (Acts 2:21). We toil for our daily bread, but all God has to do is open His hand when He hears our cries and meet whatever needs we have. When He supplies one need, we must praise Him, and we must praise Him when He supplies the next need! "Casting all your care upon Him, for He cares for you" (1 Peter 5:7 NKJV). (See 104:27–28 and Matt. 6:26.)

*Praise God from Prayer to Prayer (vv. 17–21)*
The emphasis here is on calling on the Lord. "Yet you do not have because you do not ask" (James 4:2 NKJV). God is righteous, so we want to come with clean hands and a pure heart (66:18), but God is also loving, so we should love Him and obey Him. Prayer is not just a creature coming to the Creator, or a servant coming to the Master; it is a child coming to the heavenly Father, knowing that He will meet the need (Luke 11:1–13). He hears us, watches over us, and supplies our every need (Phil. 4:19). When He answers prayer, we must praise Him, and when He answers another prayer, we must praise Him. "My mouth will speak the praise of the Lord," wrote David, and we must follow his example. The sad thing about the wicked, whom God will destroy, is that they have nobody to thank when a blessing comes their way! We need to tell them about our wonderful Lord who died for them and desires to save them.

# Psalm 146
The last five psalms are the "Hallelujah Psalms" that focus our attention on praising the Lord. This psalm begins with a vow to

praise God throughout life. The next psalm tells us it is "good and pleasant" to praise the Lord, and 148 reminds us that when we praise God, we join with all creation, for heaven and earth praise Him. In 149, God's people are admonished to worship joyfully, and the last psalm tells us where and why and how "everything that has breath" should praise the Lord. These five psalms are a short course in worship, and God's people today would do well to heed their message. Sanctuaries are turning into religious theaters and "worship" is becoming more and more entertainment. The author of this psalm understood that God was not just a part of life but the heart of life. Paul had the same conviction (Phil. 1:21; Col. 3:4 ).

### Life Means Praising God (vv. 1–2)
God gives us life and breath (Acts 17:25), so it is only right that we use that life and breath to praise Him (150:6). To receive the gifts and ignore the Giver is the essence of idolatry. The writer promised God he would praise Him all of his life, and certainly this is wise preparation for praising Him for eternity (104:33). To live a life of praise is to overcome criticism and complaining, to stop competing against others and comparing ourselves with them. It means to be grateful in and for everything (I Thess. 5:18; Eph. 5:20) and really believe that God is working all things together for our good (Rom. 8:28). A life of praise is free from constant anxiety and discouragement as we focus on the Lord, who is mentioned eleven times in this psalm.

### Life Means Trusting God (vv. 3–6)
Most people trust in "flesh and blood," themselves and others, instead of trusting the Lord to use "flesh and blood" to accomplish His will (118:5–9; 44:4–8). What nobody else can do, God can do for us and through us. These verses suggest that the psalmist was concerned that Israel's leaders not enter into ungodly alliances, but that they turn to God for help. Beginning with Abraham (Gen. 12:10ff) and the exodus generation (Ex. 14:10–14; 16:1–3; Num. 14:1–10), the people of Israel turned to Egypt for help instead of trusting the Lord, and this was true even

during the days of Isaiah (Isa. 31) and Jeremiah (Jer. 2:18; 37:1–10; 42–43). To trust in human wisdom and strength is to depend on that which cannot last, for all people die, and the brilliant ideas of one leader are replaced by the not-so-brilliant ideas of a new leader. In the Hebrew text, "man" is *adam*, which comes from the word *adamah* which means "earth." We came from the earth and return to the earth (Gen. 3:19).

"But will the Lord help me, as weak and failing as I am?" many believers ask. Well, He is "the God of Jacob" (v. 5), a title used at least a dozen times in The Psalms. (See 20:1; 24:6; 46:7, 11.) Jacob was far from being perfect, yet God honored his faith and helped him in times of need. Jacob trusted God's promises, for his hope was in the Lord, but too often he depended on his own schemes to see him through. The beatitude in verse 5 is the last of twenty-five in the book of Psalms, starting with 1:1. But Jehovah is not only the God of Jacob, He is also the "God who made heaven and earth" (v. 6; 115:5; 121:2; 124:8; 134:3; Ezra 5:11) and has the power to act on behalf of His people. When we pray, we come to the throne of the universe to ask our Father for what we need. Finally, He is the God who "keeps faith forever" (v. 6 NASB). Israel knows Him as the God of the covenant, and Christian believers today know Him as the God and Father of our Lord Jesus Christ who initiated a new covenant by giving His life on the cross. Jehovah is a God who can be trusted to keep His Word.

### Life Means Loving God (vv. 7–9)

This list of God's gracious ministries to needy people has at its heart "The Lord loves" (v. 8). He loves the church (Eph. 5:25), a lost world (John 3:16), and His people Israel (Deut. 4:37), and the greatest proof of that love is the cross (Rom. 5:8). Paul wrote, "He loved me and gave Himself for me" (Gal. 2:20 NKJV). All of the sins that help to produce these sad conditions were dealt with on the cross, but their existence in society is proof that the law of sin and death is reigning in this world (Rom. 5:12–21). During His ministry on earth, Jesus revealed God's love by helping people who were hungry, sick, crippled, blind, bowed down, and otherwise unable to help themselves (Luke 4:16–21; Isa. 61:1–3). We love God because He first loved us (1 John 4:19), and if we truly love God, we will love those who need God's help and will do all we can to help them (1 John 3:10–24; James 2:14–26). Living in love means more than enjoying God's love for us (John 14:21–24). It also means sharing God's love with others. We may not be able to perform miracles to heal the afflicted, but we can help them in other ways.

### Life Means Reigning with God (v. 10)

This statement comes from the song of victory that Israel sang at the Exodus: "The Lord shall reign forever and ever" (Ex. 15:18). "The Lord reigns" is found in 93:1, 96:10, 97:1, and 99:1. Think of it: the sovereign Lord of the universe is our loving heavenly Father! Not only does the Lord reign over the nations (47:8), but we can "reign in life" through Jesus Christ as we yield to Him and walk in the Spirit (Rom. 5:17). We are now seated with Christ in the heavenlies (Eph. 1:18–23; 2:4–10; Col. 3:1–4), and the throne of the universe is to us a throne of grace (Heb. 4:14–16). We "reign in life" as, by faith, we draw upon our spiritual resources in Christ and together with Him make decisions and exercise ministry. We do not need to wait for the kingdom to come to start reigning with Christ (Matt. 19:28; Rev. 22:5), for God's grace is reigning (Rom. 5:20–21), and we can reign with Christ today (Rom. 5:21). Then we can have a life of praising God, trusting God, and loving God, a life that will glorify God.

# Psalm 147

When Nehemiah and his people finished rebuilding the walls of Jerusalem, restoring the gates, and resettling the people, they called a great assembly for celebration and dedication, and it is likely that this psalm was written for that occasion (vv. 2, 12–14; Neh. 12:27–43). The verb "gather together" in verse 2 is used in Ezekiel 39:28 for the return of the captives to Judah, and the word "outcasts" in verse 2 is used for these exiles (Neh. 1:9). One of the unique characteristics of this psalm is the large number of present participles in it—"building, healing, binding, counting, lifting up," and so on—all of which speak of the constant and dynamic working of the Lord for His people. The psalm presents three reasons why the people should praise the Lord, and each section is marked off by the command to praise God (vv. 1, 7 and 12).

### Praise the Lord—His People Have Been Restored (vv. 1–6)

The Medes and Persians captured Babylon in 539 B.C., and in 537 B.C. Cyrus issued a decree permitting the Jews to return to their land. Led by Zerubbabel, a large band of exiles went back to Judah the next year and the temple was rebuilt. Nehemiah came in 444 B.C. to restore the walls and gates of Jerusalem. Both Isaiah and Jeremiah had predicted the captivity of the Jews as well as their release and return, and God's prophetic Word proved true, as it always does. But the psalmist did not simply notice the event; he also noticed the way the Lord tenderly cared for His people. Many lost loved ones in the invasion and during the time in Babylon, and all returned to a devastated land and ruined houses. No wonder they were brokenhearted (34:18; Isa. 61:1). The "wounds" (v. 3; "sorrows") were in their hearts, not their bodies, for many had repented and confessed their sins to the Lord, and through the Word, the Lord gave them the comfort they needed (107:20; Isa. 40). Our God is so great that He knew each person and each need (John 10:14, 27–28). The God of the galaxies, who knows the name of every star, is also the God who heals the broken hearts of His people (Luke 4:16–21). He builds up Jerusalem and lifts up His people, for nothing is too hard for Him. (See 20:8; 146:9; and Isa. 40:26–29.)

### Sing to the Lord—the Land Has Been Refreshed (vv. 7–11)

The exiles returned to a land that had been left a war zone for seven decades, and they needed the early and latter rains in order to get a harvest. The Lord gathered the clouds over the land and emptied their life-giving rain on the newly planted seed. He even caused grass to grow on the mountains where nobody had planted any seed! He gave food to the wild beasts so they would not attack the humans, and He even sent food for the noisy young ravens. (See 104:1–24.) The ancients believed that young ravens were abandoned by the parent birds and had to find their own food (Luke 12:24). It was essential that the men and their farm animals stay healthy so they could work toward a harvest and be able to feed themselves and their families. But as important as that was, the most important thing was trusting the Lord, fearing the Lord, and giving Him delight as He beheld their devotion and obedience (33:16–17; 146:3–4; Matt. 6:33). It is an awesome thought that we can bring pleasure to the heart of the heavenly Father (35:27; 37:23; 149:4).

### Extol the Lord—the Word Has Been Revealed (vv. 12–20)

God's prophetic Word made possible the rebuilding of Jerusalem (Neh. 3:3, 6, 13–15; 7:1–4; Lam. 2:9), and then the Lord added His blessing to the city and its people. In the Hebrew language, "peace" (*shalom*) is much more than the absence of war. It describes total well being, including material prosperity and physical and spiritual health. Peace at the borders means peace in the nation, for invaders have to cross the borders before they can attack. Peaceful borders, strong walls, locked gates—it adds up to safety and security. Because of their disobedience, the nation had forfeited the "finest of the wheat" (81:16; Deut. 32:13–14), but now the Lord would give His people the very best. After all, the Lord controls the weather with a word (33:9) and He can do as He pleases. Hail storms and snowstorms are very infrequent in the Holy Land, except in the higher altitudes, but the Word of God accomplishes what He purposes. The Word brings the winter and then it brings the springtime, for all creation obeys the will of the Lord.

This truth prepares the way for the final thrust of the psalm: God gave His Word to Israel, and they must obey it even as creation obeys it (vv. 19–20; Deut. 4:7–8, 32–34; Rom. 3:1–2; 9:4). What a privilege it was for the people of Israel to be the bearers of God's Holy Word and to share it with the world! After the fall of Jerusalem, Jeremiah wrote, "The Law is no more" (Lam. 2:9), but God's Word was not destroyed with the city and temple. God's Word endures forever (1 Peter 1:25). The church today is blessed by having the Word of God, but we must obey it and share with a lost world. The Jewish nation took great care to protect the manuscripts of God's Word and their scholars carefully counted the letters and words, but they did not look beyond the text into the truth being taught (John 5:38–40). When their Messiah came, they did not recognize Him (John 1:26; 1 Cor. 2:6–12). How easy it is for us to respect the Word of God, bind it in expensive leather, and explain it with exhaustive notes, *and yet not obey what it tells us to do!* "Every Bible should be bound in shoe leather," said evangelist D. L. Moody, which is another way of saying "faith without works is dead" (James 2:14–26).

## Psalm 148

The word "praise" is used thirteen times in these fourteen verses. The psalm begins in the highest heavens and ends with the little nation of Israel. If any psalm reveals the glory and grandeur of the worship of the Lord, it is this one, for it is cosmic in its dimensions and yet very personal in its intentions. How anyone could trivialize the privilege and responsibility of worship after pondering this psalm is difficult to understand.

### The Heavens Praise the Lord (vv. 1–6)

We do not praise a god who was manufactured on earth; we praise the one true and living God who reigns from the highest heavens, the God who created all things. Solomon was right when he said, "Behold, heaven and the heaven of heavens cannot contain You" (1 Kings 8:27 NKJV; see Deut. 10:14; Neh. 9:6; 2 Cor. 12:2). The "hosts [armies] of heaven" include the angels (103:20–21) and the stars and planets (Deut. 4:19), all of which praise the Lord. He is "Lord of Sabaoth—the Lord of Hosts" (Rom. 9:29; Isa. 1:9; James 5:4). Scripture gives us a few descriptions of worship in heaven (Isa. 6; Dan. 7:9–10; Rev. 5:11–14), and we are cautioned not to worship the angels (Col. 2:18; Rev. 22:8–9). The sun, moon, and stars also praise God simply by doing what they were commanded to do (8:1–3; 19:1–6; 89:36–37; 136:7–9). We cannot see the angels in heaven, but we can see the heavenly bodies by day and night, and they tell us that there is a God and that He is wise, powerful, and glorious (Rom. 1:18–20). The pagan nations worshiped the creation instead of the Creator and Israel often fell into the same sin. The waters above and below take us back to Genesis 1:6–7 and 7:11, and see Psalm 104:3. Why should the hosts of heaven praise the Lord? Simply because He made them and gave them the privilege of serving Him and His people and bringing glory to His name. We have many more reasons for praising Him, and yet too often, we do not do it.

### The Earth Praises the Lord (vv. 7–13)

The sea creatures from the ocean depths head the list (104:6; Gen. 1:21), followed by the demonstrations of God's power in the atmosphere (107:25). Remember David's psalm about the storm (29)? "Fire" in verse 8 is probably lightning, although some opt for volcanic disturbances. Lightning often accompanied hail storms in the Holy Land. To us, the storms are unpredictable and seem out of control as they do extensive damage, but we are assured that they are accomplishing God's will. The psalmist then moved from the sea and atmosphere into the land where God placed trees for food and trees for building, wild animals and domestic animals, small creatures ("creeping things"), and birds. But men and women are the highest creatures in God's creation, because they were made in the image of God (Gen. 1:26–28). If any of God's creation has good reason to praise the Lord, it is mankind, because we have the privilege of knowing God more intimately, and we have the promise of one day being like Christ. Angels rejoice when sinners are saved, but they cannot experience the grace of God (Luke 15:7, 10). We wonder how many world leaders take time to thank and praise God. Whether we are male or female, young or old, famous or unknown, we can all know the Lord and praise the Lord. *We know His name!* What a privilege to be a child of the King!

### The People of Israel Praise the Lord (v. 14)

In Scripture, a "horn" is a symbol of power and dignity, a king or a kingdom. To "take away the horn" means to deprive a nation or person of authority and prestige (79:10; see also 89:17, 24; 132:17; Ezek. 29:21). When the Lord brought His people back from exile in Babylon, He "raised up a horn" for them. This cannot refer to a king, for David's dynasty had ended with the capture of Zedekiah and the returned remnant had no king. But they did have a nation, a temple, and a priesthood, and they had preserved the sacred Word that the Lord had given them through their prophets (147:19–20). But Luke 1:69 gives us the right to apply this image to Jesus Christ, the Son of David, for He is the only person qualified to sit on David's throne (Luke 1:30–33). "Salvation is of the Jews" (John 4:22), and the Jews are a people who are still dear to the Lord (Ex. 19:6; Num. 16:5; Deut. 4:1–8).

If you read this psalm again with Jesus in mind, you can see how much greater He is than anything or anyone mentioned, for He is the Creator of all things (John 1:1–3; Col. 1:16–17). He is Captain of the hosts of the Lord (Josh. 5:14), the Sun of Righteousness (Mal. 4:2; Luke 1:78) and the Morning Star (Rev. 22:16). When ministering here on earth, He demonstrated power over storms (Matt. 8:23–27; 14:23–33), trees (Matt. 21:18–22), and wild and domestic animals (Mark 1:13; 11:1–3). He is far above the angels (Heb. 1; Eph. 1:18–23 and 3:10–11). He revealed the Father's name (John 17:6) and glorified that name in all He was, said, or did (John 1:14; 2:11; 11:4, 40; 12:28; 14:13; 17:4). In all things, Jesus Christ has the preeminence (Col. 1:18).

## Psalm 149

Everything that God's people do in serving and glorifying the Lord must flow out of worship, for without Him we can do nothing (John 15:5). The most important activity of the local church is the worship of God, for this is the activity we will continue in heaven for all eternity. This psalm is a primer on worship and gives us the basic instructions we need.

### Worship the Lord Intelligently (vv. 1–2)

Worship is something that we must learn to do, and we will be learning all of our lives. In times of corporate worship, the saints do minister to one another (Eph. 5:19; Col. 3:16), but the primary focus must be on the Lord, glorifying and extolling Him. Yes, we may worship the Lord in solitude, and we should (v. 5), but we must not forsake the assembly of the saints (Heb. 10:25). As members of the body of Christ (1 Cor. 12:12–13, 27), we belong to each other, affect each other, and need each other. We need both the old songs and the new songs (see on 33:3), which suggests an intelligent balance in worship. The church family has young and old, new believers, and seasoned saints (1 Tim. 5:1–2; Titus 2:1–8; 1 John 2:12–14), and nobody should be ignored. The old songs bear witness to our steadfastness in keeping the faith, but the new songs give evidence that we are maturing in the faith as we grow in the knowledge of His Word and His grace (2 Peter 3:18). A maturing faith demands mature expressions of worship, just as a maturing marriage demands new expressions of devotion, but we do not abandon the old and major only on the new. "Let us press on to maturity" (Heb. 6:1 NASB). The old and the new must be integrated or we will not be balanced believers (Matt. 13:51–52). We must walk in the Spirit (Eph. 5:18–21) and grow in knowledge of the Word (Col. 3:16), learning new truths about the old truths and having new experiences of blessing from both.

The church today can join with Israel in saying, "God is our Maker and our King" (95:6; 100:3; 10:16; 24:7–10; Eph. 2:10; Rev. 15:3; 19:16). How He has made us is His gift to us, and what we do with it is our gift to Him. We must remind ourselves that we came from the dust, but because of God's grace, we are destined for glory! "Soon and very soon / We're going to see the King."

### Worship the Lord Fervently (vv. 3–4)

A very expressive people, the Jews used musical instruments, songs, and dances in their worship of the Lord. The dances, of course, were not modern ballroom or disco dances but rather interpretive dances that pointed to the Lord and not some person's talent (see Ex. 15:20; Jude 11:34; 1 Sam. 18:6; Jer. 31:4). We find no evidence that the New Testament church patterned its worship after the Jewish temple. Their pattern seems to have been the local synagogue worship, with its emphasis on prayer, the reading of the Word, exposition and exhortation, and singing hymns. However, spiritual fervency must not be confused with fleshly enthusiasm. There are false worshipers as well as true worshipers (John 4:22–24; Col. 2:16–23), and some people who think they are filled with the Spirit are really being fooled by the spirits. Bringing false fire into the sanctuary can lead to death (Lev. 10:1–11). Our purpose is not to please ourselves or to demonstrate how "spiritual" we are. Our purpose is to delight the Lord (147:11), and humility is one virtue that brings Him great joy (Isa. 66:1–2). The Lord gives spiritual beauty to those whose worship brings Him delight. Worship ought to be beautiful, for we are beholding the beauty of the Lord (27:4; 29:2; 90:17; 96:9) and becoming more like the Lord (2 Cor. 3:18). Worship must focus on God, not on us, and it must be enrichment, not entertainment. The experience of true worship can help us experience deliverance from the bondage of sin and the world.

### Worship the Lord Gratefully (v. 5)

"Let the saints rejoice in this honor" is the *New International Version* translation, the "honor" being the privilege of worshiping the true and living God. God gave His Word and His glory only to the nation of Israel (147:19–20; Rom. 9:1–5), and this Word and glory have peen passed on to the church (John 17:8, 14, 22). When the believer's private worship and the church's corporate worship become routine, the Spirit is grieved and the blessing is gone. Worship ought to mean so much to us that we sing even on our beds! The word is "couches" and could refer to someone reclining at the table or resting in bed. Singing at the table or in our bed can bring joy to the Lord. Instead of the bed "swimming" with tears (6:6 NKJV), it is filled with "songs in the night" (42:8; 77:6). Even while lying in a sickbed, we can look up to God and worship Him. Without private worship, we are but hypocrites at public worship.

## Worship the Lord Triumphantly (vv. 6–9)

Worship and warfare go together, as the book of Revelation makes very clear.[3] Satan has always wanted to be worshiped (Isa. 14:12–15), and he is willing to pay for it (Matt. 4:8–11). Satan is constantly at work enticing the world to worship him (Rev. 13), for he does not mind if people are "religious" so long as they leave out Jesus Christ and the truth of the gospel. In recent years, some denominations have eliminated the "militant songs" from their hymnals and their worship, and this is disappointing. Whether we like it or not, the church is an army, this world is a battlefield, and there is a struggle going on for the souls of lost sinners (Matt. 16:17–18; Eph. 6:10ff; 2 Tim. 2:3–4; 2 Cor. 10:3–5). Jesus Christ, the Prince of Peace (Isa. 9:6), is also the Conquering Warrior (45:3–7; Rev. 19:11–21), and like the workers in Nehemiah's day, we must have both tools for building and swords for battling (Neh. 4:17–18). Our weapons are prayer, the sword of the Spirit, the Word of God (Eph. 6:17; Heb. 4:12), and hymns of praise to the Lord. Worship is warfare, for we are singing soldiers! Did not our Lord sing before He went out to the cross to do battle against the devil? (See Matt. 26:30; John 12:31–32; and Col. 2:13–15.)

God has declared in writing that "the day of the Lord" will come when He will send judgment to a world that has rejected Christ and chosen to worship Satan (Rev. 6–19). God's people will appear to be the losers, but in the end, they will conquer the enemy and reign with Christ (Rev. 19:11ff). Today, the sword belongs to human government and its agents (Rom. 13), and God's servants do not wield it (John 18:10–11, 36–37). But the day of the Lord will come "as a thief in the night" (1 Thess. 5:2ff), and then Christ will "gird His sword … and ride prosperously (45:3–5). Until then, the church must take worship very seriously and realize that worship is a part of the believer's spiritual warfare. To ignore worship, trivialize it, turn it into entertainment, or make it a routine activity is to play right into the hands of the enemy. It is an honor to serve in the Lord's army of worshiping warriors!

# Psalm 150

When you read and study the psalms, you meet with joys and sorrows, tears and trials, pains and pleasures, *but the book of Psalms closes on the highest note of praise!* Like the book of Revelation that closes the New Testament, this final psalm says to God's people, "Don't worry—this is the way the story will end. We shall all be praising the Lord!" The word "praise" is used thirteen times in this psalm, and ten of those times, we are *commanded* to "Praise Him." Each of the previous four Books of Psalms ends with a benediction (41:13; 72:18–19; 89:52; 106:48), but the final Book ends with a whole psalm devoted to praise. Like the previous psalm, it gives us a summary of some essentials of true worship.

### The Focus of Worship: The Lord (1a, 6b)

"Hallelu Yah"—hallelujah—"Praise the Lord!" Jehovah (or Yah, for Yahweh) is the covenant name of the Lord. It reminds us that He loves us and has covenanted to save us, keep us, care for us, and eventually glorify us, because of the sacrifice of Jesus Christ, His Son, on the cross. The new covenant was not sealed by the blood of animal sacrifices but by the precious blood of Christ. "God" is the "power name" of God (El, Elohim), and this reminds us that whatever He promises, He is able to perform. Worship is not about the worshiper and his or her needs; it is about God and His power and glory. Certainly we bring our burdens and needs with us into the sanctuary (1 Peter 5:7), but we focus our attention on the Lord.

### The Places of Worship: Heaven and Earth (v. 1b)

The "firmament" is the great expanse of heaven (11:4; 148:1; Gen. 1:6) where the angels and "spirits of just men made perfect" (148:1–7; Heb. 12:23) worship the Lord. The "sanctuary" was the Jewish tabernacle or temple where the priests and Levites led the people in praising God. We know that the Lord does not live in the structures that we design and build (Acts 7:48–50; 17:24–25), but there is nothing sinful about setting aside a place totally dedicated to worshiping the Lord. The early church met in the temple, in upper rooms, in private homes, and even in synagogues, and when persecution began, they met in caves and underground burial chambers. People who excuse themselves from public worship because they "worship God in nature" need to be reminded that the God of nature has revealed Himself in Jesus Christ and commanded us to gather together with other believers (Heb. 10:25). We can lift our hearts to the Lord from any geographic location, for our God fills heaven and earth.

### The Themes of Worship: God's Acts and Attributes (v. 2)

The Old Testament is a record of "the mighty acts of God" as performed for the nation of Israel, the chosen people of God. Especially notable are the exodus from Egypt, the conquest of the Promised Land, the expansion of the Davidic kingdom, the deliverance of the Jews from Babylon, and the restoring of the nation. In the four Gospels we see the acts of God as done by Jesus Christ, the Son of God, and in the Acts and Epistles, we have the record of the Holy Spirit's mighty acts accomplished through the people of God. The acts of God reveal the character of God, His holiness, love, wisdom, power, grace, and so on— what the psalmist called "His excellent greatness" (NASB). The nation of Israel had a calendar of special feasts to help them remember who God was and what God had done (Lev. 23), and there is nothing wrong with the church having a similar calendar for the great events in the ministry of Christ. However, we must beware lest the routine use of the calendar becomes more important than the meaning of the days, or that the observing of these days is a means of salvation (Rom. 14:1–15:13; Gal. 4:8–10; Col. 2:16–17). We cannot plumb the depths of all that God is or all that He has done (106:2; 145:4, 11, 12). This is why our eternal worshiping of God will never become boring!

### The Means of Worship: Musical Instruments and Human Voices (vv. 3–6)

When it is used correctly, by God's grace and for God's glory, the human voice is the most perfect musical instrument in the world, but we find no prohibitions in Scripture against using man-made instruments in the worship of God. Instruments will be used in heaven (Rev. 5:8; 8:6–12), and there will also be singing (Rev. 5:9–14; 6:12; 11:16–18; 15:1–4; 16:5–7; 19:1–9). The psalmist seems to be describing an orchestra that has string instruments, percussion instruments, and wind instruments. The trumpet was the *shofar* or ram's horn that the priests and Levites used (47:6; 98:6) along with the harp and lyre (1 Chron. 25:1). The timbrel was probably what we know today as a tambourine. It was usually played by the women to accompany their sacred dances (Ex. 15:20–21). There were two kinds of cymbals, smaller ones that gave a clear sound and larger ones that gave a loud sound. But the final verse sums it up. Whether you can play an instrument or not, no matter where you live or what your ethnic origin, male or female, young or old—"Let everything that has breath praise the Lord!" After all, that breath comes from the Lord (Acts 17:25), and if things that do not have breath can praise the Lord (148:8–9), surely we can, too!

Praise the Lord!

# Book IV

1. Heb. 4:7 ascribes this psalm to David. The NIV and NASB both read "through David," while the KJV and NKJV both read "in David," that is, "in the Psalter." This is the preferable translation.

# Book V

2. Some students connect these "degrees" with the fifteen degrees on King Hezekiah's sundial (Isa. 38:8; 2 Kings 20:9–10). See Old Testament Problems by J. W. Thirtle (Morgan & Scott, 1916); Appendix 67 of *The Companion Bible*; and chapter ten of *Mark These Men* by J. Sidlow Baxter. There are some interesting parallels between Isa. 36–38 and Pss. 120–134, but modern evangelical scholarship has not accepted Thirtle's interesting theory.
3. See chapters 13–15 of my book *Real Worship: Playground, Battleground or Holy Ground?* (Baker Books) for a more detailed discussion of Satan's desire for worship.

# BE EXULTANT

*A study guide for personal reflection
or group discussion.*

# Questions for Personal Reflection and/or Group Discussion

# Book IV: Psalms 90 – 106

## Psalm 90

1. Who wrote this psalm, the oldest of al the psalms? How does it comfort you to know that no matter where you live God is your "dwelling place"?

2. Abraham was the father of Israel. How many generations were there from Abraham to Moses? How can you invest your life rather than just spend it?

3. What sad decision did Israel make at Kedesh Barnea? What big decision confronts you today? How will you bring the Lord into that decision?

## Psalm 91

4. What two addresses did the psalmist have (vv. 1, 9, 10)? Which one is everlasting? How should you live, knowing which address is everlasting?

5. Do you agree or disagree that the believer who does the will of God is safer in a war zone than in a house in the suburbs? Explain.

6. Which is better: quantity of years or quality of years? Why?

## Psalm 92

7. What is the major theme of this psalm? How can this theme be the theme of your life?

8. The psalmist compared the wicked to grass and the righteous to a palm tree? Why are these comparisons appropriate?

## Psalms 93

9. Who permitted the Jews permission to return to their own land after their long captivity in Babylon? Do you long for your heavenly home? Why?

10. How are nations like raging seas and pounding waves? Where do you find stability in these calamitous times?

11. What practical benefits do you see in the fact that the Lord's "statutes stand firm"?

## Psalm 94

12. Unjust leaders in Israel triggered prayers for the Lord's revenge. Do you see a correlation between injustice and disregard for the Lord? If so, what is it? When will the righteous be vindicated?

13. What keeps you from cheating and abusing others?

14. Why does the Lord allow unjust leaders to retain their power?

## Psalm 95

15. What is your concept of genuine worship? What standards should our hymns and praise choruses meet?

16. Worship can become routine and meaningless? How can we keep our private and public worship focused on the Lord and pleasing to Him?

17. What attitude should fill the heart when we "kneel before the LORD our Maker"?

## Psalm 96

16. This psalm calls upon its readers to sing to the Lord. What songs do you most enjoy singing to the Lord? Why do you like singing those songs?

17. Why is the Lord worthy of our praise?

18. What changes in nature are you most eager to see when the Lord reigns over all the earth?

# Psalm 97

19. What false gods do people worship? What distinguishes God from false gods?

20. Verse 10 states that "those who love the LORD hate evil." What expressions of evil do you find most offensive?

# Psalm 98

21. What popular Christmas carol is based on this psalm?

22. Why is the Christian life such a joyful life? How can you let your joy overflow to others?

# Psalm 99

23. How does knowing the Lord reigns affect your family life, your job, your worship, and your general outlook on life?

24. Describe how you feel, knowing that you can approach God's throne "with confidence" (Heb. 4:16)?

# Psalm 100

25. How has the Lord shown His goodness to you?

26. In what specific ways will you respond to His goodness?

# Psalm 101

27. David was determined to maintain a blameless life. What difference do you see between blameless and perfect? What resources can help you lead a blameless life of worship and service?

28. What worthy goals do you want to attain? What steps lead to your goals?

# Psalm 102

29. What word describes the writer's mood as he composed this psalm?

30. How does confidence in the Lord enable you to rise above changing circumstances? Can you say sincerely, "I have learned to be content whatever the circumstances" (Phil. 4:11)?

31. What constants strengthen you in rapidly changing circumstances?

# Psalm 103

32. Praise characterizes this psalm. No requests are made to the Lord. Do your prayers usually include more requests than praise? What adjustments, if any, should you make to your prayers?

33. What practical advantages in old age does a believer have that an unbeliever lacks? What do you most admire about elderly believers?

## Psalm 104

34. What evidence of the Creator's handiwork do you see in nature? In your life?

35. The psalmist credited the Creator with wisdom (v. 24). In addition to His wisdom what divine characteristics do you deduce from creation?

36. If modern science and Scripture are at odds, which is credible? Why?

## Psalm 105

37. What does Israel's history teach us about God? What victories did He grant Israel? What victories has He given you recently?

38. Israel's deliverance from Egypt was due entirely to God's grace and mercy. Do you believe your redemption is due entirely to His grace and mercy? Explain.

## Psalm 106

39. This psalm rehearses Israel's history of sinning. Ingratitude and grumbling seemed to have been habitual sins. Why are these habits so destructive?

39. How does verse 21 explain Israel's lapse into idolatry? What application to your life can you make from this episode?

40. What measures did the Lord take to discipline His rebellious people? What measures might He take today to discipline rebellious Christians? How can a believer avoid such discipline?

# Chapter Three
# Book V: Psalms 107 – 150

## Psalm 107
41. God's people often encounter hardships, just as the Jews did while returning home from Babylon. What kind of journey should Christians expect on their way to heaven?

42. Why might God allow an enemy to afflict a believer? Why should we trust Him in difficult times as well as in good times?

## Psalms 108–109
43. What new challenges are you facing that only God can help you meet?

44. David's attempts to return good for evil failed (109:4, 5). How should a believer respond when his or her kindness is repaid with evil?

45. The word "accuser" (v. 6) gives us our word "Satan." What accusations do you think Satan hurls against believers? Read 1 John 2:1. What defense do we have?

# Psalm 110

46. Name two New Testament men who attributed this psalm to David. What characteristics and actions mentioned in this psalm identify Jesus? How do those characteristics and actions strengthen your faith?

47. What three significant offices does this psalm mention? How does Jesus fulfill each of those offices?

# Psalms 111–112

48. What does it mean to you that God's name is "holy and awesome" (111: 9)? Do you think unbelievers disrespect His name today occasionally or frequently? Where is His name most likely disrespected?

49. What does it mean to fear the Lord? What practical value do you see in fearing the Lord?

50. What heritage would you like to pass to your children or to the younger generation? How would you like to be remembered after you die?

# Psalm 113

51. What three reasons does this psalm give for praising the Lord?

52. How do you perceive God when you read that He "stoops down to look on the heavens and the earth"? How does this perception of God out space exploration into proper perspective?

53. How do verses 7–9 highlight God's compassion? How have you been the object of His compassion?

## Psalm 114

54. The Lord separated Israel from Egypt, and He also separated Israel unto Himself. What has the Lord separated you from? How is your life better because the Lord separated you unto Himself?

55. Where does the Lord dwell today? How can you reveal the Lord to others?

## Psalm 115

56. The people of Israel gave the Lord the glory because of His love and faithfulness. Read 1 Corinthians 10:32. What specific kinds of deeds can you perform today to glorify the Lord?

57. What was Israel's most habitual and costly sin? How does worshiping God "in spirit and in truth" (John 4:24) transform us?

58. Which of the following opposites best differentiates between unbelievers and believers: irreligious/religious; ignorant/enlightened; dead/alive? Defend your choice.

## Psalm 116

59. What was "the cup of salvation" (v. 13)? What did it represent?

60. Why is childlike faith so significant? How might a highly intellectual person lead a life of childlike faith?

61. What spiritual decisions might a sincere follower of the Lord appropriately make public?

## Psalms 117–118

62. What is distinct about Psalm 117? Have you "bragged" about the Lord recently? If so, what was the occasion?

63. How has the Lord manifested His love to you recently? How often do you praise Him for His love?

64. What is most likely the historic background of Psalm 118?

65. What never changes in spite of the many changes we observe in modern times? How does this unchanging feature comfort you?

66. What messianic pictures do you see in 118:22?

## Psalm 119

67. How is this psalm uniquely structured? What is its main theme?

68. Critics often accuse believers of worshiping the Bible. Why might they think this? How would you respond to the accusation?

69. What practical help for daily living do you derive from the Bible?

70. What role, if any, should the Old Testament play in the lives of Christians?

71. How might leaders of a congregation foster a love for God's Word on the part of the members of the congregation?

72. How can parents pass along to their children knowledge of and love for God's Word?

73. How does the Bible give you a "heads up" about world conditions and future events?

74. How do you differentiate between reading God's Word and meditating on it? Do you maintain a daily schedule of both? If not, how will you arrange your schedule to accommodate these important habits?

75. Which verse in Psalm 119 best indicates your need for God's word? Which verse best indicates your devotion to God's Word? Explain your choices.

## Psalm 120

76. What occasion prompted the writing Psalms 120—134? What three responsibilities do we have to fulfill if our burdens are supposed to become blessings?

77. In what ways do some believers live like unbelievers? How do you feel when believers close to you live like unbelievers?

## Psalm 121

78. How secure do you feel in an insecure world? Who keeps you secure no matter how dangerous your surroundings become? Can anything harm the believer who walks with the Lord?

79. The Lord is your "shade at your right hand" (v. 5). Does this assurance guarantee nothing will hurt you? Explain.

## Psalm 122

80. Do you agree or disagree that churches must provide entertainment to draw people to them? Should we attend church primarily to get something or to give something? Explain.

81. What does it mean to pray for the peace of Jerusalem? When will Jerusalem enjoy permanent peace?

## Psalm 123

82. What burdened the writer of this psalm? How do you explain the existence of Israel after centuries of persecution?

83. What should a believer do when criticized or physically abused for his or her faith?

# Psalm 124

84. Have their been occasions in your life when you were under attack but the Lord proved He was on your side? How did He come to your assistance?

85. How does Satan resemble a lion stalking its prey? How can you maintain vigilance against him?

86. Have you ever escaped Satan's snare just in the nick of time? Recount that experience.

# Psalm 125

87. What differences do you see between the faithful and backsliders? Between backsliders and apostates?

88. How are believers like Mount Zion?

89. Why will "the scepter of the wicked" not remain? Ultimately, who will destroy the scepter of the wicked and raise His own scepter? Why will "peace be upon Israel" (v. 5) at that time?

# Psalm 126

90. When God returned His people to their homeland after the Babylonian Captivity, even the Gentiles neighbors confessed, "The Lord has done great things for them" (v. 2). What has the Lord done in your life that might bring a similar response from unbelievers who know you?

91. How can you apply the principle of sowing and reaping (vv. 5–6) to your ministry of drawing others to Christ?

92. Why do you agree or disagree that we need to faithfully sow the seed of God's Word and leave the results with Him?

## Psalm 127

93. What do you believe distinguishes a home whose builder is the Lord?

94. Do you agree or disagree that the traditional family unit is under attack today? What ideologies threaten today's families?

95. What "materials" make a household strong?

96. What blessings do children bring to their parents? How might parents love their children without spoiling them?

## Psalm 128

97. What measure of success would you have if it were not for the Lord's blessing?

98. How can a person prosper without becoming wealthy?

99. What does it take to be content in one's old age?

# Psalm 129

100. How hard is it to bless those who persecute you? How should believers respond to unbelievers' taunts?

101. What ABCs of this psalm should we remember when people malign and mistreat us?

# Psalms 130–131

102. Have you ever cried to the Lord when you felt that you were drowning in trouble? What was the occasion? What happened when you cried to the Lord?

103. When you ponder the vast contrast between your sin and guilt and God's salvation and forgiveness, what word best describes how you feel? How does God's intervention in your life reinforce the fact that the Gospel is Good News?

104. As Christians, we enjoy spiritual freedom now, but how will our freedom be complete when Christ returns?

105. What qualities did David exhibit in Psalm 131 that you wish to emulate?

# Psalm 132

106. What suggests this psalm is not a post-exilic psalm? Briefly state why the ark was so significant to Israel.

107. What two great ambitions did King David have? What are your two highest ambitions?

108. Where did the glory of God reside in Old Testament times? When Jesus ministered on earth? Today?

109. Believers today enjoy a covenant relationship with God. Who made this covenant, and how did He make it? Why is this covenant unbreakable?

110. Do you agree or disagree that someday Jesus will rule from a throne in Jerusalem?

111. How long did David rule in Hebron before the Lord gave him a united kingdom?

112. Do you agree or disagree that someday Jesus will rule from a throne in Jerusalem? Defend you answer.

# Psalms 133–134

113. What impact is a church feud likely to have on a community? How can you help to build and safeguard the unity of your local church?

114. What pleasant benefits arise from church unity?

115. What subject does Psalm 134, the last "Songs of Ascent," address?

116. How might you enrich your personal worship?

## Psalm 135

117. Why did God choose Israel? Why did He choose you? Could Israel take any credit for the choice? Can you? How does belonging to God affect your gratitude? Your willingness to serve God?

118. What does God's care of Israel during her the wilderness wanderings teach you about His power? His ability to take care of you?

## Psalm 136

119. When was this psalm sung? What Christian songs do you associate with special occasions?

120. Repeatedly in this psalm the statement occurs: "His love endures forever. Compare this statement with the teaching in Romans 8:38, 39. and tell how His enduring love sustains when you suffer, when doubt clouds your mind, when you sin, when you feel lonely, and when you get discouraged.

## Psalm 137

121. "Remember" and "forget" stand out in this psalm. What did the Jewish exiles in Babylon remember? What did they ask the Lord to remember?

122. What should you remember? What should you forget?

123. Why does it seem so hard to forgive and forget? How does knowing the Lord has forgiven and forgotten your sins help you to forgive and forget?

124. What memories strengthen your faith?

## Psalm 138

125. The Lord had given David a united kingdom, but neighboring nations wanted to fracture the kingdom. Who tries to thwart King Jesus' rule over the lives of His followers? What sinister methods does he use? How can believers oppose him?

126. The Lord gave David boldness to confront his enemies. Under what circumstances has the Lord given you holy boldness? For what causes do believers today need boldness?

## Psalm 139

127. How does this psalm lead you to conclude that God is omniscient (all-knowing)? How does the fact that God knows you intimately encourage you? Does this fact inspire a healthy self-esteem?

128. How does the theory of evolution collide with the teaching of this psalm?

129. How does this psalm support the pro-life position?

130. Why does it make no sense to try to run from God and hide but perfect sense to run to God?

131. If like David, you asked God to search you and know your heart, what do you think He would find? What should He find in the heart of every believer?

# Psalm 140

132. Apparently some of King Saul's officers had it in for David and therefore spread lies about him. Have you known an employment situation in which ungodly coworkers ganged up on a believer by lying about him or her? What should a believer do in such a situation?

133. How freely can you confess your faith at work? Should Christians witness while they are on the clock? How might you share the Gospel with a coworker without stealing time from the boss?

# Psalm 141

134. How are choices and character related? What do you think of the comment, "He is just a good kid who fell in with the wrong crowd"? How can parents teach their children the value of wise choices?

135. Why is it unwise and ungodly to return slander with slander? When is it extremely hard to keep your mouth shut?

136. Why is it better in a tough situation to ask, "What can I get out of this?" instead of asking, "How can I get out of this?"

137. Since God is the "Sovereign LORD" (v. 8), why should we trust Him in every situation? What difficult situation will you commit to the Sovereign Lord?

# Psalm 142

138. David might have written this psalm in a cave while hiding from Saul. He wanted the Lord to free him from his "prison." What kinds of "prisons" might believers find themselves? How can they rise above the hopelessness this confinement creates?

# Psalms 143

139. How often do you think believers would pray if we never encounter trouble? How earnestly would we pray?

140. Does believer ever have a valid reason to maintain a negative attitude? Explain. What signals does a believer's negative attitude send to unbelievers?

141. David asked God to teach him His will. What measures will you take to know His will?

# Psalm 144

142. What difference does it make to your life that God loves you personally?

143. Describe the abundance God has lavished on believers in North America? Do believers in third world nations enjoy abundance from the Lord that can't be measured in dollars or number of possessions? Describe that abundance.

# Psalm 145

144. This psalm is an acrostic. Build an acrostic identifying God's characteristics based on the word "GREAT."

# Psalm 146

145. What are the last five psalms called? What do you learn about God's benevolence in this psalm? How might believers practice benevolence and thereby demonstrate that God is kind and loving?

# Psalms 147

146. Why is praise to the Lord so uplifting? Why should every day be a thanksgiving day?

# Psalms 148

147. How do the heavens praise the Lord? How does the earth praise the Lord? When will the Lord receive universal praise? How keenly should we anticipate that time of praise? Why is it impossible for a believer to live endlessly in defeat? How can we apply Psalm 60:12 to our lives?

# Psalm 149

148. How can a new song escort you to God in refreshing worship? How can we keep from falling into a rut when it comes to corporate worship? David longed for the Lord's presence. How should your life reflect the truth that the Lord is with you always?

149. Should worship be mostly emotional or intellect or a good balance of the two? How do you balance the two elements of worship?

# Psalm 150

150. How does this psalm conclude the Book of Psalms in a grand crescendo of worship? How has your study of Psalms helped you to worship and serve the Lord more joyfully and thoughtfully?